Unexposed Film:
A Year on Location

Rob Harris

A DEDICATION:

This book is dedicated to all the fathers and sons, mothers and daughters who sacrifice a part of their lives so that movies can be made. It is a passion, a privilege and probably a punishment for past-life sins.

A YEAR ON LOCATION

PART I: THE CIRCUS LIFE

PART II: GODFATHERS AND SONS
BONANNO: A GODFATHER'S STORY

PART III: PRIORITIES
THE THOMAS CROWN AFFAIR

PART IV: WARRIORS
GLADIATOR

PART V: SEX AND DEATH
GLADIATOR

PART VI: INTERLUDE
RATED X

PART VII: CLIMATE CHANGE
THE PERFECT STORM

PART I
THE CIRCUS LIFE

CHAPTER ONE

ON THE ROAD

Movie crews refer to location life as "the circus," though it just as often begs comparison to summer camp or boot camp. Like the world under the Big Top, it's full of artists and con artists, midgets and giants, craftsmen and creatures so suited to this environment they couldn't survive in any other. They work day, night, often to exhaustion, often drinking themselves to sleep alone in fancy hotels they could never afford on their own. They eat in the same lunch tent as the world famous and go home to their personal obscurity when the movie wraps.

And there they dwell: no bounce to glamorize their living room lighting, no craft services refilling coffee cups, no video playback to remind them how they've passed their day.

Unemployed crew, adjusting to civilian re-entry... until a call comes, inviting them back for one more display of sword swallowing, somebody saying "nobody juggles chainsaws the way you do" and "this show is really too big to miss." *Hey, ya gotta make a living,* they tell each other – all the while complaining they don't have a life.

They repack a suitcase that still has some mismatched socks from the last job, kiss the dog, pet the kids and leave their home to report to their department: props, grip, electric, camera, set decoration, catering, construction, costume, makeup, special effects, visual effects....

I'm in the communications department: job title, unit publicist. The job description: liaison between the studio and the filmmakers, the film and the public, the press and the actors (and their publicists) and whoever else needs access to or information about some aspect of the movie being made.

Mine is a much-caricatured profession. Movie Publicist conjures images of sell-his-own-mother Sidney Falco in *Sweet Smell of Success* and the studio flack harassing Jean Harlow in *Bombshell.* If your film education doesn't include these titles, I'll summarize: a publicist is a shameless puppeteer, a conjurer of image without conscience.

But movie publicity has evolved from setting up scandals to make a gay client look straight or gathering press to deny the non-existent rumor about your leading lady liaising with the leading man she loathes. Self-released sex videos and what-were-they-thinking shoplifting slip-ups make manufactured notoriety less a publicist's stock and trade these days. That was never what the *unit* publicist job was about anyway.

So what exactly do I do?

I'm a Zelig, a visitor to imagined times and invented lives, materializing among the famous in both real and recreated places. I write about what's being filmed and tell people why they should be interested.

But I never write about what's *most* interesting: the laughs and drama between scenes, hubris and humanity behind the scenes, lives we live unseen.

This is partly my story, partly the story of all of us - gaffers, grips and go-fers alike – who spend our lives traveling with the circus, cleaning up after the elephants, making movies. The famous with whom we work and brush shoulders – George Clooney, Russell Crowe, Charlie Sheen, Pierce Brosnan, Joaquin Phoenix, Mark Wahlberg, Diane Lane and others – are also part of our story.

You don't have to be born into the movie business, though it's hardly a secret that many are. It's a family trade - like black-smithing or mortuary work – handed down, father to daughter, mother to son. My father delivered bread to the studio commissaries. His connections to the kitchen staff were of no help to me.

Film schools may be closing the nepotism gap but I wouldn't know. I took one course in college studying the experimental works of Stan Brakhage, Kenneth Anger and Bruce Conner. I only learned that some films were better to watch stoned.

It never occurred to me that people made a living from movies in capacities other than acting, directing, writing and selling concessions. But in the summer of 1969, I came down from Berkeley - where I was majoring in Revolution at the University of California - to spend a few weeks with my beautiful Flower Child sister in Los Angeles.

One of the guys in the apartment next door to hers was an aspiring movie director who'd directed a couple of *Night Gallery* television episodes. His short feature, *Amblin'*, was just making the rounds at the festivals.

A lean, kinetic young man, about a year my senior, he was most animated talking about films, mainly the greats from the past – some of which I'd seen, most of which I hadn't – and stories of how they were made. I told him I'd like to learn more about the way movies were made. He took a paperback from his shelf.

"Read this," he said, handing me a copy of Arthur Knight's
The Liveliest Art.

It was a book that changed my life.

The transformation didn't happen overnight.

I continued through my hippie high times at Berkeley, graduated into dropping out of graduate school and headed to Nashville
to become the next Kris Kristofferson. Hit a dead-end in
Tennessee (Kristofferson later told me, "Ya gotta stick it out more
than six weeks"), moved back to California and survived three
years as a social worker until I met a woman who knew a lot about
horses and we bought a small ranch in the northern San Fernando
Valley. I learned a bit about horses and more about women. Left
her and the livestock for a starving writer's life. Wrote anything I
could get paid for and more I'd never get paid for.

Then through a former social work colleague who'd become a
low-level publicity executive at 20th Century Fox, I began getting
freelance work editing badly written press kits for their movies. I
would pick up assignments in person, a drive-on pass left at the
guard gate... a gate behind which the Liveliest Art came to life.

After that it was simply a matter of finding my way around
this enchanted village – and the not-so-simple matter of finding
where I fit in.

I soon learned that the real excitement of moviemaking wasn't
found on a studio lot. The adventure of film production was on
the road. That's where I wanted to go.

That's where we're going.

The crew van is leaving for set. Buckle up.

CHAPTER TWO

1999

It was "The Year That Changed the Movies," according to *Entertainment Weekly,* "...the first real year of 21st Century filmmaking."

The Internet had reached its tipping point: Pixels had replaced paper for forty percent of America - twice that many in the film business - and the Y2K meltdown loomed like a serial killer around the corner.

It was a year of reckoning for movie marketers, confronting an information apparatus they didn't trust and couldn't orchestrate. Or could they? *The Blair Witch Project* came out that year, earning $240 million worldwide on a largely internet-based campaign. The race for cyberspace promotion was on.

Computer-Generated Imagery – CGI – had moved light years beyond light saber battles. It was a voracious beast, swallowing entire productions, stretching the limits of time, place and imagination and ultimately demanding the re-emergence of 3-D. The *Lord of the Rings Trilogy* began filming in October and would take the art of graphic imagery to another level.

Releases that might have been cult hits a decade prior went mainstream: *American Beauty* swept the year's Oscars. *The Matrix, Fight Club, Being John Malkovich* were cinematic acid trips that found big audiences. *The Sixth Sense* launched a new wave of phantasmic fright films.

The new millennium's new direction was further signaled by movies being produced in 1999: Darren Aronofsky shot *Requiem for a Dream*; Ang Lee finished the balletic *Crouching Tiger, Hidden Dragon*; indie director Steven Soderbergh was readying two major studio pictures, *Erin Brockovich* and *Traffic*, which would make him the first director in six decades to earn two Best Director Oscar nominations in the same year.

Epics re-emerged: *The Perfect Storm* was about to enter the vernacular, harnessing groundbreaking effects to rising star George Clooney for his first blockbuster hit. A little-known Australian actor was working on a milestone epic that would bring him fame and his first Academy Award, *Gladiator*.

Nineteen ninety-nine was also an important year in my personal life. I worked twelve consecutive months on three continents, five movies, one marriage and two pre-teen boys. It was a year of challenge and change.

This then, is the story of an exceptional year for both the film industry and the author. Yet in the most fundamental ways, it's about a year like any other, traveling with the movies.

CHAPTER THREE

THE SPACE BETWEEN RETURNINGS

Ithaca, New York was approximately a four-hour commute from Manhattan: across the George Washington Bridge to the Palisades Parkway, along two-lane roads through the tiny towns of Upstate. I didn't mind the drive. I enjoyed the sense of being on the way *to* someplace – especially to my wife, Margaret, and our sons Casey and Sam. It was the leaving that left me hollow. And the space between returnings.

What was a guy who made his living in the movies doing in Ithaca?

I'd grown up in Los Angeles and couldn't wait to get out. A childhood friend had moved to western Washington in the late 1970s and, visiting him, I succumbed to the spell of the Cascades, the clean air, the mystique of Puget Sound, even the inconstant weather. I thought I could have it all: a beautiful place to live, a beautiful family and a career in the movie business that I so loved.

After five years in the magnificent Northwest, Margaret and I were on the brink of divorce from too much time apart. They didn't make movies in Seattle: "Honey, I'm going to work" always meant the beginning of a journey. I had underestimated how much I'd be working, as my career was just taking off. Clearly, one cornerstone of my model existence – marriage, career or scenic wonderland – would have to be refitted.

I suggested we move back to L.A., where work in the film industry merged with the prospect of more nights in our conjugal bed. But Margaret had put down roots in Seattle and she was not an easy woman to uproot.

However, she had a sister and brother-in-law, along with some other relatives, in the little college town of Ithaca. Living in Upstate New York meant a weekend commute from films shooting anywhere between Philadelphia and Toronto. Weekends were better than nothing. And the three pillars of my perfect life could stay intact.

Some jobs, though, were too distant for a weekend visit. And as I started getting hired for bigger movies, our separations got longer.

It was time for reinvention as we began our fifth year in Ithaca and I accepted an offer to become an executive for a small film company in Manhattan. I could come home every weekend and, if things worked out, we'd move closer to the City. But I came home exhausted. And I came home depressed.

One day, my boys asked, "Dad, when are you gonna get a long time off again?" Those long times off that other people call periods of unemployment.

Well guys, this job isn't like that. I get four weeks vacation, a week at a time.

"We hate this job," declared one for both. "You should go back to your other job."

But… I'd bought ties!

I gave my notice the following week.

And so we were back at square one, still needing to figure out how to organize our collective life so I could take a greater part in it.

"We got married to be together, didn't we?" This wasn't an argument; it was a recurring theme in the episodic comedy of Margaret and Me. "You knew what I did for a living when we got married. We always planned to travel together. You used to love traveling. When did you change your mind?"

When our first child, Casey, was born, she would say. We both knew that wasn't the whole truth. She'd had her fill of it early in her working life. As a solo singer and instrumentalist, she went where the work was: North Carolina or Norway didn't matter except as a change of venue. She traveled because she had to.

I traveled because I wanted to.

We hadn't really known that about one another back then.

I fell in love with Margaret's voice before we even said hello. She was at the piano in a small club in West Los Angeles; honey blonde hair cascading down a graceful neck, eyes closed as *Come in from the Rain* poured out lush as a whisper.

Well hello there, dear old friend of mine
You've been searching for yourself for such a long time...

Her performer's smile met me at my table during a break. We were introduced. We shook hands.

It was only a year after Ann's death and I'd finally started dating again. Ann was my first love, who died of complications from breast cancer at age 29.

I'm not good at dating. I suffer from good relationship role modeling, a disability I've had to live with since adolescence. Women have always wanted to be my friend. The Holy Grail of uncomplicated sex has always eluded me.

Yet a night later the sultry singer and I ended up in bed together. I only had a week in town before flying off for five weeks on location in Alabama but we spent that week keeping constant company. She was smart, she was sensitive, she had a great laugh and she was a traveler. Three weeks after returning to L.A. I asked her to marry me.

Home for another precious weekend. Margaret and I decided to see the movie *Living Out Loud*, in which Holly Hunter is jettisoned back into the dating scene after being dumped by her philandering, traveling husband.

During our 13 years of marriage, roughly two-thirds had been spent apart. And not unprecedented in the history of wedlock, it appeared Margaret had misplaced her sex drive sometime during her first pregnancy and had pretty much given up looking for it. It suddenly seemed odd to me that neither of us had ever brought up The Question. So, I pointed out the elephant in the room. "Do you ever wonder about my sleeping with other women when I'm traveling?"

She was silent for a moment. Then she admitted it had crossed her mind.

"But you've got it so great with me and the boys, you'd have to be crazy to throw that away by falling in love with somebody else."

Had she changed the subject? I was talking about casual sex; she was talking about love. The former was increasingly on my mind, the latter never in question.

Margaret was my Rosetta Stone. Her kindness could decode any character strength I might possess. I found direction in the bend of a small line on her face and definition in the intimate appellations she offhandedly tossed my way.

I treasured each hour we were together. In low sex drive or overdrive. But we didn't have so many hours together. Or days. Or nights. And the road offered lots of opportunities to live in a Stephen Stills song (*if you can't be with the one you love...*).

"I know," I told her. "I was just curious if you were curious."

It was Sunday night and I had to get to bed early to get up early to get to my job on this movie. We didn't make love. Again.

I'd been working on the romantic heist-thriller *The Thomas Crown Affair* in Manhattan for the past two months. Production had recently moved to a makeshift studio in the suburb of Yonkers and in three days, key crew and stars were flying off for a week of filming in the Caribbean island of Martinique. But a snafu on the part of the production had left the publicist's name off the travel list. In the breach, I'd accepted an offer from Showtime Networks to spend the next two weeks in Sicily and Rome. I would get a paid trip to Italy and still have my job in exotic Yonkers when *Thomas Crown* returned from Christmas hiatus in January.

Best of all, Margaret was considering coming to Rome with our boys. It would cost everything I earned on the job but we'd all be together for an Italian Christmas.

I just had a few more publicity chores to breeze through in New York.

CHAPTER FOUR

ACTORS

It happened on *Gremlins*, my first movie.

Late one cold L.A. night, I was standing with the stills photographer on Universal's back lot, bored and hungry, waiting for the film's complex puppetry to be reset for the Big Explosion. It was a master shot of decimated storefronts along a small-town Main Street and the local theatre (featuring *Snow White and the Seven Dwarfs*) was about to blow.

The film's leading lady, Phoebe Cates – schoolgirl heartthrob from *Fast Times at Ridgemont High* – was standing next to us.

"Wonder what happens to all that candy after the shot?" she mused, watching a set decorator scattering crates of chocolate bars through a confections store.

"Hey, let's just run over and grab a handful of what's in the (smashed) window," joked my crewmate. The candy store display was a "hot set." Everyone on a film crew knows you don't mess with a hot...

"OK, I'll do it," said Phoebe.

We watched her run past grips laying dolly track, electricians setting lights and art department personnel artfully strewing debris. She reached into the broken plexiglass, pulled out two handfuls of candy bars, stuffed them in her jacket pockets and flew back, light as a lark, giggling between gulps of air, to where she'd left us.

As she chewed on a Milky Way, teasing the caramel into long gooey strands, she twice glanced back at the scene of the crime: what a thrill to run through a movie set and do something naughty! No guile, no cool, no fear.

That was when I fell in love with actors.

I'd recently had a bonding experience with Pierce Brosnan.

We were at a photo session in Manhattan where MGM was paying photographer Greg Gorman an enormous sum of money to shoot Pierce and Rene Russo for the poster of *The Thomas Crown Affair*. I was being paid a lot less to oversee and troubleshoot.

While waiting for Rene to get her final makeup touches, Pierce approached the catering table where I stood nibbling crudités. What began with small talk metamorphosed into a thing of substance when he mentioned his late wife. They'd been married for 11 years, the last five of which had been spent battling her cancer.

I'd also lost a wife to cancer, I told him.

Sorry.

Same.

Difficult.

Hmm.

Devastating.

Yes.

We talked about our roles as support spouse, the helpless-
ness, the holding back, the desperate sadness that others mistake
for strength. We talked about the lessons learned from our late
wives, about the real courage that comes from clarity - when death
is no longer abstract. We talked about recovery after the loss. We
shared the celebration of having found new partners who provided
us the peace to finally hang memory like a lantern that forever
lights a lovely, quiet room.

The warmth in his parting handshake, when it came time to
return to his place in front of Gorman's camera, bridged a chasm
of professional caste.

Days later, Pierce snapped at a journalist I'd brought on set
for asking "stupid" questions. O.K., maybe the questions were
a little unoriginal but mainly he was getting tired of doing interviews. He'd already done about a dozen, which is more than
a lot of stars would put up with during production. Contrary
to popular belief, movie stars don't really *like* talking about
themselves – at least to the press. But it's in every actor's contract (except maybe Jack Nicholson's) that they must do some
publicity for the film.

Because actors go on to other projects, often the only time
they have for interviews is between scenes while working on a
movie. And everyone agrees that the best stories are the ones that
capture the excitement on set, the filmmakers collaborating, pro-
cessing, creating; the star still fresh in his role.

So if everyone agrees, a) these stories are better, b) the star
is more engaged in *this* movie - instead of the two others he's
done between the date you wrap and the date you release - and c)
the timing is not only more convenient during production but
often impossible afterwards, it might seem odd that actors so
often make publicists feel like playground police chasing truant
children.

In defense of actors, publicity is the department that adds the least *apparent* contribution to making the movie and is therefore an annoyance to nearly everybody.

I'd scheduled a behind-the-scenes crew to cover one of the film's biggest action moments. The production had built a wing of the Metropolitan Museum of Art on our sound stage in Yonkers and the big scene involved Pierce stealing a painting, setting off an alarm and rolling under a security gate as smoke bombs went off. The sequence had everything one wanted in behind-the-scenes coverage: stunts, effects, drama and our leading man.

My crew arrived on set before the first shot and I got them in position to cover a stunt man demonstrating the roll to Pierce. Good stuff.

Then our union shop steward approached and asked to see the union cards for our video camera and sound operators. The sound-man wasn't in the right union. He was ordered to leave.

Alright, the video camera operator would record what he could with his built-in mike. He got in position to shoot the first scene.

"Everyone off the set who isn't involved in this shot," the first assistant director demanded.

Surely he didn't mean...

"You too," he barked at my cameraman.

I tried for the rest of the morning to get him back in there but was met with the same answer each time.

"It's too complicated a shot. I don't want any distractions."

Distractions? There were already three film cameras covering the scene from different angles.

Complicated? Like that which makes behind-the-scenes coverage interesting?

A word here on behalf of film publicity, film production's stepchild: as much money is spent in marketing a movie as in making one. Most of that goes to advertising – which creates the "awareness" that your product is out there. Publicity, as its partner, not only stretches the ad dollar, it creates the "want-to-see."

Our assistant director obviously didn't want to hear it – let alone see it – from that perspective.

But there's more to it than that. I wanted to ask if he'd ever read a film history book? *Any* history book? *Ever watch an old newsreel?*

You see, a unit publicist's job isn't just about promoting movies. It's also about preserving the moments that tell the story behind the story: two stars in a revealing off-camera interaction; the director *in* action. How did they make Van Nuys look like Casablanca? It's worth something beyond box office to have a well-written news article describing young Orson Welles directing himself in *Citizen Kane* or footage of Dustin Hoffman making Anne Bancroft laugh between scenes in *The Graduate*.

The embarrassing secret almost no one in the movie business will admit is that we're *all* in it to be a part of film history. Sure, it's manufactured glamour; so was Art Deco. And to the pompous auteur who says his finished work of art is all that matters, *no one should know how sausage is made,* I say, "psst, you wanna see some behind-the-scenes clips of da Vinci painting Mona Lisa?"

I stood watching Pierce dive under the descending gate, take direction, then do it again a different way, wishing we could be documenting some of this.

Our video camera was finally permitted on set that afternoon – to cover the less "complicated" shot of Brosnan staring at a painting.

Peggy Robinson, our pig-tailed production assistant who was assigned to the area around the actors' trailers, had a rule about working with actors.

"Get comfortable - but don't put your feet up."

I should have that sewn onto a pillow to take with me on every location, so it's the last thing I see before closing my eyes each night.

Pierce's personal publicist, Dick Guttman, had called to ask me to relay an important message to his client: a politician in New Zealand was claiming the actor's endorsement and Guttman had been contacted to see if there was truth to the claim. Dick had been phoning Brosnan all night but the actor couldn't be reached.

So, I got to the set early and waited outside his trailer to give him the message the moment he arrived.

Pierce's black limo pulled into the parking lot and as it turned toward the trailer area where I was standing, I could see the actor in the back seat. He saw me too.

He exited the car with buffed Italian leather flattening the gravel, head and shoulders erupting from behind the door - neck and chest imperially uplifted. A precise box step, then two fingers of his left hand flicked the door closed. Behind dark glasses, his eyes scanned the horizon, stopping in my direction. I took a short step forward.

His lips spread outward, teeth bared, nostrils flaring.

"The last thing I want to see when I get to work in the morning," he snarled, "is the publicist standing outside my trailer."

The publicist?

Wait a minute, I started to say, I'm the guy you shared your heart with over celery sticks a couple of weeks ago. I'm a person, not a publicist!

But in the instant his arrows struck, my inner ear heard the sound of suction cups. Of course! He was joking! I lifted an invisible palm upside my head. And I laughed.

It didn't take him a full second to respond.

"I'm fucking serious," he glared.

I stood there trying to remember when I'd put my feet up.

Waiting for the car service that would take me to the airport the next day, I ran into Pierce coming out of the soundstage. This was the last of his filming in Yonkers. After completing work in the Caribbean he was going straight on to his next movie.

"So, I'll be seeing you in Martinique," he noted my suitcase.

No, I'm not going.

"Oh, well. I guess this is goodbye then. I'm...," he looked me in the eye. "I've enjoyed working with you."

I, uh...

He has four kids, one with his current partner, one with his late wife and two adopted from her previous marriage. And he would barely have time to unpack before starting his next picture. It's not an easy life - even for a movie star.

"Well, maybe I'll see you on another one," I shook his hand.

Just around the time my plane took off, I thought of Margaret preparing dinner for the boys. Casey would have plain pasta with butter, drowned in salt. His brother Sam would want ham and cheese on a plain bagel - the same thing he'd had for breakfast and lunch.

Margaret would be wishing I were home, if only for motivation to have more than a cup of yogurt.

And I'd soon be eating airplane food.

It was a fairly typical family meal.

PART II
GODFATHERS AND SONS

Bonanno: A Godfather's Story –
Showtime Networks

CHAPTER FIVE

POWER PERCEIVED

"It was obvious that he was awed by his father, and while he no doubt had feared him and perhaps still did, he also worshipped him."

Gay Talese on Salvatore "Bill" Bonanno
(*from* Honor Thy Father)

In the northwest corner of Sicily, the Doric Temple of Segesta dominates a hilltop overlooking family farms and olive groves. "Segesta's temple yields in beauty to none," writes Dr. Helen Hill Miller in *Sicily and the Western Colonies of Greece*.

Except for the paved road leading to the parking lot, which was filled with equipment trucks on this day, the Temple appears

almost exactly as it did when its builders abandoned it midway
through construction in 424 B.C. It is a pristine monument to a
God they didn't believe in.

Perpetually under threat from the eastern empire of Syracuse,
Segesta turned to its ancient enemy Greece for protection. These de-
scendants of Troy began a courtship of Athens that played like a Marx
Brothers sketch in which Harpo and Chico help Groucho romance an
airheaded heiress - Greece taking the part of Margaret Dumont.

First, the civic leaders gathered all the golden goblets and
silver platters in the vicinity. Then they invited some Athenian
ambassadors on a tour of Segesta's most impressive homes. The
communal collection of 24-karat cutlery and gem-encrusted serving dishes was shuttled to each hosting abode just ahead of the
guests, where it was exhibited as subtly as Jane Russell's cleavage.
It was hoped the ambassadors - who may not have been the highest intellects on the Hellenic shelves - would return home believ-
ing the Elymians were wealthy enough to pay for a Greek military
expedition against Syracuse.

The capper to this charade was the majestic hilltop temple.
Built to convince the Greeks that Segesta had gotten that old
time religion or simply as a tribute, it had to look impressive.

But like a backlot facade, it was never what it seemed.

From the temple floor during a filming break, I ran my hand
over the surface of a two-thousand-year-old alabaster column and
scanned the sprawl of pastureland above the rocky edge of Golfo
di Castellammare to a silver-haired man in cowboy boots on a
grassy knoll above the temple grounds.

I was in Sicily with a real Mafia Godfather. How weird was
that?

Salvatore "Bill" Bonanno had been expecting me.

"Tom told me you're a straight shooter," he said when I
reached the top of the hill. "Anything I can do to help you out,

I'm always available. I'm either here or you can call me at the hotel. Whatever I can do, I mean it."

"Tom" was the screenwriter, Thomas Michael Donnelly, who had spent two years writing the 300-page, six-hour adaptation of *A Man of Honor: The Autobiography of Joseph Bonanno*. Donnelly had logged over thirty hours of interviews with the 94-year-old patriarch at his home in Arizona. He was circumspect in his judgment of Papa Joe but enthusiastic in his assessment of Bill, who'd followed Pop into the Godfather business.

"He's a regular guy," Tom told me over the phone from L.A. "He wants to make a tribute to his father. This movie is his way of saying 'Thank you for all you've given me.' Naturally, I had to include good and bad. We fought about some things. But overall, Bill was happy and I was happy. Guess we'll see how happy the Old Man is."

Reading the script, it seemed to me the Old Man should be downright delighted.

Bill embraced his father's culture and made no apologies for its excesses. But his vision for this story was more Zane Gray than Mario Puzo.

"As a boy, my father would ride into the mountains, across the family farm over there, and dream his romantic dreams," Bill pointed to a hill west of the temple.

Bill was born in New York and grew up mainly at a boarding school in Tucson, Arizona. Though he hadn't set foot in Sicily until his honeymoon – and this was only his second visit - he took pride in an archival knowledge of his father's land and traditions. My research confirmed him to be impressively accurate - give or take the odd date or details of incriminating methodology.

In 1930, New York's Castellammarese War redefined the American Mafia. When the smoke cleared, 26-year-old Joseph Bonanno became the youngest of five godfathers to share the spoils. In the following decades, names like Luciano, Genovese,

Colombo and Gambino would rise and fall. Bonanno would endure.

In 1964, Joseph Bonanno was kidnapped – nobody knows by whom, how or even, for certain, if. Bill took over leadership in his father's absence. In October of that year, a breakaway faction lured Bill into an ambush. He shot his way out and made it back to a safehouse in Brooklyn. From there, he waged a two-year battle the New York tabloids called *The Banana War.*

The war ended with Joe's reemergence – appearing as mysteriously as he had vanished. Shortly thereafter, father and son decided to retire to Arizona. Unlike the founders and heirs of the other Five Families, no pallbearers attended their retirement.

"The secret to our longevity is olive oil, garlic and pasta," laughed Bill. "Plus God's will."

Now his 94-year-old father would live to see an authorized television epic made from his autobiography.

I had some moral qualms about this job.

Castellammare's citizenry had numbered approximately 15,000 for the last 100 years. Since the late 1800s, the devoutly Catholic town had practiced a form of population control that flew under the radar of Papal concerns about contraception.

According to *The Cadogan Guide*, "Its present tranquility belies its sordid Mafia past, when feuding inspired Mario Puzo to write *The Godfather* and an estimated one in three men in town had committed at least one murder."

The echo of gunshots resounded from the dark edge of sunset through the early morning outside my window at the Punta Nord Est Hotel. It was a sporadic popping - usually three to a sequence, spaced as a half-note followed by two quarters. A syncopation of return fire frequently rejoined.

"I think you should know," the woman booking travel for Showtime had informed me, "The U.S. State Department issued a travel warning about Castellammarre. It's on their list of Most Dangerous Places. At least it was last year when all the Mafia bombings were going on. Let me see if it's still listed. I'll get back to you."

She never did.

The next morning, a pair of swarthy gentlemen from Palermo stopped by the production office, announced themselves as being from "the film commission" and specified a payment that would enable the production to continue under their protection. Our production manager discussed the matter with producer Kevin Tierney and the gentlemen were paid.

"Power perceived is power achieved," Bill was fond of saying.

Bill was a likeable guy. We had drinks after wrap one night. He talked about his father. He also asked about mine. I'd been thinking a lot about my dad. He would've been about ten years younger than Joe had he not passed almost a decade ago. The two even spent different parts of their youth only a few miles away from each other in Brooklyn. Joe's neighborhood soon filled with other young men from Castellemmare, tough kids who forged careers in bootlegging and racketeering in the employ of mob boss Salvatore Maranzano.

My father also grew up tough. On his side of Rockaway Parkway and Kings Highway was Murder Incorporated - though in the early days, they were simply known as Benji, Meyer and Lepke (Siegel, Lansky and Buchalter). I told Bill that Dad used to play soccer with some of the younger members of that gang. I recalled him saying he'd broken his nose three times playing soccer. I'd always thought it was from the ball.

Bill got a laugh out of that.

The following day's filming began with actor Tony Nardi standing on a beach, playing middle-aged Joe Bonanno as he gets news that rival boss Albert Anastasia has been assassinated. It was

1957 and Joe was on native soil for the first time since he fled the fascists here at age 16.

Tony had talked to me earlier about his frustration with this role.

"I thought it would be exciting to play a man who was so contradictory," the actor confided. "You know: he regards himself as a man of peace but he doesn't hesitate to have people killed - or at least threatened with death - for violating his 'Code of Honor.' What is that about? How does a 'peaceful' man justify that level of violence? But those kinds of contradictions are what make Joe a rich character.

"Unfortunately, Bill won't let any of that into the script."

What must Bill have been thinking, watching an actor recreate this important event in his father's life? Did Nardi's dignified, slightly imperious portrayal capture the man Bill knew – or was it the statue of a man? Do sons want to remember their fathers as they really were or is personal history always revisionist? Aren't we all in creative conflict about whether to make our life's movies from myths or memories?

My father was my hero. If I could make a movie about him, I'd want to show him in the best light.

Was Bill any different?

I could think of one way.

My father was a frustrated entertainer. Sort of Henny Youngman without the meanness – which is to say, not funny.

Within the first two sentences of any dialogue exchange – with anyone: friend, stranger, tollbooth agent – he would crack wise. He would also sometimes take a word or phrase from the last thing a person said and tie it into a song lyric:

"I was desperate, I had to do it."

...*Birds do it, bees do it...*

He was a constant embarrassment to his children.

His only actual stage experience was a time in his youth when he wanted to sing for his mother.

There was a local Yiddish theater in his Brooklyn neighborhood, which held a Variety Night. Locals who thought they were the next Al Jolson or Sophie Tucker would compete for a $5 prize.

My dad wore his good pair of pants.

He greeted his mother at the door, helped her to a front row seat, two of his brothers beside her, and raced backstage.

He was the third act, as he recalled it. Neither of the other two were any good. He felt he could win it all.

He came out from the wings with his head hung and a borrowed, rumpled hat pushed low over his eyes. He took off the hat, held it to his heart and announced, "This is for you, Mama."

He began to sing.

Once I built a railroad, made it run
Made it race against time

He got down on one knee and increased the drama through another chorus.

... Hey don't you remember,
They called me Al,
It was Al all the time

My father, from the stage, could see his mother squirming in her seat, looking at something below his eye level.

... Say don't you remember,
I'm your pal.
Brother, can you spare a dime.

His mother leapt to her feet.

"Get up off the floor already. Those are your good pants. I'll give you the dime!"

My dad was my hero because of his ability to laugh at himself. Bill would never allow any of that into his script.

Showtime had flown a video cameraman and sound mixer in from Paris to shoot behind-the-scenes footage and record the actor and filmmaker interviews it was my job to organize. Newly arrived New Yorker Deborah Goodwin had come to do the interviews and produce the electronic press kit - the EPK - a key marketing tool distributed to all major broadcast outlets around the time the movie is released.

The company was filming inside the high-ceilinged garage of a two-story house where a gang of mustachioed actors in woolen overalls sat around a card table as the cinematographer checked his light meter against the mustard walls.

Bill was waiting outside to do his EPK interview.

"Whenever you need me, just holler. I'm at your service. When you're ready, you let me know. I've got nothing else to do here," he laughed. "That's off the record."

The Video Frenchmen went away to set their lights and camera in a vacant house the art department was renting. After about half-an-hour, they sent word they were ready for Bill. But Bill was nowhere to be found.

"I had to have cappuccinos with some of the town elders," Bill explained when he returned, hours later. "They wanted to talk about members of my family. They wanted to ask how things were going. It was a goodwill gesture. I didn't know I'd get stuck so long."

His tour as ambassador completed, he was again ready for his interview.

But we'd lost our interview space to set construction and now the Video Frenchmen had to find somewhere else to reset.

Bill waited in the blocked-off street with idle production assistants and grips who had just finished rigging the next shot in the cramped café. He asked what we were presently rehearsing. It was a scene in which Grandpa Salvatore – played by the young TV star Costas Mandylor - confronts his brother's killers.

"Costas overturns a table, stabs a guy, shoots another guy, then turns to Felice (head of the rival Family) and says something like, 'You will remember this moment!'"

Bill went ballistic.

"The hell he does!" the goodwill ambassador metamorphosed into The Terminator. "He says 'Salvatore Bonanno's hand doesn't shake.' He's showing Felice that he has the nerve to kill. If he doesn't say 'Salvatore Bonanno's hand doesn't shake,' there's no point in even doing the fucking scene."

He stormed off before I could get the word "paraphrase" out of my mouth.

Inside the adobe café, Bill conveyed his concern to our Quebecois director, Michel Poulette (*"Mais non. Zis iz not vat I 'av 'im zay!?!"*) and the dialogue question was quickly resolved. When Michel called *"coupe`,"* the Godfather stepped in to instruct the young man playing his grandfather. Taking the dagger from Costas, Bill grabbed the intended victim and demonstrated what each man would be doing when the blade went in.

"I wanted to make sure that at the moment the stiletto was plunged into the heart of the assassin, the person plunging the knife looked right into his eyes," Bill shared later. "So, at the moment of death, the assassin would know that justice had been done. Because justice is a very personal thing. For us anyway."

Costas played the scene the way Bill instructed. No one changed a word.

Bill stayed on set beside camera the rest of the day.

With a look – and only a few words – the EPK producer reproached the publicist.

"You promised, after the last two times…"

Was it my fault that after we'd set up an interview in the town cemetery this morning, perfectly framing the subject between tinted portraits on his grandparents' headstones, Bill had to go off to pacify the Mayor?

"Nobody even contacted him to ask his blessing," Bill steamed after returning from that three-hour diplomatic ordeal. "Then, apparently, he came by the set the other day and everybody ignored him. I mean, a guy puts on a sash and a medallion, you gotta figure he wants some attention."

The harbor, where the company relocated in the afternoon, was a better place to do Bill's EPK interview anyway. With its fishing boats and the old Castillo in the near distance, it was a perfect setting. But Deborah was expanding her objectives. Before the sit-down interview, she wanted a stand-up of Bill outside the church of Joseph Bonanno's baptism, several blocks from the set.

So, Bill, Deborah and the Video Frenchmen drove off.

Bill had two "friends" who accompanied him everywhere. To call them "bodyguards" would conjure the wrong image. Though their companionship was eerily constant, neither looked particularly intimidating. Gary, a soft-spoken man in his mid-fifties was a former nightclub owner whose muscle tone suggested he'd never lifted anything heavier than a roll of quarters. Anthony, whom I'd earlier mistaken for Bill's son, had a choirboy face and a cannonball body. Bill described him as "practically a member of the family," with no explanation as to whether it was a genetic or organizational reference.

When Deborah hastily spirited Bill away, Gary and Anthony had been left behind with instructions to meet him at the church.

I was standing near the playback monitors with Bill's daughter Gigi and a couple of the Bonanno grandchildren when Anthony and Gary rushed up, breathless and frantic.

"Where is he? He wasn't at the church."

Gigi, so American, so out-of-the-loop, made a joke: "Maybe he was kidnapped."

Neither bodyguard cracked a smile.

Jogging up the steep street behind the harbor that led to Corso Garibaldi and the church of Joe's baptism, we confirmed Bill and the EPK crew weren't there.

Running towards the other end of the avenue, which overlooked the film set, scanning the crowd for a towering head of silver hair... he wasn't there either.

Dashing back in the other direction, a policeman near the church was questioning a shopkeeper who was making wildly despairing gesticulations. We sprinted towards them.

That's when the EPK van drove up and Deborah rolled down her window.

"Could you ask that policeman if we can park here just for a few minutes?"

Bill peered out from the seat behind her.

On the way to the church he'd pointed out the house where his father was born. Deborah thought it would be a swell idea to stop for an impromptu taping there first.

Production wrapped along the waterfront at dusk. Wine and beer were brought in for toasts. Bill circulated, thanking each member of the crew in English, French or Italian, as darkness descended over the little piazza.

There had been rumors of a transportation strike beginning tomorrow. Producer Steve Hewitt urged me to change my reservation so I could leave with the filmmakers on the last Alitalia flight for Rome that night.

Packing my bags at the Punta Nord Est, I heard the sound of gunshots again. I stepped onto the balcony and looked out towards the east side of the Piazza Petrola, where a pair of nightclubs faced the Hotel Al Madarig across the broadest expanse of public space in Castellammare.

Two boys were lighting firecrackers. Pop. Pop-pop.

One of them threw rocks at a lamppost until the glass finally shattered. The two ran away, disappearing into the shadows where their arsenal assumed more fearsome, anonymous authority.

CHAPTER SIX

HONORABLE MEN

It had taken some persuading but a five-hour drive from Ithaca to JFK airport, a five-hour flight to Paris, then five more hours of combined airport and airplane time to Rome delivered my family to me, limp as laundry.

Sam and Casey napped at the Sofitel while Margaret and I walked to the Spanish Steps. White clouds waltzed on cobalt skies and a crisp breeze snapped at us to huddle closer. Rome tantalizes the solitary but it embraces those who explore it in pairs.

We strolled to the Trevi Fountain where gypsies selling rubber squeeze toys descended like mosquitoes on any stationary tourists. The only persons seemingly immune to this infestation were kissing couples. So for purposes of pest control, we kissed.

All Margaret's concerns about this trip – which ranged from: "it's a long way to go for only a week" (though my trial balloon of making it two weeks, including Sicily, was popped before I could inflate it), to the tragedy of the boys missing a Christmas party with "haywagon rides" (let me weigh that out: haywagon/Rome, haywagon/Rome...) seemed to have disappeared.

All except one.

On the walk back to the hotel, we paused at the base of Trinita dei Monti. Leaning over the balustrade, looking out at a cityscape that placed the Mausoleo di Augusto between us and the Tiber, my wife unfolded a note from her purse and put it in my hand.

It was a report from Casey's teacher for the visually impaired: his Braille reading skills had declined in the last year. Further, she reported, he wanted to discontinue studying Braille.

Casey is blind - not totally but nearly so. He was born with a retinal condition that blocks 90 percent of his vision. A specialist once described his eyesight as "looking at the world through a straw with wax paper on the end," though it was better up-close and with greater contrast. Vistas were mostly amorphous colors. But he'd learned how to adapt a computer so he could see large white lettering on a black background - thus his lack of dependency on Braille.

I refolded the report and Margaret returned it to her purse. The sun was setting as we leaned on the waist-high wall and our gazes floated across the City of Caesars.

Margaret gave sound to our silence.

"Do you think we'll ever be able to completely enjoy a view again?"

The warmth where our shoulders touched substituted for an answer.

My professional duties here were practically nil, so this would be the closest we ever got to a real family vacation. The following afternoon we marched on Rome.

At Piazza Navona, Sam spent his allotment of lire on an arcade shooting game and had to beg a single candy from the roll Casey bought with pocket change to spare. Following the ninety seconds it took Sam to put holes in a paper target and thirty minutes for his brother to finish his game of sibling torment, I dragged my jetlagged legions to the Pantheon so Casey could look up at the oculus where the white beam of afternoon sky provided brief entertainment ("I'm getting a stiff neck").

My checklist of the day's destinations wasn't half done but one look at our sagging sons and we took pity, returning them to the hotel to watch Italian music videos. They were asleep in ten minutes.

Margaret needed some catch-up sleep herself and begged off accompanying Steve Hewitt and me to our production wrap party, which we were having on our last Saturday night in Italy.

Wrap parties are a dance around the fire after a hunt, a Dionysian rite of closure with those you've run alongside and depended upon for a significant portion of your year. The temperate let their hair down, the intemperate let it all hang out and young production assistants shed tears like their parents were divorcing. I'd only been on this movie for ten days. And most of the crew were speaking French or Italian.

A sumptuous buffet was laid out at the hillside Tuscan-style restaurant, which was overflowing with vaguely familiar faces whose names were all Buddy or Darling. After picking at the buffet and circling the room twice – once for "it's been good working with you" and a return pass for "see ya on the next one" – it was time to go.

As Steve and I began easing our way out, Bill cornered me at the door.

"Before you leave," he put his hand on my shoulder, "we should get our families together."

"Family is everything to him," Steve underscored on the cab ride home.

The subtext was clear: this wasn't a Hollywood, "we should have lunch" – a courtesy without substance. It was an invitation to share what was ostensibly most valuable to each of us, and refusal – or avoidance – would be hugely insulting.

My most recent meeting with Bill hadn't gone so well. We'd argued over how I might turn *A Man of Honor* into a man of interest for the press notes – Bill being as inflexible with the promotional materials as he'd been with the screenplay.

"I'm not buying it," he'd flatly shot down all my ideas for putting a spicier hook into our descriptive paragraph – and changing the title from *A Man of Honor*. "This is a movie about a great man who has lived his life by an ancient tradition. What about 'A Tradition of Honor?' I like that. Or how about 'A Tradition of Respect' - if you don't like 'Honor?'"

"That's the same thing!" Had I really raised my voice?

I'd read enough to know that the flip side of this Honorable Man was a cold-blooded bully. But I wasn't wrestling with ethics here. As Tony Nardi had said, at least that made Joe interesting. However, neither the title of Joe's book, *A Man of Honor*, nor Bill's alternative, *A Man of Respect*, were going to inspire hardboiled journalists to drop their half-smoked cigarettes into their lukewarm cups of coffee in a mad dash to beat the competition to a front page exclusive.

I made my case. Bill declared case closed.

Notes from *Publicity for Dummies*:

* Don't second-guess the producer.
* Coming up with titles is not in the job description.
* Never argue with a Mafia Don.

And maybe I shouldn't have used any variant of "violent" in my positioning paragraph.

Like I said, the meeting didn't go so well.

But he'd obviously forgiven me. We scheduled a dinner the next day.

Margaret and I, along with Steve Hewitt and his girlfriend Nancy, met Bill and Rosalie Bonanno, along with bodyguards Gary and Anthony, in the rooftop lounge at the Eden Hotel for cocktails Saturday evening.

The Eden had been the Via Veneto's glamour spot during the *Dolce Vita* '60s. Everyone from Marcello to Brando used to drink there. It had been remodeled and continued to boast one of the best terrace bars in the still swank district.

The first round of drinks loosened things up. Rosalie had barely sipped from her first glass before everyone else ordered a second. Anthony was drinking Coke.

Then Bill started telling stories.

Bill's resume is prefaced: "I am the product of an ancient tradition... My life was determined before I was born." It continues with a list of his jobs: San Quentin State Prison as *Chief Clerk, Captain's Office*, then a two-year stint at McNeil Island Correctional Facility as a *law clerk in residence*, then three years in the Federal *Correctional Institution, Terminal Island, California...*

"I was President of the Inmate Council from '72 to '73 and I had somehow earned the trust of all the different factions," Bill began. "One day, the warden calls me into his office. I ask him 'What's the trouble?' He tells me, 'We have a new guy coming in. His name is Liddy, y'ever heard of him?' Well, of course I'd heard of him: G. Gordon Liddy. Watergate was all over the news then. The warden tells me, 'I don't know if I can take a chance on letting him out in the yard with the other inmates.' This is a very high profile prisoner. The warden can't risk something happening to him.

"So, I told the warden, 'Lemme talk to some people.' I checked with the white gangs first because I knew they'd be o.k. about it. I asked the Mexican gang leader. No beef with him either. Then I went to the head of the Black gang. I said, 'Look, the warden has a problem. There's this new prisoner named Gordon Liddy. Used to work for the White House. Warden can't take a chance on something happening to him. Can I assure him this guy will be o.k.?'

41

"The head of the Black gang asks, 'Is he a rat?' I say, 'No. In fact he's in here because he wouldn't rat.' 'In that case,' he says, 'tell the warden he's got no problem.' And that's how Liddy got yard privileges."

At the end of this story, I glanced over at Rosalie. Perhaps, in previous encounters, I had misinterpreted the thinness of her smile. For all her obvious distaste at the direction of the conversation, there was no tension in those pursed lips. She had endured these stories before. She was married to a man who had no shame about who he was, no embarrassment about his past and even a measure of pride in what he'd learned from it.

Joe had never done hard prison time. He'd left that to Bill. But Bill would never blame his father for the years he lost. Instead he would create this testimonial to the man who gave him life. *Thank you for all you've given me.*

Whatever the sins of the father, Bill had paid for them many times over. He'd earned the right to call this movie whatever he wanted.

And the stories continued into the night.

We walked to Vatican City the next day - Casey complaining "how much further?" - where we experienced the overwhelming opulence of St. Peter's Basilica. We perused the art in the Vatican Museum and sat in the crowded Sistine Chapel staring at the famous ceiling.

As sighted people ooh'd and ahh'd, Casey said he was bored and Margaret reprimanded him for forgetting to bring his monocular. He forgot it on purpose. It brings distant objects into range but it doesn't enhance clarity. What would he have seen? Blurs of paint like puddles in a lava lamp? Psychedelic maybe - but not quite what Michelangelo had in mind.

Back at our hotel, I made a phone call to the only Roman citizen I knew and arranged a time for her to meet us the next day.

Though we'd had a French-speaking video crew and an English-speaking interview subject, Deborah Goodwin had deemed it wise to hire an Italian translator for our one day of EPK shooting here. Simone, a slightly built young woman with a fine-boned face crafted around big brown eyes, arrived on her motorbike, displaying the trick-riding skills of Annie Oakley. She was a University of Rome graduate student specializing in 5th Century archaeology and history.

I knew Margaret would like Simone. There was nothing not to like about Simone: earnest, engaging, polite, pretty-but-not-threateningly-so. Simone and Margaret shook hands and introductions were made to Sam and Casey as if this were the start of a normal day.

Simone listed the architectural wonders she planned to show us today - beginning at the Theatre of Marcellus, continuing through the old Jewish Quarter and so on. Margaret, no history buff but an intellectually curious, educated westerner, listened politely, helping Simone conjugate a few tricky verbs in English.

It was not until Simone pulled the spare helmet out of the storage compartment of her motorbike that the veins in Margaret's neck tightened to the point of strangling further conjugations in any language.

Sam, at a tender age, had been dangled by his foot in a playful moment by his practical joking Uncle Ralph and had decided, perhaps in that instant, he'd approach the thrills of jungle gyms, roller coasters and kamikaze skateboarding with caution.

Casey, for whom the routine of walking required inordinate caution, wanted nothing more from his recreation than to experience the exhilaration of speed, slalom, freefall or any other form of dare-deviltry.

Simone buckled the helmet under Casey's chin.

The veins in Margaret's neck plucked the banjo theme to *Deliverance* as Casey mounted the *motorino* behind Simone.

I think the bike's first left turn, scooting in front of a panel truck, nearly grazing a pedestrian's briefcase and almost

separating a young couple from their baby carriage, got
Margaret over the hump. With a look at me that could have
been interpreted a lot of ways besides a death threat, she followed Sam into the cab.

"Il Teatro Marcello," I told the driver, searching my phrase
book. "Guidi adagio ma non troppo adagio, per favore."

At a café beside the Theatre of Marcellus, Simone sipped
espresso while Casey played with the straw in a juice drink. The
look of satisfaction on his face - and relief on his mother's as she
exited the taxi - outshone anything else we saw all day.

Our final night in Rome, Margaret and I scavenged fruit and
nuts for the boys, instructed them how to dial the front desk and
met Steve Hewitt and his girlfriend Nancy at a quaint osteria.
With Tony Bennett crooning from speakers, confidences and his-
tories were exchanged. It was the time for summation.

Steve and Margaret discovered a commonality in having been
raised by serial housekeepers: Margaret after her mother died
when she was nine, Steve after his mother became ill, even before
his father made the difficult choice to leave and devote more time
to his career.

Margaret and I learned that Nancy's father was an industrial
whistle-blower whose life had been ruined by going public with
what he knew.

"He did the honorable thing," Nancy said to her glass. "But it
destroyed him."

Margaret discovered what I already knew: the identity of
Steve's father.

Don Hewitt was one of the pioneers of television news programming. He produced *The CBS Evening News with Walter
Cronkite* and the first televised Presidential debates, between John
F. Kennedy and Richard Nixon. Then in 1968, Hewitt helped
develop the weekly news magazine show *60 Minutes* over which
he'd maintained dominion these 31 years.

A few months ago, I'd received a call from Paul Bloch, head of one of the big p.r. firms in Hollywood, about working on a movie that his client Michael Mann was directing. A young Australian named Russell Crowe would star as a whistle blower from the tobacco industry. The veteran Phillip Don Baker would play Don Hewitt.

It was the story of how a whistle-blower was sold down the river by a beacon of American broadcast journalism. One a man of honor; one a man of respect.

The city seemed nearly silent as we four walked back to the hotel in huddled pairs. Passing piazzas that honored saints, along streets named after Popes, under arches commemorating the reign of emperors, we carried our separate thoughts. Mine circled around testaments and monuments, legacies and idolatries, fathers and sons.

The press kit I write at the end of every job includes brief biographies of key players. The length of the bio is usually a measure of the subject's value relative to the project. It requires a shameless hubris, condensing a person's life into a paragraph or two, a page or two if he or she is exceptionally famous.

As we walked, I wrote this one:

Irving Harris - An eighth-grade dropout truck driver who died broke and unknown except to the family who loved him. Never made a million, never produced a television show. Bought a tract house on the G.I. bill, stayed married to the same woman for 46 years and fathered two children - one of whom got his grandson a ride on a motorcycle through the streets of Rome.

Don't stay up late waiting for the mini-series.

PART III
PRIORITIES

The Thomas Crown Affair – MGM/UA

CHAPTER SEVEN

PICTURE THIS

The original *Thomas Crown Affair*, directed by Norman Jewison, starring Steve McQueen and Faye Dunaway, was done using a split-screen technique – showing multiple parts of the action occurring simultaneously on different sides of the screen. The results, by consensus of the critics, were somewhat muddled and largely ineffective.

This new version, it seemed, was being done with split personalities. Less a technique than a circumstance, the reviews were not yet in.

"What am I paying my personal publicist for?" director John McTiernan demanded as we walked to his trailer during a break in filming on the first day of our final month in Yonkers. I'd just asked if he'd read the latest in a long line of press release drafts needing his approval.

Some directors and most actors work with personal publicists to filter press requests when they're making a movie and to insure they're not forgotten when they're between pictures. I was obliged to defend his personal publicist, Bumble Ward, head of one of the better boutique agencies in the business, telling him she'd already approved the release pending his ...

"Does anyone at MGM have a plan for how they're going to sell this movie?" he interrupted.

Before I could explain what I thought to be the studio's marketing plan, Jay, McT's new assistant, began his unsolicited analysis.

"It doesn't seem like they have a concrete plan at all," said the rangy, Ivy League MBA pain-in-the-ass who appeared to believe his input was indispensible on an array of topics above his paygrade. "I don't think they realize the contemporary approach you're taking with this movie. For all we know, they may be selling it as a 'remake.' They're leaving everything for the last minute. I don't even know what magazine covers they're pursuing. They haven't sent concepts for what the poster is going to look like. I doubt they even know what angle they want to take. There's certainly been nothing that's come through me that indicates a plan of any sort."

"Well, Jay," I told him calmly, "perhaps that's because the studio isn't required to run anything by you," you fatuous phony, "but McT has seen ad concepts, the studio has been in regular contact with McT's publicist and they're in regular contact with me, whose actual job it is to know about such things as pending magazine covers."

"Well, I should have copies of all those memos," Jay whined.

"How are you coming with the John Wayne thing?" McTiernan, who appeared to be paying no attention to anything either of us had said, suddenly asked Jay.

John Wayne thing?

Here's where it got interesting.

It seemed that sometime between filming in Martinique and resumption of production in Yonkers, John McTiernan had been visited with a vision.

McTiernan was Irish and Pierce was Irish. Pierce's company was even called Irish Dreamtime. Following, so far? Denis Leary was certainly Irish. It was a bit of a stretch for Rene Russo but producer Beau St. Claire was a bonnie Irish lass, as was costume designer Kate Harrington.

The listing of the Irish went on: first assistant director Bruce Moriarty, casting director Pat McCorkle, cinematographer Tom Priestley, editor John Wright, key grip Jim Finnerty, Jr., even the Eastern Local's most famous soup and sandwich guys running the craft service table, Mike and Frank McKenna. What a coincidence! What kismet! Imagine all these Irish people right here in New York!

But what did this have to do with *The Thomas Crown Affair*, which to the best of my knowledge had no Irish characters, setting or theme and no more backstage blarney than most movies? Ah, here's where inspiration came in: John Wayne and director John Ford were both Irish! Get it?

McTiernan – with Jay chiming in "great idea," I'd venture to guess - had decided he wanted to create a double-truck (two-page) concept ad announcing the completion of principal photography on *The Thomas Crown Affair*. He would get a copy of the famous photo of Johns Wayne and Ford posing in Monument Valley and run it opposite a shot by some famous - preferably Irish - photographer showing "all the people of Irish descent on this movie!" The text would read something like, "The Irish still have a lot of influence in Hollywood."

This would run in *Daily Variety*, *The Hollywood Reporter*, maybe *Premiere*, *Entertainment Weekly* and who knew where else, if the studio only had a little imagination and was willing to back it with the bucks.

It sounded so bizarre all I could think to say was, "Well, I imagine you can get the Wayne and Ford photo from the Academy library."

"It's not that easy," Jay sulked. "I've been looking for three weeks."

I crossed the parking lot base camp and descended the muddy hill to the showroom of the former Buick dealership that had been our makeshift movie studio since November. The showroom floor now featured production secretarial desks, the sales offices now accommodated our executives and the old copy room had become the publicity office. The copy room had recently been home to four cats, which one of the producers purchased to address a pre-production rat problem. The rats were gone and some of our staff had adopted the cats - but the stench of soiled litter lingered for the run of the show.

I hid in the cat office most of the afternoon but producer Beau St. Clair caught me on a trip to the kitchen for coffee and a scented candle.

"Do you know anything about this Irish thing McT is going on about?" she asked once we were behind closed doors.

Pierce was against it, she told me, because being Irish, he knew that people from Ireland regarded Irish-Americans as Americans, not Irish.

What about the fact it has nothing to do with this movie?

She didn't even want to go there. With Pierce back in London beginning production of *Tomorrow Never Dies*, she could do nothing but play along and hope McT forgot the idea as suddenly as he'd gotten it. Meanwhile, the director had asked her to find a top quality "Irish" photographer.

"Whenever I'm away from the set too long, I feel like he punishes me by sending me out on errands."

I offered two Irish-American photographers with whom I'd worked: my pal Ken Regan who was a noted portrait and documentary photographer and famed advertising photographer Albert Watson. Beau said she needed a list and asked me to keep thinking.

I had only two more weeks in which to play Hide-and-Seek from McTiernan. It wouldn't be terribly difficult. He was, once again, preoccupied with filming his movie and Jay was preoccupied with advising anyone who asked that the NASDAQ market was accelerating like a rocketship but there was still time to jump aboard before it soared completely out of sight.

Film crews are always looking for places to invest their money. There is no job security and the big paychecks can fool you. Since crew mostly get their financial advice from other crew, they mostly end up broke. But if you're not a gambler, you're in the wrong business.

There's a top to bottom roll of the dice in the film industry: a producer gets an idea or script he/she likes and puts some money into developing or buying it. The producer then gets funding for the movie and has to get a production and creative team on board. For the creative team – stars, director, writer, certain producers and often the cinematographer – there are always elements to be tweaked. But meanwhile a crew has to be hired. As crew, you're told you'll be starting on a certain date. So you turn down other jobs that conflict. But the creative tweaking turns into turf wars, the distributor won't sign off, a funder drops out, the stars can't agree with changes made by the director-writer-producer and they drop out. And everybody watches their bets swept off the table.

Occasionally a movie clears all those hurdles and is green-lit. The principal cast is signed and sealed, the producers flesh out the supporting cast and the production is launched. Then begins the hard work of keeping everyone rowing at full speed and in the same direction. This gets harder the closer you come to the finish line. And too often the finish line moves – as it had on this one.

The stages of life on a film crew are not dissimilar to the stages of a love affair: you thrill in the first blush of being wanted, the initial period of courtship seems so carefree and everyone seems so nice. Then maybe the director yells at you or you work a 16-hour Friday and the bloom is off the rose. Then it begins to feel like a grind but you bear up affably because you've made a commitment; then less affably as you question your own judgment. Then at some point you mentally threaten mayhem on the next person who won't give you a straight answer. Then the last Martini shot sneaks up on you, it's finally over and – eventually - all you remember are the good times.

I was somewhere between feeling less genial and wanting to punch somebody.

Spending so much time under the yellow neon of an office that had once been a litter box was affecting my sight, smell and sense of humor. The silliness of my job - persuading petulant actors like Denis Leary to stop playing video games in his trailer and come do the interview he'd blown off twice already; trying to guess what mind-space our director was coming from on any given day; praying the union shop steward didn't ban another television news crew because their sound man was a member of NABET and not IATSE - was starting to wear me down.

Or was it the years-long routine of long drives home on wintry roads to catch a few weekend hours with my family?

Rene Russo had also been wearing down. And withering away.

The former fashion model was about to turn forty-five. Still beautiful, still slender... but getting a little too slender. She was worrying she was deluded playing a seductress at her age, she was worrying if she was failing as a mother to her five-year-old daughter, she was worrying about hurting the feelings of those in her employ, she was worrying about the plight of sugarcane farmers in Cuba. You name it, Rene was worrying about it.

It was all worrying to McT. It was worrying to costume designer Kate Harrington. It was worrying to everyone around our female star. Here was a very decent human being who was literally eating herself up with worry.

The solution came in the form of a hairdresser named Enzo. Rene's former hairdresser who also did her makeup, her career counseling and her photo kills had been fired a few weeks before the Christmas break. This was because she had also begun encroaching on the director's and producers' jobs - suggesting not just what perks the actress should consider essential for her trailer but even how she should play a scene.

"One of the three of us has got to go," McTiernan finally announced.

In some ways, the replacement of Rene's former all-purpose attaché with the Milanese mop maestro didn't make a lot of difference.

"Dees are 'orrible," Enzo declared about a pair of Armani sunglasses Kate Harrington had selected for the actress. "Dey clash wis her skin."

But along with multiple opinions, Enzo brought multiple skills: in addition to being an expert with a curling iron, he was a master chef.

The smell of garlic and oregano wafted like opium smoke from Rene's trailer daily, mid-morning 'til late afternoon. Even if the skinny star wasn't visibly fattening, she seemed at least sufficiently distracted by the procession of platters placed before her to have calmed down a bit. Wouldn't have surprised me if the sassy saucier had slipped a potion in there. But whatever it was, it was working. And it was keeping Rene working.

I had discovered my own favorite place to eat: Delfini, on Columbus near 85th, a few blocks from the studio apartment I was renting from photographer Ken Regan. It was relatively new, relatively reasonable, with relatively good food and a pleasant ambiance. What took Delfini out of the realm of suitable, into the stratosphere of compelling, was that it came with my own favorite waitress - a blue-eyed, black-haired actress named Elisa.

Between off-off-Broadway performances, acting classes and otherwise living on fame's Outer Banks, she served dinners on Tuesday, Friday and Saturday. It wasn't her beauty, which was considerable, but a Midwest candor dished up with apple pie amiability and a most unactress-like quality of not needing to top an anecdote of yours with one of her own that drew me back to Delfini this snowy night in mid-January.

Here I freely confess how frequently I crave the company of women. A waitress, a bank teller, a dental hygienist, doesn't matter. I just like sharing space with them. Women are a puzzle; guys are a conclusion. I don't consider it a transgression. If Margaret were around, she'd be my company of choice. But she wasn't around. And it was snowing.

I sat at the bar near the service station. Scanning the room for a glimpse of Elisa gliding between tables, laughing at bad jokes, I caught the eye of the hostess.

I asked if my favorite actress-waitress had gotten to work yet. "She's off for the next two weeks."

But I'll be gone in two weeks, I barely refrained from shouting.

Suddenly a voice rang out from the Happy Hour crowd at the bar, "Hey Mr. Publicist!" Peering through the pack of pre-dinner drinkers, I saw a shining white smile below smoky brown bullets aimed in my direction. She was waving me over.

Her name was Anne Marie. She had been an extra in *At First Sight,* a melodrama starring Val Kilmer, and we'd struck up a conversation one day at Washington Square where she was positioned as a jogger, effortlessly, endlessly loping past the camera, take after take, in tight shorts.

I plowed through packs of loose-necktied men and fashionable women to the barstool where she sat, surrounded by Upper Westside actor types. She beamed up at me and crossed her legs, revealing three more inches of thigh beneath a short denim skirt.

"Remember me?"

Sure. Whatcha been doin'?

"I got a lead in a play. I'm a killer lesbian."

Congratulations.

She introduced me to the others in her group and we talked about her play, the sudden wealth of "good new material by really sharp, avant-garde writers" off-off Broadway and, inevitably, about the Clinton impeachment.

"Over a blowjob? Geezus, those Senators really need to get some," she tossed a wicked wink to one of her pals. "Any of 'em good lookin'?"

So... still jogging?

"Too cold. I've been hanging out at a lot of lesbian bars, studying my character," she laughed, re-crossing her legs. "There's a really interesting one in the Meat Packing District. A lotta leather but you'd be surprised who goes there."

I was sure I would be.

"What are you workin' on?"

I told her.

"So, ya gonna be in town March 5? Come see my play. I'll comp you."

I'll be in Morocco or Malta by then, I explained, on my next movie.

"Wow. I've always wanted to go to Malta. Do you need an assistant?"

Always wanted to go to Malta?

I'd love to have an assistant but I don't think it's in the budget.

"Well, maybe I could come visit."

Alright, you tell me: what's the polite response a married man gives to that?

Sure, I said, should be an interesting movie – stealing another glance at her thighs.

"Great. Lemme give you my number."

And she did.

One of her friends asked about *Crown* star Denis Leary.

"I did standup on the same night as him once. He was funny. How's he doing?"

I gave the politic response.

"Don't know if he'll remember me but tell him I said 'hi.'"

I said I would. Then I said I had to go. I wished Anne Marie luck with her research.

"Promise you'll call me."

I promised.

I didn't keep the one about saying "hi" to Denis Leary either.

I'd just settled in behind my desk with the morning's *New York Times* when the phone rang. It was Beau St. Clair.

"McT wants Albert Watson."

It took me a minute: McT wanted Watson... to shoot his 'Irish' photo! Ahh. What was going to be required of me beyond trumpeting the sagacity of this decree?

"Nothing. Just thought you'd wanna know."

And that was it. I hung up bewildered as when I'd first heard the idea.

I opened the sports section. The phone rang again.

"McT wants to see you as soon as possible," said Jay in a flush of urgency.

Despite my suspicions about the messenger, when the director says, 'as soon as possible,' one in my position makes it immediately possible. I folded my newspaper, tucked it under my arm and headed for the set.

An hour later, *The Times* fully read, I got a moment with McTiernan.

"Oh, yeah," he had to think awhile after I said I'd gotten an 'urgent' call from Jay. "Tom (the propmaster) has some 'spy' shots of Rene in The Dress. I think they'd be good for the cover of something."

The Dress had been one of the most inspired stylistic contributions to what was shaping up as a very stylish movie. For the Ballroom scene, in which gorgeous Guess Jeans model Esther Canadas appears as a mystery woman who seems to be a rival for Crown's attention, Kate Harrington needed to put Rene in a frock that would dazzle.

Canadas offered a few suggestions for her wardrobe from the racks of couture she had on hangers at home. One of the gowns she brought to our costume designer was a semi-transparent, black sequined number. Kate showed it to McT who convinced the 6'4" model that if she wore this to the ball the wrong actress would be the focus of the scene.

Kate fitted the dress for Rene who did indeed dazzle. The "spy shots" taken during the filming, in grainy black and white as if through a surveillance camera, exposed all her feminine assets sidelit from the bandstand.

At lunch, McT had only one comment when he looked at the photos again.

"Ask Barry (the stills photographer) if he can make this nipple a little more prominent."

Barry said that wouldn't be a problem.

I could've argued. But I didn't.

During the decade I'd known Rene, we'd talked very little about her religious beliefs. She was not one to proselytize but I was aware that her Christian faith was deep and abiding. Was it stereotyping to think that also meant being a little prudish? I mean, swapping dirty jokes with Mel Gibson on the set of *Lethal Weapon* was one thing but...

My curiosity had been building: she'd already bared her breasts in a beach scene in Martinique but she was supposed to be on a private island with her lover, so it made sense, and she'd tussled nude in a bedroom with Pierce but that was also integral to the story. Still, allowing her nipples to be photographically fiddled with for purposes of *press exploitation*...? Where does a good Christian girl draw the line? Had to be here.

The next day, I waited outside Rene's trailer until the Italian Taste Police stepped out to give his grocery list to a driver and snuck inside the moment he was gone.

I joined Rene at her dining nook and extracted the photos from a manila envelope.

McT loves these, I explained.

"Yeah, he showed me one of these yesterday. I think this was the one."

She picked the shot with the augmented nipple.

"Was this retouched?"

I told her it had been.

She studied it awhile longer.

"I'd like to see the un-retouched version again."

I hiked back to the props trailer and asked Tom for a copy of the un-retouched print. He ruffled through drawers of forged paper currency, cigarette lighters, knives, watches, keychains, eyeglass frames, wallets and badges until he came to a stack of photos. He pulled out one of the grainy black and white 8x10s.

"I want this back," he grumbled.

I rushed back to Rene's trailer.

McTiernan was inside. Enzo was cooking him a steak.

McT put his hand out and I gave him the picture. He glanced at it, handed it back and I walked it over to his actress who was seated not ten feet away.

She looked at the photo for what seemed like a very long time.

"I'd like this retouched," she said - pointing to the photo's *un-enhanced* nipple.

Enzo peered over Rene's shoulder.

"You look berry 'ot," gushed the chef.

I left to tell Barry what the lab should do with Rene's left nipple.

Alright, so maybe I'm the prude. But I still didn't get it.

Our lady of the modified-mammaries passed me on her way to the set and I stopped to say goodbye, telling her I wouldn't be here for the last day of filming tomorrow.

She gave me a hug, pressing her un-retouched chest tightly against my own.

I couldn't help myself.

"I've gotta ask," I sputtered. "There's been a fair amount of nudity in this movie. And now the photo thing… I mean, you're o.k. with… I mean, you know, as a Christian? And all?"

She smiled.

"I don't remember the bible saying you can't be proud of the body God gave you."

She gave my hand a final squeeze before scurrying off to the waiting cameras.

Amen to that.

And bless the photo lab for helping the Lord in His work.

CHAPTER EIGHT

DON'T GO

My father, before The War, had a job buying canaries for Hartz Mountain Pet Products. His work required extensive travel, particularly to the Orient.

Like many men his age, the range of his travels expanded with the U.S. invasion of Europe. He brought home a Lugar pistol taken from Omaha Beach, a colored pencil drawing of the Seine bought from a starving artist in Paris and memories of foraging for eggs in the Norman countryside. Upon his return from service in 1945, his old job was waiting for him. So was my mother. Without hesitation, he made his choice. They were together 'til death did them part 46 years later.

One day, when his son wondered aloud - and unkindly - why his dad had chosen thirty years of driving a bread truck around

Los Angeles over following songbirds to faraway places, he said simply, "You get tired of so much traveling."

I don't think my dad ever really got tired of traveling – he just stopped wanting to get on planes without my mother.

The mighty Susquehanna shimmered under starlight as I skirted its banks through the historic town of Owego where I picked up Route 96 north, the last leg of my weekly journey home. I continued past trailer parks, farms and a lumber mill until I could gaze across our front four acres at the big yellow house in the woods.

This was my last weekend with family before leaving for five months overseas.

The new job excited me. Big canvas, interesting locations, classic subject.

The prospect of being away from my sons so long saddened me.

Most of the parenting books say kids can deal with anything as long as it's consistent: four days a week at Mom's house, three at Dad's; weekend visits if that was all the court allowed; holidays and summer vacations if that was all logistics permitted. Unfortunately, consistency was the one thing I couldn't give my guys. So, my contribution to their lives required a little creativity - and a certain amount of begging their mother to visit me on location.

This next one was going to be a test.

January 24 was Casey's 12th birthday. The fact I was home for it was like winning a lottery. As any traveling parent knows, personal events are too often victim to deadlines, board meetings, extended deployments, tsunamis, hurricanes, earthquakes, airline schedules, train delays and traffic signals. I'd spent the past twelve years running red lights to make it home for one event or another. Still, if I started listing the number of friends' weddings, funerals, holiday parties – not to mention my own family's birth-days, first days, traumas and triumphs – I've missed because I've been in another state or another country, there'd be enough tearstains on these pages to render them unreadable. Suffice to say, forgiveness of oneself is as essential to this life as wheels on a suitcase. And each celebration you are able to attend becomes more joyous for its rarity.

A dozen kids went screaming down slides into piles of multi-colored plastic balls and we all had a good time celebrating Casey.

After the party, I accompanied Sam to the last basketball game I would ever see him play. Whatever that aggressive gene that made athletes battle like Trojans, Sam didn't have it. My heart ached for my reticent warrior as I watched him put up the final shot of the game, which bounced on the rim, then off.

But it was only dawning on me that Sam's athletic shortcomings were a dress rehearsal. He always *looked* good on the court or field - just missing the play with a dramatic dive or crashing the boards after someone had already gotten the rebound. Sam was an actor. That was his budding talent and aptitude. Like most parents who know anything about the entertainment business, I had trepidations about the thick skin my sensitive son would need to pursue this path. Still, as a sensitive father, it was my duty to foster his natural gifts.

That night I gave him a copy of the script for *Gladiator*.

"Maybe you'll wanna read this," I said as I tucked him in. "Maybe you'll wanna be a screenwriter."

The boarding call for my commuter flight scolded as I held and kissed Margaret in the lobby of tiny Tompkins County Airport.

I bent to the boys, who bound me in iron.

"I don't want you to go," pleaded Sam.

"Don't go," ordered Casey.

I freed myself, attached to the earth now only by the span of small palms.

"I'll call you when I get to England," I said softly.

"Remember England?"

I may as well have asked, "Remember Mars? Remember Atlantis? Remember Death?" They were one and three-years-old at the time of their only visit there. The last time Margaret traveled with me.

"I'll show you some pictures," Mom offered, taking their hands.

I turned as the conveyor swallowed my laptop. When I turned back, they were walking away.

PART IV
WARRIORS

Gladiator - DreamWorks

CHAPTER NINE

WHERE THERE'S SMOKE

The first day of production is like the first day at a new school: you search for friendly faces, you see who's in with the In-Crowd, you try not to do anything stupid.

It's awkward stepping onto a film set the first day - until you're surrounded by hand clasps, embraces and back pats from old mates. Suddenly, the world is bright - no matter that you're filming nights in an alley. You are where it's happening. A member of an elite team. Shaping the zeitgeist.

Of course, if you don't know anybody, it can feel like prom night without a date.

A driver was waiting outside the Royal Garden Hotel to shuttle me to Farnham in Surrey, a green and brick hash of shutters, shingles and tweed about an hour outside London. At its center were the Bourne Woods, thousands of hilly acres honeycombed with hiking trails.

Today, guards were posted at the forest's vehicular gates and hikers were routed around meadows packed with caravans and lorries. Footpaths now ended at a swath of felled, scorched Scots pine and shrubbery that had been trampled for set dressing.

Nearby, Roman Legionnaires stood in queues with tunics lifted above trousers waiting to use the port-o-potties lining a service road.

Figuring sixteen years, times an average of three movies per year, I'd had roughly forty-eight First Days on movie sets.

I hadn't worked with a British crew in nine years but the cheery face that greeted me at base camp was a familiar one.

Mark Somner had been a production assistant on the CIA-themed action-comedy *Air America*. He'd since moved into the locations department, the route his father, Basil, had followed to the middle-management post of unit production manager. Basil had been UPM on *Air America*. I asked how he was doing.

"He passed on about two years ago," Mark said, as one who has done his grieving skips such information like a stone on a pond.

Politely suffering my condolences, he quickly offered, "My brother Adam's the 'second' on this. D'ya know him? C'mon, I'll introduce you."

Second assistant director Adam Somner swayed his compact body like a track star loosening for a sprint, listening to instruction from burley first assistant Terry Needham. The a.d.'s job is to mobilize manpower into colors on the director's palate. It's a formidable task on any movie but this one would involve more than 10,000 background actors and an exacting director who frequently used four or five cameras in a single shot. This was Adam and Terry's fourth film with Ridley Scott.

Terry trucked his thick torso away on knees he'd been cursing since his soccer career ended three decades ago. Mark and I met Adam at the bottom of the hill.

"Hey Adam, this is Rob. He knew our dad."

Adam took me in like one of the family.

"Ya met Ridley, yet?" he asked. "C'mon, I'll introduce ya."

On set for half-an-hour and I was already about to crack the inner circle.

At an age when contemporaries pass leisure hours motoring around country clubs, it would be impossible to imagine Ridley Scott in a golf cart unless he were tied to it. Hands that belonged to a taller man absently rolled a cigar as he stood shoetop-deep in mud with frost on his moustache, surveying the battlefield of Germania.

His mien was relaxed and his smile inscrutable as Adam introduced us and I sputtered something hyperbolic about the scope of this project.

"Umm, well *'1492(:Conquest of Paradise)'* was about this size," he said without flinching. This had been one of Ridley's few flops.

I just widened my eyes and nodded. Films are the fruit of a director's womb and nobody has ugly children.

Adam darted off to place background soldiers for the first shot and Ridley headed to a chair at the playback monitors, giving me a pleasant nod of dismissal. I turned to go.

Standing five feet in front of me was Russell Crowe. His lips pursed in a tight smile, his head titled slightly while his eyes flashed suspicion. I introduced myself.

"Good ta meetcha" he said, like it was a dare. I passed along greetings from a journalist, the friend of a friend – risking that I wasn't naming someone he hated.

"Oh, yeah, I like Alex." And no more. He was called to set.

I walked away thinking that was a pretty good start – considering all I'd heard.

Costume designer Janty Yates had been among the first to have a run-in with Russell. No wilting flower herself, a member of her department told me that during one frustrating, early presentation of wardrobe possibilities, she had let loose her inner Valkyrie on our star who, exercising his own flair for the operatic, slammed his fist on a table and unleashed an ear-splitting alpha-male roar. After this, she vowed she would "never speak to that... (epithet under contention) again" and insured herself of this by assigning one of her staff to handle all future dealings through the (expletive's) personal dresser, Michael Castellano.

Amiable armorer Simon Atherton fared no better. Told Russell wanted to see him at production headquarters, Simon tore himself from his busy pre-production workday to bring Maximus' sword to the boardroom at Shepperton Studios.

"It's long because Maximus is probably a cavalry officer," explained Simon, whose career began as an apprentice gunsmith at age 16, then a weapons museum curator, then weapons expert on *Raiders of the Lost Ark.* "I didn't see him as a poofy sort who'd have a lot of decoration, so I told him the grip is a solid carving of a lion's head, simple lines, that's it. He says to me 'Well, I don't see it that way at all. That's not the kind of character I play. Haven't you seen any of my movies?' I looked him straight in the eye and said, 'To tell you the truth, I've never heard of you.'"

In one of his first meetings with Ridley, Russell reportedly threw the *Gladiator* script across the office, declaring it a "piece of shit." In a subsequent meeting, he narrowed his critique to a proposal that there should be history between his character and the Emperor's sister, Lucilla, played by Connie Nielsen. Ridley agreed. Russell liked that in a director.

Later I introduced myself to our Croatian-American executive producer, a robust septuagenarian named Branko Lustig.

"Have you met Russell?" he rolled the "R."

I said I had.

"He's a bit of an asshole," Branko shrugged.

A movie crew is a mélange of co-dependent relationships: the camera department is reliant on the electricians, the electricians on the grips; stunts rely on special effects, art directors on set decoration, the transportation department on locations, makeup has to work with hair and everyone depends on the assistant directors. The publicist is joined at the hip with the photographer. A confident, competent photographer can halve a publicist's labor load and make him look good. The opposite also applies.

Most unit photographers, having started in photojournalism, are a wily lot. He or she must work invisibly around actors who are distracted by a light breeze, camera assistants who claim workspace like it was a place in the lunch line, producers who feel qualified to kibbitz because they've contributed to the family photo album and, most dreaded of all, happy-snap seekers in the cast, crew or crowd who bring their point-and-shoots into an already pressurized mix. A motion picture set is neither a news event nor a studio session. It is not a natural place for a stills photographer.

Normally, photographers are among the easiest personnel to identify - what with a hundred pounds of Nikons draped bandelero-style across multi-pocketed flak jackets. It took several hours before I spotted mine, crashing out of the forest like a gangly fawn. The lanky, square-jawed youth introduced himself as Jaap (pronounced Yaap). He carried a single camera with a wide lens - though he assured me the rest of his equipment was "around here somewhere."

Jaap had started his movie career on low budget, independent films only about three years ago and was recommended for this job by Ridley's son Jake, for whom he'd shot stills on the small feature *Plunkett & Macleane*. He was frighteningly inexperienced to be working on such a big movie.

Jaap practically pranced with excitement as we walked towards the lunch tent, talking about ratios of color transparency to negative, quotas of production shots, headshots and other photo-related aspects of my job that, I confess, bore me to narcolepsy.

As charming as he was, I warned myself not to get too attached. If he didn't have talent to match his zeal, I'd be breaking in a new photographer before we left England.

"Actor Oliver Reed Arrested," a small, page-three headline announced the next morning.

The story went on to say that Mr. Reed had been drunk at Heathrow airport and taken into custody after becoming involved in an altercation with a man at whom he allegedly hurled a beer can. I was slow to realize that the modesty of the headline, its innocuous placement and brevity of text meant that the papers were treating it with all the rarity of a weather report. *Ollie Reed made a drunken public nuisance of himself again. And now for tomorrow's forecast...*

The good news was that Reed wouldn't start work until Morocco. This was especially fortunate because Richard Harris, our Emperor Marcus Aurelius, despised him - and Harris only worked in the English part of the production. There were, of course, no shortage of stories about Harris's own drunken antics.

I'd once met Bahamian neighbors of his who recounted the night when police finally said they would no longer respond to complaints about his nocturnal patrols outside his beach house - usually involving him naked and ranting, waving a bottle of vodka in one hand and shooting a semi-automatic pistol into the surf with the other.

"Call us when he starts shooting at your house," they were told.

Then there was the story about him drunkenly stumbling out of the Beverly Hills Hotel, leaving a sound-asleep famous actress handcuffed to a bed where she was found, struggling and cursing, by a startled maid the next morning.

Though professing sobriety these days, tales of his irascibility persisted. One pertaining to this movie had him not responding to any of Ridley Scott's - or his own agent's - inquiries about the part Scott was offering. The frustrated filmmaker was about to offer the role to Anthony Hopkins when he decided to take a final assertive stab and go to the Savoy Hotel where Harris lived.

The thespian greeted him in the hall, dressed in a nightshirt at mid-day, saying "Nice of you to pop by. I'm looking forward to being in your movie" as if there'd never been a doubt. Perhaps there hadn't been in Harris's mind. But more likely he wanted someone important to come ask him personally, nicely, thank you very much.

Mostly, though, there was Russell.

On the way from the set back to London, I shared a ride with a co-worker who repeated a variation of the "script flinging" meeting. In this version, Crowe stormed out saying something like, "Don't waste my valuable time."

A few days later, he was hired anyway. To my source, it was shocking for Ridley to have tolerated this from any actor, let alone one who'd been in a handful of Australian films, a string of American flops and was only the second lead in his lone notable U.S. movie, *L.A. Confidential*. He was awaiting release of a Disney hockey film called *Mystery Alaska* on which the buzz wasn't good and had just finished a lead as a chubby business exec in the currently-untitled *Michael Mann's Whistle Blower Project*, about which no one knew a thing.

The allure for Scott was Russell's performing, not his fame. In *L.A. Confidential,* he burnt up the screen; in Aussie features like *Proof* and *Romper Stomper* he was riveting. Even in the techno-tanker *Virtuosity,* Denzel Washington – not known for loose compliments – declared he was watching a "special" talent in co-star Crowe. Russell knew how good he was. But, thus far, he was a STAR only in his own mind.

This was always the warning bell for me. I am regularly asked who are the most difficult actors I've ever worked with. I invariably cite names few remember: actors who thought they were more famous than they were.

Ridley later confided that he'd written in his journal before the first night of filming, "I wonder if Russell is going to be trouble?"

Like this was even a question?

I arrived at the office the next morning to find that bouncy James Bowman from the *Farnham Herald* had called again.

"Hel-lo, Rob," he used the extended syllabic separations of a sympathetic mortician. "How ahhh things going today?"

They were going better before a series of photos of the burnt woods showed up in today's *Herald*.

The main reason we were here was that Ridley had been told a section of the woods needed to be cut for reforesting. The director said, "I'll do it." While this may have been a public service, the photos looked to the world like a public menace.

Our redheaded Forestry Service elf, Colin, had been fielding calls since early morning from concerned citizens all over Surrey, worried that "these Steven Spielberg people" were ruining the landscape.

That was another thing. Despite repeated corrections and admonitions, journalists continued to refer to *Gladiator* as Steven Spielberg's movie. The recurring use of this possessive had begun to chaff Mr. Scott's thick hide.

"Spielberg doesn't have a fucking thing to do with this picture," he snapped after I showed him the latest of several stories that had appeared in the British press.

At least James Bowman had cited Ridley as the film's director. He couldn't resist, however, throwing in a reference to "...the Steven Spielberg owned company."

It's an awkward relationship that production publicists have with local press. Suburbs and small cities are training grounds for big city reporters, meaning most are in these places to learn from their mistakes - which are numerous and often large. Also, "publicist" is a bit of a misnomer. We're not interested in the "free publicity" (all publicity is "free"; advertising you've gotta pay for) the press offers during production since we don't yet have a product to promote. For local press that means waiting until we're no longer local news. So, where's the elusive middle ground? Depends who's answering the question.

"Whaddaya want, James?"

What he most wanted was to be able to hang around the set all day, everyday, interview Ridley Scott, Russell Crowe and Richard Harris and help his newspaper fill column inches with the biggest news to hit Farnham since the train station came in.

I respected that. I also couldn't give him that.

"So, when can I visit the set?"

"You can't, James."

"Can I get a short interview with Ridley Scott?"

"Nope."

"How about Russell Crowe, then?"

We agreed that he could call me anytime and I'd give him quotable answers to relevant questions. My judgment as to the relevance. There would be a time when we'd invite press to visit our set: this was not the time or the set. We were not yet in Rome. That was our movie. That was the image we wanted to sell.

But James was only one of many blips on my media monitor.

The BBC story that aired last night, which included purloined battle footage and unauthorized interviews with some of our extras, repeatedly referred to this as "The Steven Spielberg movie." They also repeated the casting of former British soccer star Vinnie Jones – a rumor that had flown all across England and seemed to be making a return trip. The Beeb further noted that Nicole Kidman and Arnold Schwarzenegger were in the cast. Wow.

Maybe the stories about our budget spinning out of control after only two days of filming really were true?

On set, however, the production had other things to worry about. The 120-meter speed-track dolly popped a belt and it was fortunate that no one was hurt when the camera cart flew off. Repairs wasted half a day.

"Fucking Spielberg had twice as much time to film his opening battle sequence as I've got on this," a frustrated Scott referred to the recently released *Saving Private Ryan*.

Meanwhile, sound mixer Ken Weston was next in line for frustrations with our pugnacious protagonist. Russell had refused to wear a radio mike under his armor.

"Fucking prick," Ken began. "We're shooting the close-ups at the same time as the master and he wants us to get a bloody boom (microphone) in there. Let him do the fucking movie without dialogue, then. Probably be better off anyway."

Ken solved the problem by attaching a mike to the armor of the soldier to whom Russell was talking. Skirmish won - but another department had declared war on our star.

The EPK producer, John Pattyson, had missed a flight connection so I supervised the first day of behind-the-scenes taping in the forest of Germania. It would be our first test of Russell's cooperation with publicity.

The production crew were rigging effects, laying camera track and setting equipment for several hours before the big scene, so I had my guys shoot some of the preparation, including test runs of a mechanical horse ridden by a stunt Legionnaire who gets knocked out of his saddle by a club-wielding barbarian.

We started towards another hill where Ridley was rehearsing a scene in which actor Tomas Arana, as Roman officer Quintus, signals the assembled archers to fire flaming arrows.

A man in heavy armor approached us with a drawn sword.

"Come closer and I'll skewer ya," Russell jibed with camera-man Paul Bernard.

Paul laughed and kept rolling.

"Lovely day for a barbeque, mate," a cheery Crowe continued, indicating with his sword the smoldering corpse of a rubber barbarian. He kept doing this shtick for another five minutes before it became obvious he was running out of material. I made Paul put down his camera and introduced him and the sound recordist to the actor.

Russell asked about the jacket I was wearing from the golfing movie *Tin Cup*.

"You a golfer?" he made an effort not to sound disparaging. Nope.

He said he got his relaxation on horseback around his ranch. I told him I used to raise horses. He looked toward the other hill and asked if we'd been over there yet.

"Lots of fantastic war toys, catapults, semi-automatic bows. Everything a boy could wish for under the Christmas tree."

I told him we were on our way.

As we parted company, I began to wonder if there wasn't some cultural dynamic between our mostly British crew and our Kiwi-Aussie star I wasn't getting. The small number of American crew seemed to get along with him just fine. Dark, volatile, intense, churlish, Crowe was all these. But an asshole? Was I missing something? It would take me most of the movie to come up with a theory.

John Pattyson led the EPK crew onto the battlefield the next day and I was taking a tea break at our base camp when a tall man in Clark Kent glasses exited Russell's trailer and headed straight for me. Bob Long introduced himself, saying he handled "various business interests" for Russell. My bulletproof shield went up.

It started to snow and Bob invited me to join him in Crowe's sport utility van where we exchanged quips about the cold and tips about London restaurants. Then we arrived at his reason for this meeting.

"Tell me, honestly," his inner being leaned confidentially close, "what have you heard about Russell?"

If Show Business is life in a fishbowl, rumors are the refracted light sparkling off the glass, magnifying the ceramic castle, rippling in the wake of a waving tail - to be regarded as a distortion while acknowledging that something has created them.

I'd heard a lot of things about Russell – good and bad.

The good included his generosity with crew gifts, his support – on and off camera – of fellow actors, and the occasional production party he'd pay for out-of-pocket.

I'd recently been told about a friend of his whose jalopy of a classic Mercedes finally broke down beyond repair. Russell feigned admiration for a similar model in mint condition, bought it and asked his friend to "keep it for me to use when I'm in town." Of course, Russell had no intention of ever using it.

The bad... well, I didn't know how much was true, how much exaggeration, how much sour grapes. All I knew was I hadn't experienced any of it yet.

"Not much," I told him.

There are those who demand more of themselves than the world can demand of them - and they're pissed off at the world for asking so little. That seemed the most logical explanation I could come up with for Russell Crowe.

CHAPTER TEN

THE MORE YOU PLAY

Sam had sent me an e-mail following a phone call in which he'd said he was feeling bad about being "the last kid picked" on a playground basketball team. At the same time, some of his old friends were starting to "bug" him because they were "so immature."

Hi Daddy,
Another thing that I forgot to mention to you was that I don't think that I help the team out at all. Oh, I haven't noticed anyone make me feel bad. But what's bothering me is whenever like Noah or Carter or Alex get picked to go on a team, everybody has a look like "Yes! So-and-so is on our team!" but when I'm picked, they look at me like, "Oh, it's Sam. I guess we can live."

... I also have another problem. Every time Stevie and I get into a silly argument like whether E=MC2 is spoken: "E=MC squared" or "E=MC two," and I'm right and he's wrong, he always physically hurts me! Like today, with the E=MC2 thing, after he had found out he was wrong, and persisted that he was right still, he pinched my nose really hard! And that's not the worst part. Afterwards, when I told him it hurt, he tried to be so cute! He kept apologizing to me in a sweet little voice. It really got on my nerves! But I didn't want to hurt his feelings.

Please help me with these problems.

Your loving son,

Sam

"There's nothing harder than feeling like you're outgrowing your old friends and not yet fitting in with new ones," I sent back cold comfort. "I don't know if this will make you feel any better but I have to make new friends on every job and one thing I've learned is that the friends I start with at the beginning of a movie aren't always the same ones I come out with at the end. Maybe you have to try on friends like they were shoes to see which ones fit."

This dull counsel bordered on sage compared to the limpness of my efforts at making him feel better about his basketball skills.

"Keep that elbow lined up with the basket," I driveled. "Shoot with your fingertips." (*Here, lemme show you.*)

I concluded with a pathetic, "The more you play, the more you'll improve."

Right, Dad.

Jaap had a toothache that was getting worse. But he still greeted me at the start of our third week together like the boyhood chum he hadn't seen in years.

"Hello, my friend," he effused from the un-swollen side of his face. "So good to see you."

There is instant rapport that's circumstantial, instant rapport that's opportunistic, instant rapport that's pure chemistry, instant rapport from discovered commonalities and instant rapport of the trenches. On a film set it can be any combination of these. Despite initial misgivings about the headaches his inexperience might cause, it was impossible not to be instantly fond of Jaap.

"When are you gonna go to a dentist?"

He made excuses about not wanting to miss work. I told him I'd talk to Ridley. He said, rather weakly, he was still hoping it would go away.

"It's probably an abscess. It can kill you - if the pain doesn't make you wanna blow your brains out first."

But I suddenly had no more time for fraternal counseling. Across the camp, I saw a group of extras posing for a photo and hurried over there.

No unauthorized personnel are allowed to bring cameras to a movie set. It's standard in everyone's contract - including the extras. Still, it happens on most productions and responses to it vary. DreamWorks – and Spielberg in particular – had a policy of firing photo bugs on the spot.

The extras had been told - according to everyone with whom I'd spoken in our London casting department - not to bring cameras. This group reacted quickly and guiltily when I asked them to put this camera away and not bring it to the job again.

As I turned, I saw another photographer – not an extra hiding his instamatic in barbarian's fur but some dude in a black leather jacket with camera straps over each shoulder and a bazooka lens in front of his face.

"*Farnham Herald,*" he announced. "Here on assignment."

Our locations manager, Terry Blyther, got a couple of his men to show the *Farnham Herald* to the public walking paths.

There had already been a half-dozen extras who'd violated the "no talking to press" mandate: one did an interview with the BBC, two gave comments and posed for photos that appeared in

The Herald, two more posed for *The Daily Mail* and another gave an interview, along with inaccurate production information, to the *Surrey Advertiser*.

On another front, there was a certain Mr. Dickus - Biggus Dickus, as he was known in cyberspace. Mr. Dickus was an extra who filed daily reports on the *Ain't It Cool News* website about what was happening on our movie set. Photographs usually accompanied these half-informed bits of misinformation.

Another web writer recently reported the sighting of Arnold Schwarzenegger playing "the lead Barbarian." Surely Vinnie Jones couldn't be far behind.

The production, however, had bigger concerns than Mr. Dickus and his clique of clandestine camera bugs: we'd run out of approved script pages to shoot. The studio had green-lit the movie based on a compromise draft that everyone hoped needed only minor tuning. Everyone was wrong. Screenwriter David Franzoni was in London writing every day, meeting with Ridley Scott and faxing his output back to DreamWorks co-president – and former screenwriter - Walter Parkes every night. There were pages that Ridley rejected, pages that Parkes rewrote, pages that Russell shredded but every day there were just enough pages eking through to give us something to film.

On Friday, however, we'd come close to losing a day's work for want of a completed screenplay. The latest in the long line of script editors, Richard Harris, did not report to set because he didn't like the dialogue he'd been sent the previous night. Ridley, Branko and the a.d.s scrambled to cobble together a shooting day from pieces of alternate scenes that wouldn't suffer continuity gaffs. Somehow, they came up with just enough to keep the cameras rolling until dusk.

Rewriting the script was at the top of everyone's priority list as we began week three. But while Richard Harris was busy rejecting pages, actor Tomas Arana was turning entropy into opportunity. In his hotel room at night, or at the desk in his phonebooth-sized trailer between breaks in filming, the former avant-garde theatre veteran and Andy Warhol protégé was concocting scenarios in which his character, Field Marshal Quintus, might live to fight in Rome.

One idea he came up with - promoting the loyal centurion to captain of the Praetorian Guard – was championed by Russell who delivered his endorsement when he introduced Tomas to Walter Parkes. Ridley decided he liked the idea of using that character in a recurring role. So, the part of Quintus expanded from a minor character who disappeared when we left England to featured player who'd be with us through most of the filming in Malta. Tomas owed a debt to our star. But Russell wasn't collecting chits; he was adding his imprimatur.

Crowe, of course, had also been doing some writing and had come up with a new part of a scene wherein Maximus describes, in wistful detail, his family farm. This monologue lent weight to his quandary over whether to accept the supreme power offered him by Emperor Aurelius. It would be a powerful scene.

Russell was offering such constant creative input that, for a time, it almost seemed his vision was steering the movie. But only to the untrained eye.

Ridley had an operating principal about working with actor/script-doctors."If I don't like it," he would later explain, "I can always find a way to shoot so there's a piece I can use. It's easier than fighting with him."

There was no doubt who was in charge.

Still, a pattern was emerging: Scott and Crowe were beginning to find common ground in the way they perceived the organic thing that was once a realized screenplay and was now again a work in progress.

They needed to work fast. The arrival of Connie Nielsen who was to begin work with Richard Harris next week produced something like the sound of hoofbeats, warning our lensing legion that the time for script decisions could no longer be deferred.

Margaret called late that night, (Casey yelling in the background "Tell Dad I love him. I'm busy on the computer now"), her full-throated voice soothing, musical even in speaking, as she delivered the community news of the day, news of our life. We'd had six inches of snowfall that day and she'd have to call the plowing service again since another dusting was due overnight.

Thought anymore about coming to England?

"I thought we'd settled that. I can't (*read: won't*) take the boys out of school. And I have my own work."

Her own "work" consisted of two days a week volunteering for the school district committee on assistance for the disabled and one night a month singing at The Carriage House, a supper club in nearby Lansing. I bit my tongue. Hard.

Tell me more about the snow.

"Well, Gershwin loves playing in it," her voice brightened talking about our 130-pound, mixed-Labrador puppy. "The other day it was about three-feet deep and he must have been digging for a squirrel or something, he came back to the house and his head was completely covered in white!"

I could hear Casey laugh in the background. Gershwin always made Casey laugh.

Sam got on the phone.

"Hi Daddeeee! I read the script! Do they have anybody for the part of Maximus' son yet?"

What have I done?

Richard Harris arrived at base camp for his second day of filming and immediately had one of the production assistants summon the publicist to his trailer.

"I read that I am in a movie 'starring Oliver Reed,'" he evenly intoned. "I want you to make one thing perfectly clear to all of these... people: I would never be caught dead in a movie *starring* Oliver Reed. Are we understood?"

Okey dokey. I'll spread the word.

Branko approached me to announce in his most solemn manner, "I must tell you something important."

I'd learned by now that the 70-year-old producer often had "important," and even "very important," things to tell me that rarely weighed in with the gravity by which they were prefaced.

"Steven is coming here. Maybe tomorrow," he said in an excited stage whisper.

Branko's enthusiasm in heralding this news was understandable. Not too many years ago this tough-talking senior citizen, who still looked fit enough to lift an oxcart, was a production manager who supplied cheap Eastern European labor for Western television movies and low budget features filming in Yugoslavia. Then in 1992, he met "Steven" while scouting some locations for *Schindler's List*. As the story goes, Branko rolled up his sleeve and showed the famed filmmaker the numbers tattooed on his arm - a souvenir from Auschwitz when he was 13 years old. Steven then anointed him one of the film's producers. Surely there was more to it but the gist is probably not far off.

Spielberg had recently been attending the Berlin Film Festival and was scheduled to stop in London on his way back to New York. Branko believed he'd come by to visit Ridley on set.

I could hardly wait until the tabloids got hold of that tidbit - which Biggus Dickus or any one of a hundred other extras or crew would happily provide: "Spielberg visited the set of *Gladiator* to give Ridley Scott tips on directing his battle scene."

Ho, boy. Ridley, can I get you a new cigar? You seem to have crushed that one.

I waited around all the next day but Spielberg never showed up.

The British press, however, kept coming.

Unexposed Film:

Another page-three story in *The Daily Mail* featured four more photos from our set. There was an aerial shot captioned "Home Counties woodland has become scene of devastation for the film *Gladiator.*" Two others appeared to have been taken from the middle of one of our battle sequences. What pissed me off the most, however, was a shot of two of our barbarians posing for the camera: "Extras told not to wash for realism."

They were everywhere, these cameras. Despite my memos and repeated calls to our extras casting department reminding, pleading, insisting they tell their Legionnaires and Germanic hordes that anyone caught on set with a camera would be fired, there had only been an increase in camera sightings over the weeks. If a war were to break out between the shutterbugs in Royal Purple and the ones in animal skins, not a soul on the battlefield would survive un-photographed.

The Daily Mail article also confirmed for its readers that Nicole Kidman was in our movie. Careless of me not to have noticed.

One new star trailer had been planted in our base camp and a visage appeared, bundled and booted, in the bone-chilling bluster of our soggy surroundings: a young actor with whom I'd last worked when he was my son Sam's age.

The second son born to John Bottom Amram and Arlyn Dunitz Jochebed, who would also have three daughters, was now 24 years old. His parents were children of Aquarius and missionaries of a religious sect who commemorated their spiritual rebirth by renaming themselves Phoenix. His mother began calling herself Heart. The youngest boy sought a Christian name with the lyrical importance of his older brother River, and sisters Rain, Summer and Liberty. He christened himself Leaf.

This might have described how he felt in his early life as he floated through his family's moves from Puerto Rico, where he was born, to Florida, through Central and South America, west through

Texas to Oregon and finally to California where they settled in Los Angeles. Adapting to local custom there, the parents found a theatrical agent who would represent all five children in show business.

When *Gladiator* was being cast, Spielberg recommended Jude Law for the role of Commodus. But Ridley knew Joaquin Phoenix from a movie he'd produced, *Clay Pigeons*, and wanted to test him for it.

DreamWorks flew the young actor - who had appeared mainly in low-budget, offbeat, independent films during his adult career - to England where they arranged a screen test with Ridley directing. The day of the test, our would-be-Emperor would not come out of his dressing room. So, Ridley went in after him.

"Please, don't make me do this," the terrified performer pleaded. "I'll give you back the money for the plane ticket. I can't do it. I'm just a kid from Florida."

Ridley dragged him out, put him in front of the camera and told him to play the part. The director then cast him on the spot.

It was during his Leaf phase when we'd met on *SpaceCamp*, a box office flop released in the wake of the space shuttle Challenger disaster.

"I'd never seen so much junk food in my life," Joaquin laughed when I reminded him of our earlier connection. His first glimpse of craft services had left a lasting impression on the ten-year-old who'd been raised on bean sprouts and soymilk in a family of spiritual seekers and devout vegans.

Joaquin was now the same age his famous brother had been when a combination of drugs and alcohol induced the heart attack that killed him.

In the most cold-eyed view, I suppose healthy ideals and Hollywood reality are often an incongruous coupling.

"This is bad," I wrote in my journal the day after Valentine's Day. "Feel like I'm back to my old drinking habits - polishing off a bottle of wine in my room every night. Is it loneliness, work fatigue, staying in to try to stay out of trouble or a combination of all three?"

In truth, my old drinking habits had been a lot more extreme. When I first started traveling, I'd keep a quart of Jack Daniels in my room, supplement it nightly with drinks at a party or bar and still have to replace it every third day. A bottle of wine was temperate by comparison. But only drunks make those kinds of comparisons.

It had been many years since I curtailed the habit of drinking to excess when I went out. The compulsion to follow one drink with another now only came once I'd locked my hotel room and decided to kill off any impulses - or invitations - that might get me back out in the world. I was sealed in. Time to incapacitate myself. The Wolfman chaining the door so his bad self couldn't make mischief under the full moon.

I talked to Margaret every night. I wished that were enough. I'm not, by nature, a pack animal. But I was restless.

I took a short walk along Kensington High Street and stopped in a little side-street dive called Club 9 where a pair of friendly barmaids, Sarah from Australia and Angie from New Zealand, both said they'd like a job as my assistant - not that I'd mentioned there was one.

I chose not to stay 'til closing, as offered. There's danger under the full moon. Back at the hotel, I drank another half bottle of wine before succumbing to fitful sleep.

CHAPTER ELEVEN

TRUTH VS. FULL DISCLOSURE

The frozen morning rain would've made the battlefield too treacherous to work on but it didn't really affect us because Richard Harris had finally gotten dialogue pages he liked and we were shooting inside Marcus Aurelius' tent this Saturday.

Art director David Allday and set decorator Crispian Sallis had arranged an assortment of aged linens with sculptures and bronze to create rustic royalty. Cinematographer John Mathieson had lit the set with little more than a few candles.

Our crew needed a day of shelter from the elements. Nearly every department had been forced to replace some victim of immune system collapse for a day or two.

The director looked in need of some rest himself. His eyes were half-mast and watery, with flecks of red that stood out like wine-spill on a bridal gown.

"I'm fine," he smiled at my inquiring. "I'm not allowed to get sick."

Fortunately, the next day was Sunday. A full day of sleep for most of the crew - who would need it for our 5:00 call Monday morning.

I began Sunday, our day of rest, with a blood pressure test over morning coffee.

The Mail on Sunday carried a full-page feature with color photos under the banner headline "Spartacus of the Surrey Woods." A reporter named Michael Burke - with whom I didn't recall speaking - wrote with the authority of an insider:

"Several acres of woodland have been felled to form a Roman encampment for... *Gladiator* which started shooting last week with a 50 million pound budget, although it is rumoured the costs are already spiraling.

"... (Director) Scott has promised to replant the area when they leave but as these first exclusive pictures show, they have done almost as much damage so far as Caesar did 2,000 years ago."

At least he didn't blame Spielberg.

Being neither ill nor accustomed to getting up at 3:30 for a car pickup at 4:00, I spent the day trying to exhaust myself so I could get to bed early.

I walked across town to the Tower of London in less than two-and-a-half hours, slowing only to contemplate the heritage of Fleet Street.

The tabloids that were born here had been driving me crazy. They'd been inaccurate, irritating and invasive. But standing in the place where cheek and bombast had coalesced to make British journalism the most read and relied-upon news in the world, I felt something resembling respect. Reformist, right-wing or plain raun-chy, the British news media are all inheritors of a hard-won freedom.

If a publicist doesn't value that, he or she shouldn't be work-ing with the press. If a publicist holds the right-to-know *every-thing* as paramount to the interests of his or her client, he or she should not be a publicist.

There's a difference between truth and full disclosure.

Word came that Terry Press, head of DreamWorks' marketing department, was becoming increasingly vocal in her hostility to-wards the bloody images she was seeing from this film.

"I don't want to see *any* publicity getting out on that movie," was her reported reaction to footage in which a Legionnaire is be-headed, shortly before a German warrior takes an arrow through the neck, directly after another Roman loses a blood-spurting arm to a barbarian axe, shortly before the barbarian gets a spear in the eye. "It's disgusting."

She might not have been completely serious – or she might have been - but the DreamWorks marketing chief definitely would not want photographs or footage from today's sequence staring at her over tomorrow morning's latte.

The nervous guards stopped our car at the forest entrance and questioned the driver about whether he was carrying any camera equipment. There had been another BBC news broadcast last night. This time, the order to purge unauthorized photography had come from Branko.

"There was a camera crew here earlier," Mark Sumner rushed to tell me in the parking lot. "You'd told us not to let anyone shoot anything unless you were with them. But they said they *were* with you and, I mean, well, I hope that was right."

I found overeager cameraman Paul Bernard inside the makeup tent, videotaping the butchery being artfully applied to nearly

1,000 extras, including a cadre of real amputees who were having their stumps bloodied with food dye.

I led the video crew out of the tent into the woods, which had by now been thoroughly torched and uprooted. From a cart piled high with plastic limbs, heads and torsos, the set-dressing department was scattering body parts around the hills and valleys.

In the amputee unit, two one-armed Legionnaires were sword fighting with their detached limbs. A one-legged barbarian twirled his prostheses like a cheerleader's baton; another balanced his leg on the tip of one finger.

In another part of the forest, Clan McGregor, burly Scottish stuntmen who fought behind Wallace in *Braveheart*, were holding a family reunion. Brawny lads with bushy beards, they roared, bumped chests and banged shoulders like footballers psyching-up before a game. Hopefully, they would remember this was acting.

An icy wind cut through my bombardier's jacket, which, under layers of sweater, shirt and thermal shirt, had kept me warm enough all month. Not this morning. My teeth sounded like a horse running on pavement.

While the EPK crew followed a German with an arrow through his chest walking beside a man holding the axe that would later be fitted into his split skull, I headed towards the wardrobe trailer to see if they might have anything (*a spare animal skin!*) I could wrap around me.

In my haste to fend off hypothermia, I almost failed to notice Jaap frantically engaged with one of the grips.

"I left them right here!" he said, waving his arms in exasperation. "They can't have just walked away."

The grip walked away without a response.

My frenzied friend explained he'd lost his cameras - all but the one around his neck. They'd gone missing before - usually carted off by a crew member clearing the shot of everything that didn't look like it belonged in a German forest. But this time, no one remembered moving or even seeing them.

He was still searching when Terry Needham called "wrap" on the last shot of the day, Maximus walking the smoky killing grounds among the wounded.

Location manager Terry Blyther proudly reported his department had confiscated 24 cameras. Sadly, none of them were Jaap's.

My companion for the evening was marvelous Megan Drummond, a staff publicist for the international distributor UIP, with whom I'd had many a flirtatious phone call since our first meeting over lunch with DreamWorks' executive Peter Dunne. The six-foot, redheaded Aussie firecracker was inhaling champagne, pacing the evening with quick wit and fueling my fantasies with sassy innuendo. It was a cold, drizzly night, the kind where longings seek succor in the lazy intimacy of a private booth with a barman pouring and a hotel bed only an elevator button away.

We'd dined at an Italian restaurant across the street and had just settled into a cushy sofa in the Royal Garden lounge when Jaap suddenly appeared.

"I found them!" he declared without explaining to my date what 'they' were. "Someone had thrown a tarp over them!"

He had a quick beer with us before making a polite exit to drive back to Surrey where he was staying. Though it added two hours travel time to an already long day, he'd just wanted to share this triumph in person.

"You seem like old mates," Megan said after I explained the lengths to which he'd gone to deliver this good news.

I went on a bit about the battlefield bonding of military men and movie crews and we waved our glasses in a chorus of *People Who Need People*, rescuing the topic from toppling into maudlin, laughing like asylum inmates.

Her blue eyes fell on mine and she smiled. The moment hung.

"It is hard to be alone, away from everyone you know," her tone withdrew to a higher ground. We watched the rain lap against a window.

I could have continued in the comfort of her company all night – and there was that elevator button a tantalizing, short stroll across the lobby. But when the barman brought our evening to a close at around 1:30, I saw her to a cab.

It was a night of good stories and a few hours of battlefield bonding. Yet, riding the elevator alone, I fell into emptiness. Maybe a touch of regret.

Back in my room, I checked e-mail and found this:

"Hey, Daddy! Okay, here's the situation: I intercept a pass from a player on the other team during a scrimmage. Our last scrimmage for the rest of the year. I hear (the coach) shouting: 'Drive, Sam, drive!' I race down the court, keeping my eyes on the basket. I lift myself up into the air for a layup. I watch the ball slowly...go...into THE HOOP!!!!!!!!!!!!!!!!!!... It was the best feeling ever! I couldn't believe it! It was the first shot I have ever made in any actual game! Everyone was saying: 'Nice shot, Sam, nice shot!' I really, really, re-ally wish that you could've been there to see it. After I made it, I got totally inspired and I was darting all over the place, intercepting passes, getting rebounds and all that other stuff. I really think I might score a lot of points in our last game. I really hope I do because, well after all, it's our last game. I really hope spring (break) comes very soon because I want to see you soooooooooooooooooooooo badly, I can't stand it. I hope I'm not too big to jump into your arms because I might have grown since you've seen me. Will we visit you in your 4th month? I want to see you as soon as I can. Well, I'm going to watch a movie right now. I love you!!!!!!!!!
Love, Sam

P.S. I think you can just send in the money to Amazon for the CD I wanted and just write down where we live.

I contacted Amazon about the CD he wanted and wrote down where we lived.

Then I had my first good night's sleep in a week, dreaming of Margaret... or was it Megan?

Had I already begun forgetting where I lived?

"Hel-lo, Rob. James Bowman, *Farnham Herald*, here. Can you give us a comment about how it feels to be wrapping things up with *Gladiator* after all this time?"

I'd grown rather fond of James Bowman by now. Too fond to remind him we were far from "wrapping things up." After filming in Surrey these four weeks, we'd probably shot less than thirty minutes of a two-and-a-half hour movie.

"We're all gonna miss it here, James. Farnham's been good to us."

Well, it had.

What?

CHAPTER TWELVE

THE DIFFERENCE BETWEEN LIFE AND THE MOVIES

Our charter alighted on the short, empty runway, as two uniformed soldiers appeared from under the jaundiced lights of a terminal that was little more than an industrial warehouse in the middle of the desert. A coterie of silhouetted luggage handlers began swarming under the wings within minutes of touchdown.

Ouarzazate - pronounced Was-is-at - meant "The Quiet Place" in Berber. It seemed very quiet, indeed.

The French Foreign Legion were once the sole standard-bearers of European civilization here. But they were long gone. Our 200-man/woman traveling film army was surely the lone symbol of western culture in this primitive outpost now. Or so we thought crossing the tarmac, windswept sand pelting our faces.

The double doors of the Berbere Palace Hotel opened to a marble sea undulating with colorful carpets in a lobby big enough to accommodate the full cast of *Aida* with elephants. Through here, fez-topped porters escorted the Gladiator crew - including Ridley, Branko and all the actors except Russell - to the hotel's registration desk.

As we were handed our keys, some among the flight-fatigued film folk headed straight to their rooms to collapse. Others, depending on present state of inebriation and desire to maintain it, went straight to the bar.

Nearly every table, chair and couch in the spacious cocktail lounge was occupied and the two-man, synthesizer lounge band was in mid-medley of Sting's Greatest Hits (the Police years). I spotted the ruddy cheeks and shock-white hair of Eamonn, one of our camera assistants, patting an empty barstool, waving me to join him.

Along with some of the other camera boys at Eamonn's end of the counter were two unfamiliar, unshaven men to whom he introduced me.

"Operator and loader on the Italian movie shooting here," Eamonn said after their names, which I couldn't hear through the din. "They're staying at the Belere but they say this is the best bar in town. I told 'em Ridley knows how to treat a crew, all right."

He hoisted a salute to The Guv'ner himself, sitting a few stools away. Ridley lifted his scotch in our direction. A bartender hurried over to take my drink order.

Jaap's head appeared above the crowd and he wended his way to my corner.

"Just ran into a grip I'd worked with in Prague," my friend reported. "He's here on a movie called *Shaka Zulu* starring..." his periscope neck scanned the room, "that fellow from the TV program. The one with the honeys in bikinis."

Eamonn had spotted him earlier. Hard to have been in the bar five minutes and not noticed. Broadly gesturing and laughing so loudly at his own jokes it took the collective efforts of the rest of the room to raise enough decibel level to muffle him, none could doubt, here was a STAR: David Hasselhoff, in the flesh.

How many movies were filming in this little desert outpost, I wondered aloud?

"Five, I think," answered one of the Italian camera crew. "And there's a Paramount picture with Tommy Lee Jones and Samuel Jackson coming to town next month. Offices are down the block. I dropped off my CV this morning."

Images of veiled hatcheck girls and men in plaid jackets reading *Islamic Daily Variety* were forming an Arabic Polo Lounge in my mind when I felt a hand on my shoulder.

"I thought that was you," the sandy-haired man said, smiling. "Karen's over there. Can you join us?"

At that moment, it didn't seem the least bit odd to see Rob Cowan in Ouarzazate - until he told me he wasn't working on a movie here.

Rob was president of production for Irwin Winkler, producer of such cinema landmarks as the *Rocky* series and *Goodfellas*. He was here on holiday with his wife Karen, whom I'd met when we all worked on *At First Sight* in New York three years ago. Rob and Karen had been high school sweethearts in Victoria, B.C., went separate ways after graduation, got back together 11 years later and have rarely been apart since.

I followed him to their table where Karen explained how, of all the gin joints in all the world, they'd wound up in this one.

"We have a lot of Moroccan furniture," she laughed. "We thought we oughta see the place where our furniture comes from."

They'd most recently been in Marrakesh where they purchased several rugs from a merchant whose eldest daughter "wants to get into special effects."

"We can't seem to escape the movie business," Rob shrugged.

Karen insisted he tell what happened on the drive here.

Crossing the Atlas Mountains, they'd stopped at a café suggested by their driver for its scenic beauty. Overlooking a lush valley in which women carried bundles of branches and men led small donkeys swaybacked with grain sacks, the Cowans breathed deeply of the rustic, rural life of the Berbers. Waiting for the torpid service, serenity settled over them like the shade of a date palm as they spun an idle glance toward the café's only other occupied table.

And there, enveloped in the same tranquility, was Lily Tomlin.

So, they proceeded to Ouarzazate.

I invited them to dinner but it was late and they begged off. They were leaving early the next morning for Agadir.

"Get away from the Show Biz crowd," Rob said, only partly joking.

"We hope," added his spouse.

The next morning on my way to breakfast, I ran into actress Karen Allen.

I'd seen her on television just last week in a re-run of *Starman*. Now here she was in the flesh at Morocco's Hollywood Hotel.

I clearly remembered a conversation I'd had with her at an Academy Awards party at Ken Regan's. She dimly remembered meeting me, if at all. She'd been married then; now, I learned, she was not. Here in this desert of limited social resources, visions of late-night cocktails by poolside with the sexiest woman ever to sucker-punch Indiana Jones began creeping like parched Legionaries toward an oasis.

Suddenly, an enormous shadow fell over us. A gigantic man with a politician's grin seemed to be blocking all escape routes.

"You're the publicist," he said before his own name. His name, Ralf Moeller, was unfamiliar.

I offered my hand, my own name and an introduction to the well-known actress.

"Yes, I've seen you before," he nodded politely to Karen but without a major shift in attention from the publicist. "I have a publicist in L.A. and another in Germany. Maybe you can give me your contact numbers so they can call you later. They'll tell you about my acting credits. I was also Mr. Universe in 1985. Maybe there's a story."

Great. Useful. Thanks.

"I just finished a season of *Conan, the Barbarian*. You know, of course, the movie - with Arnold? I worked with Arnold on *Batman and Robin*. Arnold and I are great friends. Ridley had wanted him to do this role but he was busy. So, he said, 'You should call my friend Ralf Moeller.' It was maybe too small a part for him."

I was beginning to notice speech patterns - like the way his voice trailed off towards the end of a story, as though he were losing interest in what he was saying. I found that strangely endearing. And slightly soporific.

Karen's driver appeared at the door. She had to go to work, starring opposite David Hasselhoff in *Shaka Zulu*. Ralf asked her to pass along his regards to David, whom he knew from Germany, told her it was nice meeting her and hoped they would work together someday - all with barely a break in his monologue to me.

"I play Vibius. The champion gladiator in Proximo's training camp. Russell and I are rivals. But I have some ideas I've been talking to Ridley about that Vibius and Maximus team up and become friends. Maybe Juba too. Like the Three Musketeers."

Three Musketeers. Candybar. Hadn't eaten breakfast yet.

"I think there was one of the drafts where Juba doesn't become such friends with Maximus and instead I talk to him about what it means to be a gladiator. I tell him, you know, the philosophy of the gladiators."

I idly returned the wave from a pair of crew acquaintances passing by.

"But you don't care," Ralf's voice trailed off.

I re-racked my focus and watched his eyes follow his cascading verbiage to his shoes.

"I do care, Ralf," I smiled. And I suddenly did find myself caring for this unexpectedly abashed behemoth.

His hand swallowed mine, crushed and ratcheted once as the big grin returned above his Joe Palooka jaw.

"We'll talk again. We can have a drink out by the pool sometime," he said before striding to the cashier's window to exchange some deutschmarks for the local dirham.

The Roman network of roads extended from Baghdad to Britain and from the northern Danube to North Africa.

However, there was no evidence the Romans ever set a stone south of the Atlas Mountains. Until now.

"This wasn't so hard," Ridley told me as we began our first day of filming. "On *Thelma and Louise* we had to cut the entire road that we used (in the climax) through to the edge of the cliff. This one we just had to widen enough to get our vehicles through to base camp."

The road in question lay behind us: about ten kilometers of crushed rock on which our trucks and vans had been crossing all morning.

The road it joined was a jagged trail, etched into the earth by centuries of tribal traders from the Ante Atlas, now lined with wooden animal carts for our first shot of the day.

This was the Caravan Scene in which Maximus, having been found unconscious by slave traders, awakens to discover he's been added to the menagerie of livestock on the way to market. Beside him in the slave wagon is Juba, the Nubian captive played by Djimon Hounsou.

I hadn't met Djimon yet but spotted him talking with one of the animal trainers by a lion's cage, so I walked over and introduced myself.

With skin so smooth it seemed to reflect the sun, perfect teeth and classic cheekbones, he could appear too handsome for the role of a prisoner languishing in the careless charge of nomadic meat merchants. Perhaps to offset this, he had a patch of what looked like industrial carpeting on his head. I thought I'd only glanced at it but he brought it into our discussion.

"The only thing I'm a little worried about is getting type cast in slave roles," he fretted, referring to his career-making turn in Spielberg's *Amistad*. "I think it's all o.k., except for this hairpiece that looks like I've just come from a Southern plantation, you know? I asked Ridley about it but he likes it for the character, so I can't argue, can I?"

Arguing wasn't in Djimon's nature. Patience was his strength. After his searing performance in *Amistad*, there were predictions of superstardom but his follow-up film had been a disappointment. He lay quiet and waited. This was his chance to be rediscovered but he would handle it the way he handled everything in his life and work: with the power of patience.

The two busiest persons at location this morning were animal unit coordinator Ian Hickinbotham and chief animal trainer Sled Reynolds.

Sled, one of a handful of American department heads on the crew, was running between cages, making sure the animals were being properly handled.

"Has somebody watered those crocodiles this morning?"

He and Ian went down the line inspecting the hyenas and vultures that had been imported from Paris, the white oxen that had been trucked over from Spain, the lions and leopards from the zoo in Rabat.

These zoo animals were of greatest concern.

"Yeah, they're more dangerous," Sled told an inquirer. "They're wild and they're not used to being this close to people. But Branko got 'em cheap. So, here they are."

Wagons loaded with bric-a-brac and straw filled out the caravan between the livestock carts. John Mathieson had his A-camera in place on a truckbed and a second camera positioned on the ground.

The stand-ins were asked to step out of the shot and Djimon took his place on one of the wagons. Coincident to this, a white Ford Explorer pulled up near the playback tent and Russell emerged. He climbed into the wagon and lay down on the rough planks.

Ridley examined the camera beside the slave cart, instructing Djimon how far to bend into frame over the prone Maximus. Russell feebly rose on one elbow, as instructed, then repeated the action until Ridley was satisfied the two actors had their movements right. As Russell reclined into starting position, Ridley returned to the monitors beside the A-camera on the truckbed.

Jamming a fresh cigar between his lips, rubbing his hands together, the director peered at the images on two small screens.

"Get the fucking pillow out from under his head," Ridley shouted through the unlit Habana. "He looks like he's taking a nap in his hotel."

His eyes danced as he removed the cigar.

"Action."

The caravan moved into its second half of the filming day and bad tempers were not limited to the snapping hyenas.

Things had started off rather slowly.

The day's scenes were no more difficult than any of those shot in England - in many ways, easier. The weather was mild, we weren't choreographing the movements of armies and Ridley had put greater distance between him and the studio "suits."

But what seemed to be worse on this first day in Morocco than ever in England was Russell's discontent. He was more unhappy with the script, more unhappy with his wardrobe, unhappy with the sun in his eyes, unhappy with the long waits between setups, unhappy with the squalls of the animals. Some of those were things he and Ridley had in common. However, our star was now more comfortable about publicly demonstrating his displeasure. This was not a director who would tolerate that sort of disrespect.

"That fucker," Ridley snarled, heading back to his trailer at lunch break. "He thinks he can pull that shit with me. I'll go back to Hollywood and bury him."

But Russell was only doing what Russell had always done.

"He does some actory thing where he behaves like the character," a crew member with whom he'd previously worked had warned me. "On L.A. Confidential he played a guy who was very protective of women so around Kim Bassinger he was always gracious and polite. In Mystery Alaska, he'd just learned to play hockey but his character was captain of the team so he started telling everybody how to run the plays."

And here he was playing a general. In his own "actory" mind, *he* was supposed to be giving the orders.

This was going to be interesting.

Pressed against the carrot-colored walls of Café Dimitri that night, were Mark Hamill, Robert Redford and Bo Derek. They weren't waiting for a table; they were in frames beside Anthony Quinn, John Wayne, Marilyn Monroe, Elizabeth Taylor and James Dean. The outpost elegance of the room, white linen, uniformly angled tables and uniformed waiters, offset the quirky collection of movie memorabilia.

In the flesh on this evening, was star of film, television and concert halls, the omnipresent David Hasselhoff. As in past encounters, he was heard before seen, shouting in German to someone seated on the other side of the room.

I'd walked here from happy hour at the Palace bar with the ladies from our accounting department and our gaffer, Roger Lowe. Our head of accounting was a sedate, middle-aged American named Crystal. She planned to have a nice dinner, retire to her hotel room with a good novel and call her husband in California.

But tomorrow was our first day off and the other women from Crystal's office were ready to leave their calculators and inhibitions behind locked studio doors. Let the real Gladiator games begin!

Entertainment choices in Ouarzazate were limited - as were women for whom ritual stoning wasn't a recommended prophylactic. Betty was of-a-certain-age and had been around-the-block, location-wise. For younger lasses Helen and Carmel, this was their first time with a movie crew on foreign soil and they were ripe for the range of possibilities. Conveniently, the satyr seated between them was an experienced guide through the lower levels of location debauchery.

Single and denying fifty with impish allure, Roger Lowe was our key lighting designer. He had come late to the motion picture game from the world of advertising account management.

One day on his way up the corporate ladder, something snapped. He saw the end of his life as though it were coming tomorrow. But instead of experiencing it in an explosive fatal moment, it came in a slow-motion dissolve, a life simply disappearing into a scene in which his character no longer had a part.

The thunderclap of the slamming door through which he exited his corporate incarnation still resounded in the halls of his psyche.

Roger had already thrown down two or four beverages at the Palace bar and was pouring his third glass of wine here when he abruptly became annoyed at the slowness of the restaurant's service - forgetting that slow service was as much a part of Moroccan tradition as prayers at sunset.

Roger spotted a lean, bespectacled man in the pantaloons, spangled vest and blowsy shirt that identified the waiters and, with a boorish fingersnap, called him to our table.

"Mr. Peepers," Roger addressed the bewildered server. "We wish to place our order. *Parles Ingles?*"

The nametag on his vest read Saeed.

"Yes, I do speak English," Saeed replied in a soft tone with a hurt look.

My father always had the irritating habit of trying to get waiters or waitresses to laugh at his cornball humor. Part of this, I'm sure, was simply showing off. Another part was because he grew up poor, never went to a restaurant as a youth, and came from a clannish family who only invited outsiders to dinner when they were serious candidates for marriage. The lesson he took away from this was, when dining with strangers, i.e., your brother's fiancée or a waiter, someone needs to break the ice.

"Sai-eed? Is that how you pronounce your name?" I asked. "This is Roger. Roger, this is Sai-eed." I continued around the table, introducing us all. "Everything smells so good, we can hardly wait to start eating. And I'll bet we can order really fast."

Saeed seemed unable to tell whether I too was somehow insulting him.

"Let's start with Roger." A look. "In English – if you can."

Saeed didn't crack a smile. He took our orders, then hurried off to the kitchen. When dinner arrived, the tagines of beef, chicken and vegetables seasoned with prunes, raisins and curry proved worth the wait. We all made a point of calling Saeed by name and praising the dishes as if he'd personally prepared them. He seemed to warm throughout the evening and bade us a courteous goodnight at the end.

"*Hashumah*," he nodded to me as we got up to leave. At least I thought that was what he said. The Berber equivalent of, "don't come back?"

Jaap and I spent our day off hiking Todra Gorge, a narrow canyon at the foot of the High Atlas, once populated by bandits and lions, now home to two hotels and countless tour groups. That night I had a lovely dinner with lovely Karen Allen in our hotel pizza restaurant and after she retired for an early-morning set call, I dropped by the lounge for a nightcap.

Roger was there, hunched over and barely able to lift his arm for a handshake.

"I threw my back out dancing last night," he winced. "I'm getting old."

The pains of an aging sybarite came as no surprise to anyone. But in the middle of the lounge, no more than twenty feet from where we stood at the bar, was a vision of something truly astonishing.

Newly arrived Oliver Reed sat at a table conversing with an actor I knew only as The Scribe, the unfortunate prisoner chained to Ralf's Vibius in the upcoming training arena scene. A pale, thin man in his thirties or forties, he gesticulated with waggling upturned fingers, searching for *les mots juste,* as the tanned, robust gent in the opposite chair leaned forward, poised to catch the phrase when it fell.

The Scribe completed his thought, lifted his cocktail glass and they both leaned back. That's when I saw it.

On the table in front of Oliver was a cup and saucer. Nearby was a short, steaming metal pitcher. At the edge of the saucer, as shocking as if it were a glass eye, lay a small, perforated tin sphere, its short chain coiled. A tea ball.

Oliver Reed was drinking tea!

At another table, Ridley was having a scotch with a man in a blazer and open-collared shirt whom I'd never seen before.

"I think that's the new writer," one of the boys at the bar guessed.

Trying out a new transportation arrangement with Jaap as our first full week here began, our shared driver, Mustafa, had taken him to the set at crew call and returned to pick me up after breakfast.

It was a half-hour drive to the Fint Valley where we were scheduled to finish the last piece of our Slave Caravan sequence. Among the highlights of the day's work would be a scene in which a Lone Traveler peers out over a vast desert and sees the serpentine procession of the slavers' march of misery. In the role of the Lone Traveler was our executive producer, Branko Lustig.

I thought it somewhat odd seeing our equipment trucks passing in the opposite direction as Mustafa's car neared the base camp. However, a few trucks and most of the actor's trailers, as well as the catering tent, were still embedded when I arrived.

I found Branko, dressed in an Arab robe, sitting near one of the trailers.

"Don't bother me now," he said as I approached. "I'm practicing looking lonely."

Jaap was dutifully waiting for me in the catering tent. Well, not so much dutifully waiting as chatting up the pretty Moroccan catering girl while waiting for a ride back to the hotel.

"We're wrapped for the day," he informed me. "Russell's sick."

I set off to get details from one of the assistant directors, when I came upon the company nurse, Nicki Gregory.

I asked about the health of our star.

"Right, Russell has a... stomach virus," she pursed her lips. "The insurance doctor has signed off and, well, there you have it. Ridley gets an extra day to work on the script with the new writer. Handy."

Nicki had spent most of the morning at Russell's villa. She described it as being even more impressive than his mansion in

Surrey: it had a large pool, of course, game room, panoramic views and no fewer than nine servants on call 24 hours a day.

"Nine servants constantly refilling my Coke glass, I didn't want to leave," she exclaimed with her usual compassion for human weakness, in this case her own.

"It was really the first time I've sat down and talked much with Russell. He was very chatty. Surprisingly candid. Wanted to know what I thought about the script. I wasn't about to go there. But he was very nice."

First a.d. Terry Needham didn't like to be asked questions. He didn't like much of anything, except a pint at the end of the workday, a round of golf on Sundays and his racehorses whom he missed like most of us missed two-legged loved ones.

So, Terry, what's our plan for the day?

"Plan? Well, our fucking actor's sick, idden ee? Plan? We plan to shoot what we can of the fucking movie without him. That's our plan."

Very helpful.

I found second a.d. Adam Sumner who told me Ridley would shoot Branko's Lone Traveler scene, then turn the second unit over to Terry for insert coverage while he went back to the hotel to work on the script.

I went back to find Jaap.

"Ready to go?" he asked.

I explained that he needed to stay to cover Branko's scene.

He went pale.

"But all my camera gear is on the truck."

"So, get it off the truck."

"It's already left camp!"

With no photographer for his scene, Branko wouldn't have to work as hard at looking lonely.

While the main unit equipment trucks - along with Jaap's equipment - were on the move to tomorrow's location and most of the first unit crew had gone to deepen their tans by the hotel pool, a few key personnel stayed behind to work with the second unit.

Sled Reynolds was wrangling the animals - and burying two of them: the crocodiles hadn't survived the desert heat. A team of locals could be seen on the northern horizon digging a large hole.

"I tried to tell 'em," was the sum of his eulogy.

Sound mixer Ken Weston had stuck around as well, though the rest of his department had already returned to the hotel on a crew van.

Ken was staring off toward the west, watching purple shadows play in the crags of the Ante Atlas, a baseball cap protecting him from cooking like the crocs.

"Beautiful, idn't it?" he asked without turning.

I'd liked Ken from first meeting. He worked hard at overcoming a tendency toward cynicism and his wrestling matches with that side of himself were open to the public. Under the tough guy shell was a poet and a sentimentalist.

Ken was here with his girlfriend, Clementine, a taciturn Parisienne whom he employed as his assistant. Ken and Clem had met in Argentina where he was doing sound on *Seven Years in Tibet* with Brad Pitt and she was doing this-and-that as a production assistant in the art department. Ken's boom operator, a Jamaican-born Englishman named Colin, had taken her out to dinner a few times and introduced the two of them.

Ken was living out the last choking days of a long quavering marriage, which he was still trying to save. His wife had visited in Buenos Aires but convinced him it was "too expensive" for him to make the trip home for the holidays.

Clementine had joined the show through an art department connection to escape a bad boyfriend and had neither motivation nor finances to return to France for Christmas.

So, while everyone else flew off towards the opposite Pole for the holiday break, Ken and Clem were left alone together at that romantic time of year.

"Hey, Colin, looks like yer boss nicked yer bird," crew members taunted when the production reconvened in January.

Now, Ken and I stood at the edge of the desert with, as he would say, "fuck all to do" for the moment.

I asked about his day off yesterday.

"Went to a friend's funeral. Enrico Sabbatini. D'ja know him?"

I knew who he was: a costume designer, former Academy Award nominee (*The Mission*), who'd recently turned to production design.

"One of the sweetest men I've ever known," said Ken. "Amazing talent. He loved this part of the world."

Sabbatini had first started coming here on some low budget Italian productions in the mid-1970s. He kept returning. As an artist, he was inspired by the light in this area and soon came to love the easy pace of life here. He had been working on the mini-series *Cleopatra* when, on the way to a location, his car went over a cliff.

"He'd probably driven across those mountains a hundred times. Then, one time coming back from Marrakesh, his car missed a turn and that was it. I s'pose it's not a bad way to go if you think about it. Doing what you love in a place you love. Here one day, the next, no worries. We've all gotta go, don't we? Quicker the better."

I agreed.

"I've got cancer. D'ja know?"

I told him I had heard.

"'Living with it' is the expression, idn't it? I've probably learned to live as a result of it actually."

His cancer had come at the same time he and his wife had decided to divorce. On top of that, both his parents were dying, he was moving and he'd just gotten an Oscar nomination for his work on *Evita*. He got news of his cancer on the same day he got news of his Academy Award nod. "Like getting a handshake from somebody holding one of those 'lectric shockers, y'know?

"Then just when it seemed like the bottom had dropped out, I met Clem and she started me on the road to recovery. Turned my whole attitude around. Got help from the Cancer Center and I started learning how to face life - whatever portion of it I had left."

The Cancer Center was a facility for holistic treatment in London where he learned to let go of his anger. Clementine had encouraged him to go there and stuck with him while he worked his way through the fear and bitterness.

"It was everything at once, really. I don't think emotions necessarily caused the cancer but the illness was certainly my body telling me to take a breather. I look back on the time before the cancer and all I remember is anger. I was especially bitter about the divorce.

"The Oscar nomination was the one good thing that happened. I thought that was a pretty big deal but cancer certainly has a way of putting things in perspective, dudn't it? My illness was really a gift in that way. I used to waste a lot of energy getting annoyed about petty things. I wasn't a bit upset when I didn't win the Oscar because I'd just gotten a good report from the doctor a little while before. Awards are just such trivial bullshit next to everything else."

Ken had been looking at me as he said all this but now he turned back to the sun-drenched mountains and lifted his head to the cool of the morning breeze.

"Day like this, place like this, yesterday and tomorrow are illusions, aren't they? All you've got is right now. And look at it."

For the first time that morning, I did.

CHAPTER THIRTEEN

WHO ASKED YOU?

A UNESCO World Heritage site, the kasbah of Ait Benhaddou was a milk chocolate citadel whose mottled towers draped sunsplash filigree over apartments in which the lives of the few remaining occupants hadn't really changed in 500 years.

It's not the U.N. or the Moroccan government but the movies that have been the principal preserver and restorer of this antiquity.

The young men lounging outside the shops across the river will tell the gullible that *Lawrence of Arabia* was shot here. The half-truth is, there was a bit of second unit filming done here but most of *Lawrence* was shot in Spain and Jordan.

However, Zeffirelli's *Jesus of Nazareth* did have scenes at Ait Benhaddou. Deborah Winger spent time filming parts of

The Sheltering Sky here and Michael Douglas walked the narrow paths inside these walls during a sequence from *Jewel of the Nile*. The guidebooks claim approximately twenty films have been shot here.

It is fairly certain that few movies ever spent as much time for as many key sequences here as *Gladiator* would. Surely none had redesigned the place to the extent our art department did for this movie, compiling 30,000 mud and straw bricks into an amphitheater that seated more than a thousand spectators and looked as if it had done so for nearly two millennia.

John Pattyson and his EPK crew had flown in last night and were on duty filming behind-the-scenes today.

"Shoot the extras, shoot the camels! I want some panoramas from the highest spot you can get to on that mountain," Pattyson pointed. "Shit, I hope we brought enough tape."

At a certain point in every movie, even the most marginal crew member pauses to assess what the project's chances for success might be. It's always nice to be associated with a winner, even if you're the third assistant plasterer working two days as a local hire.

Despite a script with more holes than a swiss cheese, a temperamental star and a studio that was lashing the filmmakers to a contentious budget, this movie felt to most of us like it had the markings of a champion.

Russell's mercurial moods in no way detracted from his performance. The supporting cast wore their screen skins like they were born in them. Production designer Arthur Max - with help from Mother Nature and centuries of indigenous architecture - had designed backdrops against which a true epic could unfold. Ridley was as sure-handed and attentive to detail as any director in the business.

But a movie is like a great work of blown glass: one hairline crack can turn it from art to junk.

Ridley and djellaba-hooded John Mathieson discussed the first shot of the day: the gladiator slaves marching to their fate in the provincial arena through a corridor dripping red-dyed yarn, hyphenated by strings of red peppers and butchered meat dangling from thatched stalls, all fogged-over by steaming vats of smoke effects.

In setting up the scene, second a.d. Adam Somner lined one section of the corridor with children sitting atop grain sacks.

But when the cameras rolled and the frightened slaves processed through the market, something looked dreadfully wrong — at least to me.

Ralf, in the middle of the pack of mordant men, strode through the corridor grinning and slapping "high fives" with the kids like he was heading for the Super Bowl. Had Ridley directed him to do this?

Surely, I thought, this was an actor improvisation gone awry and the director would correct it on the next take.

But Ralf continued this anachronistic Americanism on all the subsequent takes of that shot, as well as the first few takes when we switched camera angles.

I exchanged looks with Pattyson.

"Does that look as bizarre to you as it does to me?"

He gave a dubious nod.

The terrified faces of the other gladiators as they marched toward impending slaughter were being totally eclipsed by Mr. Universe mugging for a World Wrestling match.

We rolled film on the scene again and, after this take, Ridley finally did tell Ralf to tone it down a bit. But the action still looked misplaced at best.

I've rarely been so depressed after watching a scene being filmed. It didn't take long to dawn on me why: it was the first time I'd really thought about how badly I wanted this to be a great movie.

I sidled up to Terry Needham. If anyone would have the balls to tell Ridley about this gross distortion, he would.

"Don't you think Ralf is overdoing the football star routine just a bit?"

"Bugger off," Terry walked away.

I found Ridley's young assistant Millie and cautiously shared my concerns.

"I totally agree. It was awful. Took you right out of the scene."

Glad to hear you say it. When you mention it to Ridley, feel free to let him know I support...

"I'm just a lowly assistant, I can't say anything," she exclaimed. "But I think you should tell him."

Okay.

I'm just a lowly publicist - but here goes.

The next night, for the first time since we'd started filming, I went to dailies. Dailies (sometimes called "rushes") are printed film clips from the previous day's work. The director watches these to note his preference of takes for the editor and to see if there's anything he has to reshoot before the sets are struck and actors dismissed.

Some directors make it tacitly - if not explicitly - mandatory for department heads to attend screenings of dailies, often catering them with drinks and sandwiches, sometimes even putting in temporary music just to make them more entertaining.

Ridley didn't appreciate a crowd at dailies. This was not a party and he definitely wasn't looking for anyone's input. If you didn't have professional concerns connected to editing or shooting the film, you were unwelcome.

The last time I offered an opinion to a filmmaker about raw footage, I was watching a rough cut of a scene in the trailer of director Ron Shelton, whom I considered a friend. The movie was *Cobb* and the scene involved Robert Wuhl and Tommy Lee Jones in an interaction that, to me, was missing a beat or two. I shared that opinion, I thought tactfully, with my friend.

"Goddamn it, don't you know what the hell a rough cut is?" the director shouted. "This is my draft. If I want your *notes*, I'll ask for them."

Pattyson, whose success as a documentary producer was attributable in large part to his fearless indifference to protocol, came with me to the conference room on the Berbere Palace mezzanine where a projector, screen and chairs were set up. We sat behind Branko, who turned once in silent questioning at the brazenness of our presence but said nothing.

There on the screen, over and over, we watched Ralf dominating the frames of a scene that - save for his overacting - had the potential to be poignant and terrifying. When the lights went up, Pattyson and I exchanged confirming glances. Somebody had to say something – for the good of the film.

But before taking our "notes" to the director, we cornered cinematographer John Mathieson outside the screening room.

"Did that look as bad to you as it did to us?"

"What?"

The big guy in the short skirt playing pattycake.

"Oh, yeah, Ralf," Mathieson chuckled. "That's a thing about Ridley: he knows what he needs and he knows what he can fix in the editing. You needn't worry. He saw the same takes we did. He's not an idiot."

Right. Knew that.

Thus absolved of my duties as film critic, I retreated to publicity anonymity juggling two thoughts: first, if Ridley had made a misstep, there was no one in that room with the guts to tell him. Second, Russell wasn't in that room.

CHAPTER FOURTEEN

CIRCLING

I went back to my hotel room to wait for a phone call from producer Gail Katz, who wanted to talk about *The Perfect Storm*. I'd already missed one call and the note slid under the door said she'd call again later. I'd kicked my shoes off and curled up with a book when the phone rang. It was Margaret.

"Oh, I'm glad I got you in."

Me too.

Communications home from Ouarzazate had been difficult. Cell phone service was spotty and we'd had a couple of rocky recent conversations when we did connect.

"Are we sure about this?" she began. "I mean can we afford it?" She was talking about her planned trip to Morocco.

We can't afford not to do it, I replied with unintended harshness.

I knew it wasn't that she didn't want to see me. I also knew her reluctance to come to Morocco had many complicated rationales. But I was being selfish.

The first two weeks on any film are a cauldron of personalities, rapid-fire data exchange and organizational juggling in which days blend into a soup of events and there's no time to think about anything but the job. It usually wasn't until the third week that missing Margaret became a misery. By the fourth week, the misery became an ache.

I hadn't seen my wife in six weeks. Not a lifetime. Not even the longest we'd been apart, not by half. But six weeks was around the time I hit the wall. Past week six, the pain doesn't intensify, it just becomes part of one's musculature - like an injury that's left you with a limited range of motion for which there is no therapy.

Still, my pains were trivial compared to those I was asking my spouse to undergo: Margaret would be at an unreachable distance from her children for the first time since they'd been born.

I need to see you, I told her.

"I know," she said. "I'm dying to see you too."

The rest of the conversation went much better.

When we hung up, I tried to return to my reading. But I couldn't focus.

I wandered down to the lounge and found Jaap talking to skin-headed, gap-toothed Fred-the-Spark, the electrical department Best Boy, about his dune buggy ride across the desert this past weekend, where he "wound up in a bloody mansion in the Fint Valley havin' tea and goin' 'wow!'" at his host's art collection. Fred looked and talked like a cockney dockworker, lived to ride motorcycles, was university educated and a serious student of classical painting.

Judi Dickerson, Russell's dialect coach joined us. This was Judi's third movie with Russell. She began coaching him in a complex mid-Atlantic accent for his role in the upcoming Michael

Mann movie. A former drama teacher at the University of Idaho, Judi was an effervescent sprite who filled conversational cups the moment they emptied.

The wine, ale and anecdotes continued as Djimon, having bid farewell to his ladylove at the airport, fell in with our gang. After an initial welcoming round, the group splintered into factions: Jaap and Fred talking dune buggies, Judi and visual effects assistant Emma talking about the "secret back room" of the jewelry store across the street, and Djimon and me talking about life, love and our movie.

Djimon's beloved was an actress-writer-producer-director named Victoria.

"I miss Victoria so much already, I can't stand it," he gave a giddy laugh. "How do you stand being away from your wife? Maybe after we've been married for a while it gets easier, eh?"

Well, yes and no.

I changed the subject.

How'd the first few days of filming go for you?

"I don't know," he began. "I know Ridley is busy rewriting the script. I don't like to bother him. I see Russell making such a fuss every day. Every day he has some other piece of dialogue to complain about. Or a scene that doesn't let him do what he wants. It's not my style to say something. But I see my part getting smaller - and it's alright if it makes the movie better. Except other people who say something to Ridley seem to have their parts getting bigger and I don't think it's all so good for the movie."

You've heard about the squeaky wheel?

"That's just not me. It's not the way I was raised. I was raised by my brother who was very strict. He would never let me complain about anything. So, I learned not to complain."

He told about his boyhood in Benin, West Africa and I asked him about reports I'd read of his being homeless in Paris.

"Whenever they interviewed me for *Amistad*, all anybody wanted to talk about was the time I was homeless," he groaned. "I wish now I'd never told anyone that story."

Djimon's time in Paris ended happily when a man saw him walking Rue St. Germain and handed him the business card of fashion designer Thierry Mugler. Days later, the homeless, handsome exile had become a model. His success in that career led him to risk it all on another: he bought a ticket to Los Angeles and began calling himself an actor.

"But I don't want to talk about that anymore," he flashed his brilliant smile. "I want to talk about Victoria..."

The telephone was ringing as I re-entered my room.

"Will you hold for Gail Katz?"

Gail was Wolfgang Petersen's longtime producing partner. *The Perfect Storm* would be my third movie with them, counting backwards from *Air Force One* to *Outbreak*. Wolfgang had just learned that Mel Gibson would not be available to star and the film's start date would now be pushed back a month to July. This would make another Australian actor available for the role. But Petersen had heard things.

"You know Wolfgang," Gail began. "He doesn't like working with people who are hard to get along with. He wanted me to ask you: how has Russell Crowe been on your movie?"

Uh, well.

"We've heard he has a habit of arguing with his directors," she continued. "We've heard he's just a generally difficult guy."

I told her there'd been "some head-butting" but offered the observation that this thorniness would also make him perfect for the part of the fishing boat captain who defies Mother Nature and risks the lives of his crew at sea.

"Doesn't sound like Wolfgang's kinda guy."

"If you can hold off for another 24 hours," I suggested, "Why doncha let me ask Ridley what he thinks?"

"Hm, interesting," Crowe's current director mulled in the lobby of the Berbere Palace the next morning. "I think you should tell Wolfgang that I said he should hire him. Tell him I think he's been working out fine."

Fine?

Fine.

Mustafa's Hyundai turned off Tichka Road onto a 17 km rocky scar leading to the company base camp at Ait Benhaddou... and almost immediately broke down.

The front right wheel had collapsed inward.

"Looks like a nut has fallen off a pin on the axle," Jaap peeked under the car. "Also looks like the axle has been welded, which means this piece of junk has broken before and instead of replacing it they just tried to patch it up."

Seventeen kilometers is a long walk across the desert. Were those vultures circling overhead?

As hallucinations go, I preferred the one that looked like the Lone Ranger's white stallion rearing up beside us... on its back tires. Steady big fella: it was a white Ford Explorer.

The driver's window rolled down and Russell's assistant Bob Long offered us a ride.

Bob had been making it rather easy for me to do business with our star. I told him when EPK crews were visiting and he alerted his boss. I gave him photos for RC to approve and he would conscientiously remind the actor to look at them until he had the kills and approvals sorted and in his hand to return to me.

Still, Bob Long was a bit of an enigma.

"I used to be a lawyer," he told us as the SUV sailed over ruts en route to the set. "But at heart I'm just a farm boy."

Born in Alberta, Canada to a well-healed real estate family, Bob practiced law for seven years before selling his practice and building his dream house in Banff. He lived there a short time before he became bored and moved back to Calgary.

"But I wasn't ready to start a new career yet. I just wanted a mindless job for awhile that would let me be around people."

He had a friend working on *Mystery Alaska*, which was filming in town at the time. All the production assistant jobs were taken, so his friend hired him to walk his four dogs. Then a more people-oriented position opened up.

"The thing I like best about movies is the popcorn," Bob admitted. "I don't think it ever crossed my mind how a film was made. But I must have started getting slightly interested because when my friend told me Russell Crowe was looking for an assistant, I said 'put my name in.'"

Though Bob described his job as "helping manage Russell's overall business affairs" that description belied the fact that he was on call 24 hours a day with responsibilities ranging from making sure Crowe didn't run out of toothpaste to making sure his dates got a taxi home before dawn. But Long didn't complain about the menial labor. Moreover, he claimed a genuine fondness for his tempestuous employer.

"Most people only see one side of Russell," the loyal assistant said. "What they don't see is a man who's incredibly generous with his friends and very sensitive to people's feelings."

He was right: most of the crew didn't see that quite yet.

There really were vultures circling overhead.

They were part of Sled Reynolds' menagerie and John Nelson's visual effects unit was on the roof of the Kasbah filming their portentous presence.

The hills overlooking the Provincial Arena pulsed with hordes of extras in multi-hued djellabas and turbans as big as flour sacks, standing beside or casually mounted sidesaddle on their camels.

In the arena below, stunt gladiators were rehearsing the Chain Fight while two cameras set up in an archway behind them to film new slaves entering the amphitheatre.

Meanwhile, outside the arena entrance, between the kasbah and a small café leading to the river, the EPK video-cam rested upon a tripod beside two director's chairs.

A darkly tanned man trailing purple robes with magenta weavings strode toward the interview setup. Shaking hands all around, he was fitted with a microphone, took his chair and patted its arm to signal his readiness for the inquisition.

"The newspapers got it completely wrong," Oliver Reed said with some exasperation as John Pattyson's crew hurried to change batteries in the middle of his interview. "I didn't throw a beer at a man in the airport.

"We were fog bound at the airport and there were a whole load of drunks in this one particular place and I thought they were being very rude. So I asked them, 'Are you Special Air Service? Is that why you're behaving like a bunch of pricks?'

"I finished my lager and it had some froth at the bottom and I said, 'I reckon you're the dregs, boys, so you might like to drink that' and I flipped the container at them. Then I went out, came back in again and sat with some others who weren't quite so rude. Ten minutes later, two policemen came in and lifted me.

"They kept me for about an hour until the plane was released, then delivered me to a hotel where I had a wonderful time. But I think that caused anxiety."

Ridley made Reed audition for the part, which established actors rarely do.

"I don't read for people," the star of *Oliver* and *Women in Love* told us. "I thought, 'if he wants to see my work, he can see it.' I've never read before. Well, once for *Richard III* but that was years and years ago."

Still, he did read for the role of Proximo. He read poorly. But Scott offered him the part anyway - with a proviso.

"He phoned me up and he said, 'We'd like you to do it. But you come with a reputation, don't you?' - which surprised me, you know. I said, 'I didn't know that.' He said, 'May I tell you something?' I said, 'Yeah.' He said, 'Straight to the chin?' I said, 'Yeah, sure.' He said, 'Don't let me down.' I said, 'No. No, I won't.'

"Nobody from the production ever called about that episode at the airport. I think they regarded it as just a private moment. I haven't let Ridley down, as far as I'm concerned.

"I admit, sometimes I make a nuisance of myself on my own time. But I try not to do it on the filmmaker's time. I think someone like Ridley respects that."

The rest of the interview was no less frank. Pattyson kept trying to steer the questions back towards the safe, standard pabulum he needed for a publicity featurette. Ollie kept responding like it was a police investigation and he had nothing to hide.

As he got up from his chair, shook hands and accepted our thanks, he asked:

"Was that okay?"

Wonderful.

"Right sort of shit?"

Absolutely.

His blue eyes sparkled as he adjusted Proximo's woven skull-cap before returning to his tarp-shaded seat near the playback monitors.

The befuddlement in Pattyson's eyes was shielded under sunglasses but for the first time in the sixteen years I'd known him, he was tongue-tied. He'd just gotten a terrific interview - if he'd been shooting for tabloid TV.

"I think there were a couple of useable soundbites," he finally said.

CHAPTER FIFTEEN

THE DIFFERENCE BETWEEN THE MOVIES AND LIFE

We had a bonus "holiday" from work in mid-week, courtesy of the Moroccan government: Feast of the Throne Day.

The work break applied to everyone but the director and the writer. Ralf worked a bit on the publicist whom he passed in the hall outside the breakfast room.

"They changed the name of my character. He will be called 'Hagen.' Ridley thought about Siegfried but..." he fluttered his hand. "They're also changing the story: Maximus and Hagen are rivals all through but at the end, the three of them team up."

Presumably, that meant Maximus, Hagen and Juba, Djimon's character. Just then, Djimon approached.

"We're going to the gym," Ralf announced. "We see you later. Oh, my publicist will call you, maybe tomorrow."

"Mine will call you today," Djimon winked. "Maybe twice." Ralf laughed that endearing, self-deprecating laugh.

The Feast of the Throne was the anniversary of the coronation of King Hassan II who had been the titular ruler of the country since 1961, nearly as long as Morocco had been a free nation. It was supposed to be, "A day when... all Morocco's cities, towns and villages are caught up in festivities," the guidebooks said.

There was a souk off the main road, Avenue Muhammad V, in which Jaap and I began our search for Feast festivities, wandering around vendor stalls where jogging outfits hung alongside caftans and ceremonial daggers shared tables with new-model electronics. We had another David Hasselhoff moment – hearing him ask over walkie-talkie if there'd been "any sightings of The Skirt?" But no evidence of a band playing, children singing, dancing in the streets.

We sat at a café on the main street, waiting for the Big Parade, sipping espresso from chipped coffee mugs. John Mathieson and some of the camera boys showed up and pulled a table alongside ours. We sucked in traffic dust for nearly two hours. Not a single flowered float passed by.

Groups of us wandered the city the rest of the day, from the main souk to the labyrinthine Kasbah. Nary a drum, flute or bleating ram's horn heralded His Highness.

As our hopes dimmed with the dusk, we finally found the party - in the main dining room of the Berbere Palace where a gala dinner, replete with high school girls' twirling team, was being hosted for the local military. We were not invited. The rest of the town was obviously celebrating at backyard barbeques.

The recognition that we were indeed strangers in a strange land, a tribe of outsiders, living here but not, was the sobering result of our holiday. No costumed dancers to sweep us along, no marching color guard to cheer, no ceremony in which to embrace the spirit of our surroundings - like there might have been in a movie.

Disappointed wanna-be festival-goers began straggling back to the hotel just past tea time and film crew festivities in the bar started earlier than usual.

Roger Lowe and visual effects Emma bought our first and second rounds of drinks. Following a third round bought by special effects boys Peter and Graham we had pretty much thrown moderation - along with dinner plans - to the wind.

Accounting babes Betty and Helen had also settled in for the night. A unit of our star's entourage was led by Bob Long, with Russell's dresser Michael Castellano, dialect coach Judi Dickerson and our massage therapist, Jill.

Jill was a vivacious brunette about 5'3" with tiny hands one wouldn't suspect of packing enough power to unbind bulky muscle in hulking men. Russell had recommended her for the job and Branko hired her with instruction that she be available for working on the gladiators as well. She could pound any of them into puddles.

A couple of drinks into the evening, Jill referred to Russell as "That Asshole." Hadn't heard that in awhile.

Last night, she and a few of Crowe's castle regulars, along with a couple of gladiators, were out bar-hopping. Jill, in probably an annoyingly cutesy but harmless way, had gotten out her disposable camera and started taking scrapbook photos of the gang. In the car, on the way to another bar, Russell got in the front seat beside his driver and Jill squeezed in beside three other party people in the back.

"Hey, why doncha let me take one of all you guys," Crowe reportedly said.

When she handed him the camera, Russell reared his arm back and heaved it out the window.

Jill exploded in protest.

"I've got fucking cameras shoved in my face all day," Russell bellowed back. "I don't need 'em when I go out with my friends."

"I thought I *was* out with friends," she snapped. "That's why I thought I could do it!"

He let her steam for most of the evening before finally producing the disposable he'd not actually disposed of.

"That asshole," she repeated, though with a tiny smile this time.

Branko entered the lounge and approached veteran art director Cliff Robinson.

"I haven't got a script for tomorrow, let alone next week!" Robinson replied in astonishment to whatever sotto voce news the executive producer was delivering.

Branko moved over to where I stood in the middle of a curious crowd.

"You know those new pages you got yesterday?"

I nodded.

"Forget about them. They're no good anymore. Throw them away."

He strode off with the hurried nonchalance of a hit man.

"I'm old enough to remember a time when you needed to have a script in order to shoot a movie," Cliff Robinson came over to share his exasperation.

The rabble rallied to mutinous murmurings about the absence of reason in the business of filmmaking. Robinson led the charge.

"It's extraordinary when you think that Ridley filmed *The Duelists* (his first picture) in the Bourgogne area in France for about 65,000 pounds (unconfirmed)," he proclaimed. "Extraordinary. But then Ridley is an artist - and I don't use that word frivolously. I don't believe film is an art. It takes more than a director to make a movie. It's a complete team effort and I don't think you produce art by committees or teams."

Art form or not, it's one thing to admire a well-made $130,000 movie, quite another for anyone present to imagine working on it. The major department heads on *Gladiator* would earn as much as *The Duelists* cost to make. Of course, there are some who point to that as the reason movies are so expensive.

"Remember whatsisname, Bruce Willis, a coupla years ago, when he became the first actor to make $10 million per picture?" said Michael Castellano, a sixty-year-old journeyman with a graying ponytail. "Boy did he get himself in hot water."

What Willis had said then was that movies cost so much because crews are overpaid. He went through the next couple of years trying to extract his foot from his mouth after encountering open hostility from every crew with which he worked.

Film crews are paid fairly well in contrast to the rest of the working population. But the expense of flights home to preserve a marriage, alimony and child support when the Friendly Skies don't cut it, room service, restaurant meals, acquired bad habits and battling boredom bring overall wealth in line with the average office worker – or less, considering the work is irregular, it's mainly a young person's game and ten-to-sixteen hour days make short careers.

What keeps Castellano going at this point are dreams of retirement.

"I've gotten to like Australia," he said. "You can get a nice condo near a beach for a fraction of what it'd cost you in L.A. Health care is good. Russell offered me a place near his ranch. I'm not sure if I wanna live that close to Russell. But I'm thinkin' about it."

Robinson, a Brit born in India, had been traveling with the movies for 37 years and had no thoughts of giving it up. "I don't mind the life, really - although I'm not crazy about airplanes," he told us. "I don't mind staying in hotels, as long as I have plenty of flowers. I give generous tips to the maids and they leave lots."

"I hate living in hotels," interjected Roger Lowe. "Hated it when I was traveling for a corporation and hate it now. I'd rather be staying in a shack where real people live."

Judi objected to being called an unreal person.

"Oh, of course I don't mean you darling," Roger said, slipping an arm around her bare shoulder.

Judi had been a dialect coach for about six years and married for only two.

"I love being on the road with a film company but I hate being away from my husband."

Her husband Neil, wrote for electronic trade publications, played tennis with his father weekly, took the dogs for walks and had little interest in traveling.

"The hardest thing about being married in this business was always the re-entry," said Roger who'd tried it for twenty years. "Coming back home and feeling like 'what the blazes are you doing here? We've been getting on quite well without you.'"

The 800-pound gorilla returns. A familiar story.

One by one, the *Gladiator* gang drifted out the door to the courtyard, wending their way back along separate paths to separate rooms. In lieu of loving arms, a welcoming pet, a favorite chair, a familiar television program, they would find a call sheet slid under their door assigning report times for the next day's work.

That other life sometimes existed in suitcase-sized mementos: a bedside photo, a favorite stuffed animal, a cricket bat, a baseball glove. Mostly, it was the invisible adhesive of a phone line that bound you to your other life. Your current one was a slipknot of nightly gatherings in the bar, shared laughs in crew vans, shared intimacies with people you'd only known a few weeks; no dishes to wash after dinner, no bed to make in the morning, no crying children to attend, no lawn to mow or snow to shovel. Not even a national festival to make you feel grounded in any reality but the movie.

And this movie still had at least three months to go.

Hi honey, your 800-pound gorilla's finally home! Wanna hear about my next job?

In the lobby next morning, I showed Ridley a couple of photos on which DreamWorks needed his immediate approval. Then I asked him how things were going with the script.

"Terrible. New screenwriter's putting a roof on his house."
Beg pardon?
"He's just doing this for the money. He's milking it. Know what he told me? He said, 'I go to bed at 10:00 p.m. and I don't take calls after that time.' I'm on set all day; I'm in dailies 'til nine, nine-thirty. By 10:00 I'm getting a second wind and he's off to catch forty fucking winks. When am I supposed to meet with him?"

When I got in the car with Jaap and Pattyson, I learned another possible reason for Ridley's grumpiness. News had come last night that Stanley Kubrick had died.

Kubrick had been something of a mentor to Scott when Ridley was first contemplating making the switch from advertising to feature films. They would talk movies for long hours over cigars and cognacs and even after Ridley became an "A-list" director with *Alien* in 1979, Kubrick was always there to help.

"When the studio (Warner Bros.) wanted to tag a new 'fairytale' ending on *Blade Runner*, I didn't have either the time or the money to do it," Ridley told me. "He gave me 50,000 feet of aerial footage that he'd had laying around which helped me finish the film. Never could have done it without him."

He also gave Ridley his assistant director, Terry Needham. When Scott was about to take on the biggest directing challenge of his life, shooting the story of Columbus in *1492: Conquest of Paradise*, he needed an a.d. who could lash a crew to the task of bringing a film, shooting in three countries, in often brutal conditions, to completion in 82 days.

Kubrick recommended Needham for the job. Terry and Ridley were both getting over difficult divorces as prep began and both were the type for whom hard work was the best therapy. They couldn't have picked a project that was much harder, shooting mainly in Costa Rica and the Dominican Republic where mud, rain and heat combined with 15-hour workdays to drive the crew to the brink of collapse. Terry was not only able to keep them going but was strong enough to stand up to the indefatigable director when he was about to push them over the edge.

Ridley's first phone call when *Gladiator* got the green light was to Terry.

I found a moment on set to offer Ridley condolences about Kubrick.

"Shame, really. Well, he didn't take care of himself very well. Never watched his diet, didn't exercise."

That was saccharine sentimentality compared to Terry.

"Yeah. Guess Cruise and Kidman done him in," on *Eyes Wide Shut*, one presumed.

Hey, shit happens and there are shots to set up. So, suck it in and get over it.

Actors back to first position. Cameras ready? Let's roll.

PART V
SEX AND DEATH

Gladiator – DreamWorks

CHAPTER SIXTEEN

TEMPTATION ON LOCATION

Saeed greeted me and my EPK crew for dinner at Dimitri's and sat us at one of his tables. I'd found a reference to *Hashuma* in a guide book: "a code of manners, including honor, respect and modesty, based on Islamic law and tribal custom." I still didn't quite know how – or if - Saeed had used it but we'd long gotten past any ill feelings from that first night.

A nightcap at the Berbere Palace bar found the accounting ladies celebrating the end of another workweek with the usual suspects from our crew. There were scattered groups of other film crews around the lounge and the electric piano combo was playing selections from *Thriller.*

Helen, our voluptuous American numbers cruncher, bared her shoulders in a dress that triangulated to the base of her breastbone,

racing sleekly along her hips to unjoined fabric around mid-thigh.
Rolling her eyes at something Roger said, which had Betty and
Carmel in stitches, she spotted me a few tables away and sauntered
in my direction. She sat on the edge of my padded chair.

The conversation was not of much consequence - or maybe she
was being profound and I was just too distracted by the whisper of
nylon lifted ever so slightly into my line of sight.

"Too bad you're married," was the only part I remembered.
She certainly said much more - and I must have been muttering
some semblance of response - because we stayed in that position
for quite some time.

Perhaps it was the length of time or Helen's repeated invoca-
tion of the phrase "you're married" that prompted Jill the mas-
seuse into action.

"You're coming with me," she declared as she grabbed my arm
and led me towards the door.

We paused there, her arm locked in mine, while she exchanged some information about Russell's schedule tomorrow
with Judi Dickerson.

As we stood at the doorway, a most beautiful woman was leaving the bar. She was in the company of a man who could have
been wearing rabbit ears and a Dracula cape for all I noticed because, as she passed, she spun her head in my direction, blue eyes
bursting zircon fairy dust, mouthed the word "bye" and wiggled
her fingers at about shoulder level.

I did that thing no guy ever wants to catch himself doing
unless he's trying to be funny: I looked behind me. She laughed
- removed all doubt - and left. I picked my jaw up off the floor
before my escort could notice.

When Jill got us out to the sidewalk, she asked, "So, what
now?"

Still a bit dazed in the wake of my brush with blue-eyed
Fatima, I shrugged and said, "Guess I'll call it a night."

"Alright."

If there was a slight hiccup in that one-word response, it didn't hit me until the key was in my doorlock.

After weeks in which, I swear, there hadn't been a female without a hump and a bridle so much as squint in my direction, I could think of only one explanation for all this sudden attention: there is an unscrupulous, international network of women who unleash a dragnet to entrap unworthy husbands on the eve of spousal visits.

As the Air Morocco twin engine touched down at precisely 2:45 p.m., Mustafa helped re-wrap my blue turban so that it sat like a perfectly packed bundle of wash-'n-fold on my head, a long veil trailing at the back.

My driver worked his way to the front of the small crowd and held high a sign that said "Mrs. Harris." I stood beside him, a foot-and-a-half taller, including my blue bonnet.

I spotted her immediately, but refrained from waving as she wound her way, bleary and disoriented, toward customs clearance. I stood motionless as she passed through customs. She was nearly upon us when her bloodshot eyes found mine and...

"You're scaring me to death," she shrieked. "Take that thing off!"

I unwrapped with one hand and held her tightly with the other.

We drove straight to the set where Jaap was the first to greet us. Margaret was quickly charmed by the winsome boy wonder. I introduced her to some other co-workers, whose names she instantly forgot and barely heard in this audio-visual salmagundi: Djimon welcomed her like a visiting royal; Ralf's puerile radiance brought laughter like flowers; Russell was gracious; Ridley polite; Judi Dickerson embracing as an old schoolmate; Ken Weston hospitable; Clementine protective.

An hour into our cinematic theme park excursion, fatigue won the battle over fascination and the weary traveler begged for the nearest hotel bed.

Mustafa drove back along the 17-kilometer dirt road, across the rocky plane beyond where our trailers and trucks were parked, as Margaret stared out the window with Benhaddou receding.

A man on a bicycle, his long cloak dangling dangerously close to the wheels, passed us coming as we passed another hooded man on a donkey going. A woman carrying a bundle of kindling on her head waited to cross the road behind two boys in western khakis shepherding a herd of goats. A dust-devil blew up in front of a group of djellaba-clad men lazing in front of a mudbrick hut. They watched it spin off into the desert, never moving a muscle even as it appeared to be heading straight towards them.

"I can't tell where the real world begins and the movie ends," Margaret said.

It didn't help her grasp on reality when we got back to the hotel and saw Omar Sharif sunning himself by the pool.

The number of extras on set the next day had dwindled to a handful. The cameras were moving in for close-up coverage of the previous days' scenes in the amphitheatre. After a few hours watching varying angles of repetitive slaughter, I led Margaret toward the ankle-deep river that ran west of the Kasbah. We took off our shoes and crossed over to the New Village, a small tourist center with a short alley of shops and three lodges, each featuring a restaurant with views of the valley.

From the restaurant patio of the biggest lodge, El Ouidane, a lunar landscape sprawled between the cocoa-colored Kasbah and distant snow-crested Atlas. The warm breeze communicated all I needed to say as I took my wife's hand.

But Margaret chose that moment to catch me up on news of our home life.

Sam's fifth grade class had a roller skating party in the school gym and Casey went along. The gym was too small for the number of kids in attendance. Casey was a good skater but hated bumping into people and finally gave up in exasperation.

Later that night, he was in the family room reading e-mail on a computer that enlarged each letter to the size of salt-and-pepper shakers. Sam was reading the screen from his sofa seat, half a room away. When Sam asked about a word, Casey realized what his brother was doing and sprang from his chair to bite him on the arm. Their mother took the appropriate action but later went up to comfort her eldest.

As she told these stories, I began to feel an inexplicable despair. In the world she was describing, I was a ghost. But here, now, I had presence.

Look, I love hearing about the kids but we're *here*. Let's take a minute.

She quieted. Not exactly hurt but not exactly sure what I was saying.

I starred across the desert beyond Ait Benhaddou and let romance blow away with the swirling sand.

"Sorry. Hey, how're Sam's tap-dancing lessons coming along?"

Re-entry. Reunion. Sometimes takes a while to get your rhythms back.

Ken and Clementine joined us for dinner at Dimitri's where conversation flitted between movies we'd worked on, movies we'd seen, directors we'd worked with, locations we'd worked in and more movies we'd worked on and seen. Margaret tried to keep up.

Ken told us a story that occurred during the filming of *Evita*.

"There were a lot of legless beggars where we were (in Argentina)," he recalled. "Nobody could explain why: landmines, polio, bad doctors, a hundred other reasons. They'd had a pretty brutal government for a long time there.

"Well, there was one boy the cast and crew got to know a bit. The crew would kid around with him, grips would lift him up onto their truck. He became something of a mascot. Can't remember his name. Call him Joey.

"Poor countries, you see people get around in all sorts of ingenious ways. One of the things we used to see was some of the cripples peddling bicycles with their hands. So, one day, some of the grips got together and made Joey a special, brightly colored, hand-peddle bike.

"He disappeared for a couple of days and the next time he showed up on the set, his face was all swollen and the bike gone. Gang of kids beat him up for it. The grips offered to make him another one but he turned them down. Didn't want any part of it. Wouldn't even take money from the crew when it was time for us to pack up.

"You see, we upset the natural human ecology wherever we go. If you want to face the truth of it, we think we're doing so much good, spending money here and there, hiring a few drivers, being big tippers at restaurants. But what happens when we leave?

"I'm not saying we shouldn't make movies on location. I'm not saying that we sometimes don't do a little good with our money here and there - though far less than we credit ourselves for. Every time I go to a place where there's a lot of poverty, oh I still toss around a few coins and such. But when I want to do some good, I think of that kid Joey. And I think, 'How bloody arrogant of me to suppose the material possessions I can give him will make his life better?' What made Joey's life better was a little kindness, a little respect - a feeling, that's all."

The table went silent for a moment.

"What the fuck am I saying? Clem, what am I talking about?"

"You're talking about how you can't save the world."

"Bollocks. We were talking about *Ishtar*," he smiled. "Piece of shit that it was."

The courtyard of our new location, the Kasbah Tamdaght, was filled with predator cats in a hundred-foot row of cages, roped off from crew and cast. Sled Reynolds patrolled the periphery.

"These are wild animals, folks," we were told, as Margaret and I stood talking with Jaap, Djimon and Judi Dickerson. "They can reach out a paw, pin you against the cage and rip your arm off faster than you can say 'Lions and tigers and bears.' Please stay out of this area."

We moved our conversation to the neighborhood of the giraffe's corral.

Tamdaght was smaller and, though probably 200 years younger, crumbling at a far greater rate than Benhaddou. While Ait Benhaddou was still a residence, no one lived in this corroding Kasbah except eight nests of storks. Legend was that when the storks left, the Kasbah would crumble. *The Man Who Would Be King* was partly filmed here around twenty years ago and that may have been the last time the place was given a face-lift.

Tamdaght was not Margaret's and my ultimate destination today. The crew were looking forward to their only two-day weekend in Morocco and we planned to begin ours a few hours early with a five-hour drive across the High Atlas to Marrakesh.

It's not the snake charmers or the acrobats in the Djemaa El Fna - the city's legendary outdoor market - not the monumental Koutoubia Minaret that superintends the spirit of Islam from 253 feet above the city center, nor even the catacombs of souks with their varietal wares and slightly sinister vendors. It's simply the sense of a gathering place for all wandering tribes that makes Marrakesh so compelling. I could've sat in the marketplace all day watching the passing parade of humanity.

But we had an agenda.

And we had a host.

Our host, Mr. Ali, came courtesy of a telephone introduction arranged by Rob and Karen Cowan. Ali was the carpet merchant whose daughter wanted to get into special effects.

Our agenda was the purchase of a carpet for Margaret to fly home with.

Ali provided us with complimentary accommodations at the Club Med ("I have a small store there") and offered to show us his carpet shop as soon as we hit town - keeping it open exclusively for us, after hours. I hoped he wasn't confusing my carpet-buying budget with the Cowans but I wasn't about to question the hospitality.

Calling Ali's rug emporium a "carpet shop" was like calling the incident on the Atlas pass, when an oncoming twenty-foot box truck squeezed us onto six inches of gravel at the edge of an abyss, "uncomfortable." It was a carpet Taj Mahal.

"I am not going to make any profit from these," Ali assured us. "We are friends."

Our host ushered us into a large parlor and sat us on pillows where a slight, elderly man promptly appeared with two cups of tea.

Two young men were telepathically summoned and carpets began to appear. Margaret's preferences came into sharper focus as a hundred rugs from all corners of the shop came flying open, then swept away the moment Her Majesty turned thumbs down. Tea flowed in and out of our cups like an infinity pool.

After two hours of this, eyes crossing, sweat beads forming and a barely controllable need to urinate, my durable darling threw up her hands. With the field narrowed to fifteen, she would defer a decision until tomorrow

Ali and his daughter Ghita met us for dinner at the Club Med that night. Willowy, black-haired Ghita was 19 and just graduated high school.

"She's a very talented artist," boasted her father, "just like her mother."

146

I asked what had gotten her interested in movie special effects and Ali helped in translation as neither Ghita's English nor my French was going to get us very far.

"I always liked monsters," she stated without elaboration.

"And movies," her father added. "She knows I used to work in the movies."

He feigned nonchalance as I registered polite surprise.

"I was a second a.d., for the great Zeffirelli," he began. "We called him 'Maestro.' I got a job as a production assistant on *Jesus of Nazareth* that was filming in Fez and around where you are in Ouarzazate.

"There was a scene in which the Maestro needed some extras to cross in front of the camera. I'd had no experience in the movies before this job and no one had told me anything but I knew, I just knew what was needed. I took it upon myself to send them just at the right time. The Maestro saw what I'd done and praised me in front of all the crew, 'bravo,' he said, '*buono lavoro*,' good job! The first a.d. gave me a promotion to second a.d. and, at the end of the movie, he said I should come to Italy and work there."

He glanced at Ghita, perhaps to see how much she understood - though it couldn't have been the first time she'd heard the story.

"I was torn. My father was old, he wasn't well and, I don't know, maybe I just knew it was time for me to settle down.

"I've been married over twenty years. I have a good business; I do very well. But I'm not happy in my work. I wish sometimes I had followed my heart. That's why it's important to me that Ghita follows her heart and does what makes her happy - not just what makes money."

He ran his hand over his daughter's hair, linking his hopes to hers.

I suggested that Ghita visit the *Gladiator* set before we left Morocco and I would introduce her to the special effects and special make-up effects teams. She looked inquiringly at her father who quickly agreed to make the trip.

"We'll stay at the Club Med in Ouarzazate," he told Ghita.

I tried to picture vacationers deciding that, of all Club Med's holiday hotspots, their fancy would be most tickled by two weeks in a former French Foreign Legion outpost with one main street.

Margaret couldn't sleep that night for obsessing on her upcoming Day of Decision but I diverted her attention long enough for us to make love for the first time in months. We were in Marrakesh, city of mystery, exotic, erotic and... fergodsakes, enough about carpets!

Our eyes sprung open at 5:30 to an announcement in Arabic that the Apocalypse had officially begun. At least that's what it sounded like: it was just the morning call to prayer - but the loudspeaker was right above our door.

Ali picked us up after breakfast and we drove to his store where the finalists were trotted out and unrolled. Margaret narrowed the field to five: she was leaning toward the blue Berber, though she wanted to see the two Glaoui weaves once more just to make sure. The two reversibles were a pipe dream out of our price range. I thought they were all great – which didn't help her much.

"I still can't decide. Now I like the two red ones," Margaret agonized.

"Let me make you a price," Ali intervened. And faster than you could do a bad imitation of Marlon Brando, he had calculated a figure for all five that was impossible to refuse.

With Mustafa's car crammed full of carpets, Margaret said goodbye and I told Ali I'd see him and Ghita in Ouarzazate.

"Yes, we look forward to that. I want her to be able to do what she wants," our benefactor repeated. "If maybe after a few years she decides not to do it, that will be fine. I want her to follow her heart - money is not important. I want her to be happy."

On Monday, Margaret flew back to her life, taking the carpets and my heart with her. It had been five days of shared adventure, intimacy, connection – with only a few bumps along the way. It was a great five days. But it was five days.

What is the elevator drop that follows such a high?

The arrival at Tamdaght of my two guests from Marrakesh was an effective distraction. Clementine took on the task of being Ghita's translator, interpreting the French-speaking cinephile's questions to English-speaking special effects, costume, makeup and art department personnel I brought over to discuss their jobs.

It shouldn't have come as a surprise that Ali knew quite a few of the Moroccans who were working with us. He did a fair amount of business in this part of the country, hired many of our drivers, bartered with some of the vendors and knew other crew who had jobs in shops and hotels when they weren't working on movies.

It would have made my life easier to leave him with these associates. But his presence on set was my responsibility and every time he stood where he shouldn't, Terry Needham would cast a lethal glare in my direction.

It's difficult for an outsider on a film set: he has no idea when he might be standing in an actor's eye line, no instincts for who may be approachable at a given moment or how a whisper carries when there's "quiet on set." The difficulty is exacerbated if one is unaccustomed to being a fly on the wall; one then becomes a fly in the ointment.

As my attention was focused on minding my meandering guest, Millie came to me with a response from Ridley to my final Moroccan memo about unauthorized cameras on set. Every stuntman, extra and half the crew were taking photos or video and most were no longer even being discreet about it. There was no way our director couldn't have seen it but even if he didn't care, I thought it my responsibility to bring it up once more, in writing - mainly so my ass was covered when pictures started showing up in unplanned, unwanted and ill-timed newspaper, magazine and internet stories.

To my astonishment, Millie's message was that Ridley "felt very strongly" about cameras not being permitted on set and he was giving me "full authority" to deal with it. Telling Millie, my ally, that I was a publicist, not a policeman was pointless. Pointing it out to Branko or Terry Needham who, aside from the director, were the only persons with any real enforcement power, was preaching to the deaf through a surgical mask with my hands in my pockets.

So, my duties shifted to running around asking people to put away their personal cameras. Meanwhile, Ali kept discovering more people he knew and chatting with them all over the set.

Ali had gone off on his own for so many lengthy stretches that I'd nearly forgotten about him in my pursuit of gladiator paparazzi. Suddenly, I caught Terry Needham glaring in my direction. His eyes panned from mine to one of our camera positions.

There, peeking over Ridley's shoulder as he was lining up a shot, was my guest. I intervened before he could start telling our maestro how the great Zeffirelli might have done it.

Minutes later, I escorted Ali and Ghita back to their car, saying I had business to attend at the office. The slightly wounded look in Ali's eyes as we shook hands did not soften my resolve in abbreviating their stay.

When they were gone, Clem shared her observations of Ghita.

"I don't think the girl has a clue what she wants to do except make money," Clementine confided. "All day long she keeps asking me 'How much does this one make? How much does that one make?' When I told her, 'I don't know but maybe 1,000 pounds per week, she turned up her nose. Her father told her, 'You could make that working in a pizza restaurant!'"

Well, maybe her heart will lead her to a special effects mushroom and pepperoni. And maybe her father will follow his heart back into the movies. Just not into this one.

My distractions had departed, work here was winding down and I was again staring into the abyss. In the words of the prophet Smokey Robinson, sometimes a taste of honey's worse than none at all. I missed Margaret even more than before and it would be a long time until I saw her again.

Loneliness on location is a siren's song against which you plug your ears with fatigue, diversion, self-medication or self-discipline. If you allow yourself to be lured, you can find love in the most romantic circumstances or you can crash each new port-o-call with hedonistic abandon. I was unavailable for the former and ill suited for the latter. This didn't make me immune to either.

Our crew was already back at the Berbere Palace when I returned from the studio after packing up my office and attending some mounting paperwork. In the lobby, I ran into Karen Allen, her nine-year-old son Nick, and his nanny returning from a stroll with the puppy that had followed Karen home that morning. The pup was only theirs temporarily, she reassured herself, watching boy and pooch bond as they trotted back to their room. Before hurrying after them, she asked me to give her an hour or so to get Nick settled in, then we'd grab a last meal at the hotel restaurant. We'd become frequent dinner companions but now we were both moving on. She was leaving the next morning for Agadir, where *Shaka Zulu* would finish filming; *Gladiator* had two more days here before heading to Malta.

I wandered into the lounge where I found Jaap and Paul Castleman from the armory department, talking about our upcoming move. Prior to a company move, a crew speculates less about questions of work than anticipated creature comforts at the next location. Paul had heard something about there being two hotels, one for the majority of the crew, the other for actors and a few key department heads.

"Hope they don't put the crew in some third-rate dive to save a few pounds."

On the positive, hopes ran high that the catering would be substantially better in Malta. It had gotten so bad here that Jaap and some of the camera crew had begun circulating a petition for the summary dismissal of the cook and his staff.

As my attention drifted from the litany of catering complaints, so did my line of vision. On a sofa by the fireplace, seated amongst a raggedy bunch of unshaven men and sweat-shirted women, was my lady with the starburst eyes - eyes that had already found me from across the lounge.

In the Petrie dish of primordial arousals there are tiny trigger mechanisms, resistance to which can damage vital circuitry. My blonde-haired, blue-jeaned Aphrodite averted her gaze and pulled an airy curtain to conceal my existence. Then in an exquisite instant, her chin rose and floated back in my direction - and she tucked one naked foot under a denim thigh, softly pressing upwards an indentation of tender flesh as it warmed her instep through her inseam. She grasped her ankle with both hands and held it there.

I lifted out of my chair and walked to the bland display of Happy Hour hors d'oeuvres where I stood deciding between the white cheese squares and the orange ones longer than a scientist studying the pasteurization process. When I looked up, she was standing across the table, harpooning olives with a plastic toothpick.

I may have said, "Do you think those are locally grown?" or "Are you working on one of the movies here?" or probably just "Hi."

She was tall, maybe 5'8, and lean, with roundnesses like a topographical map of heaven. Her name was Tatiana and, yes, she was here working as a set dresser on a multi-national mini-series, *The Bible*. The project had been filming in southern Morocco for seven years. The crew came for up to five months a year, went home or onto other jobs and kept their schedules flexible so they could come back the following year. She had been doing this for two years and had an informal agreement with her department to return for another three.

She was German but lived in Rome. She spoke German, French, Italian, "a little Scandinavian," "some" Arabic and lightly accented, nicely nuanced English. A few sun-kissed coronas at the edge of her azure eyes placed her age in the mid-thirties.

"Why don't you come by the studio where I'm working sometime and I'll show you around," she smiled, "if you like."

As she walked away I could hear the pair of electronic keyboards playing *Temptation* - though I knew the band was still on a break and the song probably too classic for their repertoire.

I stopped by Karen's room to see about dinner. Nick and the puppy were playing tug-of-war with Nick's shoe while the nanny was helping Karen pack. She apologized for the mess and asked if we could delay our date for another hour.

I don't know why I used the excuse of having an early set call - not knowing when or if, I'd see her again. But she said she understood and I understood her need to pack and get Nick settled and so we parted with those understandings, a warm hug and a see-ya-soon-I-hope.

I may have also understood I'd been developing a bit of a crush on Karen. Reciprocal or not, there could've been nothing casual with her. And falling in love wasn't what I needed.

I ordered take-away from the hotel pizza restaurant and sat in my room with a bottle of wine and my thoughts, listening to a little Tim Hardin, a little Ben Webster and too much Sarah Vaughn. The expanse of bed where Margaret had slept, nearest the telephone and reading lamp, seemed like another country.

Most of the gladiators had already been dispatched either to Malta or, like Jeff-the-Giant, back from where they came by the time I arrived at Tamdaght the next morning. The giraffes, hyenas, impalas, flamingoes, ostriches and lions were also gone - crated and trucked off like feathered and furry grip stands. The hour of wrapping the background was upon us.

Saeed had made me promise to come to Dimitri's for one last dinner before leaving town. Djimon and Judi accompanied me. It was obvious from the flatness of his greeting that Saeed was not himself. I asked what was troubling him.

"Next weekend my brother is getting married in Agadir," he explained. "But my boss just told me he won't let me have time off to go to the wedding."

I took up his outrage: surely there must be someone else who could fill in for one weekend! What kind of heartless slave driver...?

"You're my friend, so I told you, that's all. Nothing can be done."

I remembered Legless Joey and curbed my urge to play the big-footed American.

At the end of our meal, it was time for "goodbyes" and the suddenness of my departure took Saeed by surprise.

"Please stay, have coffee, one moment, please," he pleaded.

Another waiter brought our coffees and teas and Saeed disappeared. He dashed back ten minutes later and came straight to our table, hands behind his back. Then he held them out to me.

"For you, Mr. Rob."

Inside the newspaper wrapping was a pair of leather slippers.

"Try them on, please."

They were about four sizes too small.

"Oh, wait, please."

So we waited a bit longer while Saeed ran back to the store to trade the slippers for the biggest size they had. Fortunately, these fit. Barely.

Saeed and I exchanged bows and a handshake and he bid us all *"au revoir."*

"What was that for?" asked Judi, as we exited Dimitri's for the last time.

"Hashumah," I told her.

I wore the slippers out of the restaurant but would've had to amputate three toes to stay in them all the way to the hotel.

The scenes on our final filming day in Morocco were of Maximus in the slave quarters and in a corridor of Proximo's Compound. The set was crowded and I had no need to hang around after checking in with Jaap. So, Mustafa drove me back to town where I had a rendezvous to keep.

Tatiana had left a pass and one of the guards directed me to the art department where a friendly woman abandoned the clay pots on which she was painting hieroglyphs to become my page.

Tatiana shone as brightly in the daytime as she had at night, hair tied back in a bandana, all in blue as she was the first time I'd seen her. Her greeting was warm, though more professional than personal.

"We're just finishing the Old Testament," she said as we toured the back lot beside Hadrian's Palace. "This is where Salome did her dance. It was quite good - though it will probably be too sexy for the Vatican censors."

She made clear that her participation in this project was not as a believer.

"I'm not a religious person," she stated. "I don't like the way the Vatican gives notes to the film's producers or that we have to be afraid how every little thing will offend them." She expected Papal intervention to be even worse when they started shooting New Testament stories next year.

We strolled a columned courtyard to a low wall overlooking an urban valley.

"This is the old part of Ouarzazate that most tourists never see," she indicated the expanse of mostly single-story sandstone housing. "We shoot through gauze curtains so you can't see any satellite dishes or antennas. It will look just like ancient Jerusalem."

The way she said "gauze" was like the back of a fingernail gliding along silk.

She guided me back to the studio entrance.

"So you see," she gestured less for illustration than diversion with the studio guards hovering outside their kiosk. "It's an interesting project - even though Ouarzazate can be very boring after so much time here."

But she would be back next year and the year after and the year after that. I suspected there was something besides the work that kept drawing her here.

I related what Ken Weston had told me about how much time Sabbatini had spent in Ouarzazate and how fond he had become of this Quiet Place. I wondered aloud if she had ever run into the designer.

"Enrico was my angel," she said with as much quizzical calm as if I'd guessed her star sign. "I came here because of him. I started my career as a clothing designer when he was already the most famous Italian movie costume designer. He encouraged me to get into the movie business. When he started doing production design on this series, he told me I should come to work in the art department."

This revelation left us with little else to say. So, I asked her to dinner.

"I'm having dinner with my department," she said with a generous serving of regret. "But why don't we meet for a drink in the lounge later. Say, 11:00?"

Ilovemywife. Ilovemywife. Ilovemywife. Ilovemywife. Ilovemywife. Ilovemywife. Ilovemywife. Ilovemywife. Ilovemywife. Ilovemywife. Ilovemywife. Ilovemywife. Ilovemywife. Ilovemywife. Ilovemywife.

It's time to introduce the adage, "on location doesn't count."

It's a production cliché, not an axiom, and probably more of a running joke than a practice. Everyone flirts, everyone hugs, few have flings. For the majority of committed or married crew, vows and virtue vanquish whoopee. Also, a film company is like a small town: everyone knows your business, so the likelihood of anonymity is nil.

But everyone faces temptation. Men and women on crews – as in life – differ in attitude, approach and opportunity: women are more likely to "get involved" with a fellow crew member. He understands and he's probably flattered that out of the massive male majority on this production, you picked him. Guys are more likely to find opportunity in the civilian world: there are plenty of ugly men who suddenly look handsome when they tell the waitress they're with the movie.

I'm convinced what keeps most of the weak strong is paralysis: what if you get involved with a workmate and it goes bad? What if you meet a local and she falls in love with you? And believe it or not, most men in relationships – who are *capable* of relationships - are too honorable to risk causing heartbreak in the girl they leave behind. They've seen enough carnage from the single guys doing it.

I'd always thought the ideal woman with whom to have a fling would be someone who understood the life and didn't mind that you were going off to a different location the next morning.

The fact this one looked like a blue-jeaned Garbo was the *coupe de grace*.

My Woody Allen fantasies about what a late-night tipple with temptress Tatiana might yield played out something like this: a sardine tin of oblivious barroom bodies, drinking, talking, cocooning us on stools so close that we could only fit with a knee between each other's legs until one of us said "Let's get out of here."

Arms linked, we would sprint with greedy desire to my room where she would peel off her tight jeans as I selected the perfect cd to slide into my computer drive. Throwing her naked torso on top of mine, ripping at what remained of my clothes, she would pant passionate phrases in six languages, arousing me from exhaustion time after ecstatic time until the sun came up and I had to drag my depleted body from the mattress that had somehow fallen off the frame, prying her fingers from my ankle in order to get away in time to catch the crew plane.

Reality played a different tune.

The celebration of *Gladiator's* last night in Morocco was in full swing when I entered the lounge. I spotted Tatiana at a table against a far wall, surrounded by a dozen of her work mates. I waved to her. She waved back with a pleasant smile. I joined some of our crew at the bar.

At 10:00, I was half-listening to new bad-boy-Russell stories - which had begun to bore me under the least diverting circumstances - and watching her from across the room. Neither her engagement nor her gaze shifted from those in her immediate circle over the next hour.

At 11:00, I could have crossed the room, said "hello" and invited her to join me for a drink. For a hundred reasons, I didn't.

Instead, I bought the camera boys a nightcap and tried not to look in her direction. I failed at that, looking frequently.

Tatiana never looked up as I exited the lounge alone around midnight. I even paused at the brochure rack in the lobby.

But this was Ouarzazate, not *Casablanca*. There would be no final scene at the airport just before the plane takes off. No beautiful friendships. Only two ships passing - as they so often do in real movie life.

And, like many things, maybe it was better in the imagining.

CHAPTER SEVENTEEN

THE ACTORS' HOTEL

H ear that?
      Of course not.

There are no birds on Malta. Practically none, anyway. Once in a while an adventurous seagull ventures overland - though never far. Once in a great while a pair of fugitive sparrows dart across a field like androids evading Blade Runners.

The reason there are no birds - no wildlife of any kind, if you don't count lizards, rats and field mice - is that a small but significant number of Maltese are gun crazy.

"They'll shoot at anything that moves," explained David, a reedy journalist for *The Independent*, one of the two English language newspapers here. "But there is nothing left to shoot. At the Saturday market, you'll see, they sell caged birds. Tiny ones. Hunters buy them to release, then, 'boom,' a few feathers. If they miss... *mela*. A Maltese sees a bird anywhere near him he runs away!"

In 1980, the Maltese government managed to pass a declaration of protection for the remaining Mediterranean peregrine falcons - the Maltese Falcons - whose last refuge and breeding ground were the Ta' Cenc Cliffs on the island of Gozo. It was too little too late. The last of these birds disappeared by the middle of that decade.

Layered in this national pathology is the history of a populace plundered, pummeled, ignored and exploited.

Still, there is something exquisite and alive about this country.

It felt like a brand new movie the moment we landed.

This was, to a degree, not just a feeling but an unfortunate fact.

Ridley had directed faster than the new writer Bill Nicholson could write pages or producers Walter Parkes, Laurie MacDonald, Doug Wick and Our Star could approve them. So we arrived in Malta with the previous movie in the can and the new one still on the drawing boards. And though Branko had seemingly marshaled the entire Croatian army corps of engineers to cobble together a Colosseum, it wasn't ready for filming.

The production was in a holding pattern we were calling "prep." Most of the British crew took the opportunity to fly home for a few days.

Reno, the driver assigned to take Jaap and me to our hotel, was a short, nervous man in his early fifties. Serving as our driver, he quickly informed us, was his first job.

"The first time I'm ever working for anyone besides myself," he said in the Maltese lilt that strikes every third syllable like a tuning fork. "Sold the family business a year ago and I thought I would relax and retire. But I was driving myself, my wife and my children all nuts."

So, through a connection, he got this job driving others.

The roads of Malta are a tangle of roundabouts, unmarked six-way intersections, amorphous lanes and aggressive drivers, many of whom, like Reno, seemed completely clueless about where they were going.

"Fuckyouandyomamayoupieceofstinkinggarbageyoushouldlearn-howtodrive!" I thought he said in Maltese, spinning in his seat to snap at a car that had hooted at him as he cut across three lanes of traffic to make a left turn. "People here, they'll run over you sooner than put a foot on their brake pedal."

Though the traffic system was designed with Britain's left-side/ curbside setup, Reno just as often drove on the right – principally, it seemed, to claim ownership of the entire road. A native of this 122-square-mile island, he got lost twice en route from the airport to the capital city where he'd been instructed to deliver us to Malta's lone landmark hotel.

The Hotel Phoenicia piped Ella Fitzgerald through its thickly carpeted lobby, giving this luxury lodge the soundtrack it might have had when it opened in 1947.

Jaap and I were halfway through six o'clock cocktails when the director and his leading lady entered the bar and joined our table. Ridley ordered a scotch and Connie Nielsen took my word on the house cabernet. They'd just come from a discussion about the script and were anxious to change the subject.

Talk hovered awhile on the topic of hotels we've all called home and, as always, wistful regrets about time away from loved ones. Ridley carries a photo of two Jack Russell terriers from which he hates to be parted. Connie longed to be in Milan with her business executive husband and nine-year-old son, Sebastian.

Ridley reminisced about his first trip to the U.S., "...by bus, the year that John Glenn orbited the earth. I sat next to a boxer straight out of *Of Mice and Men*," he said. "Saw all the poor trailer towns. I remember thinking most of Pennsylvania looked like Manchester."

He'd just started working at the BBC, along with a young Ken Loach and Ken Russell, and decided he wanted to see Hollywood.

"I suppose I had some notion the whole town would be like a studio back lot. Actually, I had no idea how it would be. I didn't know a bloody soul there. I remember trying to find '77 Sunset Strip' and being disappointed to discover it didn't exist."

After about twenty minutes, Connie and Ridley retreated to a dinner table in the hotel dining room. Their conversations about the script only paused, not concluded.

The next morning, after another hair-raising ride through sinuous streets with our mad-motoring Joe-Pesci-on-goofballs again getting lost twice, Jaap and I arrived at Fort Ricasoli to get a look at the location where most of our filming would take place over the next ten to twelve weeks.

Reno told the guards at the gate he was carrying "important 'Glad-i-a-tor' people" - squeezing the "a" like a rubber air horn. We passed through the gate and drove directly to the entrance of the Colosseum.

It wasn't as overwhelming a sight as I'd imagined: less than a third the circumference of the real thing and only two tiers high. Without decoration, it looked like, well, an unfinished movie set.

It also looked like we might have more than a week off: neither the Colosseum, nor the Emperor's Palace, nor any of the other sets seemed close to being completed. In some places, however, that was difficult to discern: production designer Arthur Max had so well integrated the constructed sets into the existing limestone fort that it appeared some of them had been ready and waiting for us for hundreds of years.

In any case, we were assured by no less an authority than Branko that we would find "something to shoot somewhere," with some script pages by Monday or, "If we don't, you listen to me, I'll swim back to Morocco."

Looking at him, half a decade past retirement age, shoulders the width of a bull, iron blue eyes on a hatless bald head surveying an army of carpenters, painters and welders who were one of three shifts he'd been lashing to maximum output since he came here a week before the rest of us, you had to think he could make good on either boast.

Jaap had a surprise waiting for me in the Phoenicia lobby when I came down to meet him that evening.

"I found this man wandering the hotel alone and I insisted he come to dinner with us. Do you mind?"

"I really didn't want to impose but he did insist," said Sir Derek Jacobi.

Jaap had worked with him on a small movie called *Love Is the Devil* in which the world's greatest living Hamlet had played Frances Bacon. Sir Derek had flown in the previous night and no one from the production had spoken to him all day - until Adam finally called to say he might not be working until next Friday.

The Phoenicia's doorman recommended a restaurant around the corner called Lo Squero, a lace-linen bistro with a wall of windows that overlooked the Grand Harbor. Derek was a white wine drinker and we all ordered fish.

Jaap asked about a Shakespearean performance Jacobi had intended to do after their last meeting. He lamented that the performance hadn't happened.

"But I hope to perform in another of Mr. Devere's works soon." Mr. Devere?

"I don't believe for a minute The Stratford Boy wrote the plays and sonnets that were attributed to him," the famed interpreter of The Bard informed his dinner guests. "I am among the growing number of scholars and enthusiasts who are convinced they were the work of the 17th Earl of Oxford, Edward Devere."

Jacobi shocked the Shakespeare Society in Washington, DC when he endorsed the Devere Society in his acceptance speech for their Lifetime Achievement Award.

"John Gielgud agrees that Devere wrote all or most of Shakespeare's works but doesn't want to go public with it."

Whether thanks to The Earl or The Stratford Boy, those 37 plays that most of the world calls Shakespearean have given Derek a good life and no shortage of good stories.

He told about a performance of *Hamlet* in Shanghai at the end of China's Cultural Revolution. "The audience was uni-sexed and uniformed and you thought you were performing to a crowd of gingerbread figures. There were five translators simultaneously translating from backstage so you could barely hear yourself say your lines. On top of that, we'd just flown in from Tokyo, which was neon hell to a place where they barely had electricity. It was eerie."

Another evening of surreal Shakespeare occurred in Split, Yugoslavia.

"It was a lovely old theatre but it was also home to thousands of starlings. So, when they turned on the lights, the starlings thought it was daylight. The actors had to scream to be heard above the cries of the birds. Also, to go from stage right to stage left you had to go outside and around the theatre. So, while half our cast were screaming their heads off on stage, the other half were wandering lost on the streets."

But the prize for the strangest place in which to perform went to Palm Beach, Florida where Derek, Michael Redgrave and two other actors were to do readings.

"Opening night, all the ladies wore their finest jewels. But the jewels had to be back in their safe deposit boxes by 9:00. So, at a little before nine all these women got up and walked out!"

After intermission, the performance was interrupted when a fight broke out.

"We learned later the fight was caused by a woman taking out a hairdryer because her hairdo had been ruffled in the wind when she left to return her jewelry. This apparently drew violent complaints from the woman sitting behind her." The evening ended with the mayor presenting Redgrave a key to the city. "Pity we didn't have one that locked the doors."

CHAPTER EIGHTEEN

THE LUCKIEST MAN

The return of Victoria during our break had made Djimon a happy man again. We were all happy to see her, basking in the fraternal satisfaction of watching her boyfriend glow.

Not all hiatus reunions went so well. Ken Weston's recent trip to England for follow-up cancer tests brought him back to us with bitterness: Clementine had left him.

"Not much you can do, can you? Been carrying on with another man, decided she wanted shut of me and get on with her life. S'pose I just have to get on with mine."

I'd not spoken with my family in three days. Didn't know how that had happened but I'd written in my journal "drinks with Ridley & Connie Nielsen; tour of Colosseum set; dinner with

Derek Jacobi; phone conference with DreamWorks." Looked like
the appointment calendar of a very important person.

"Dad, I'm really getting into rap music. Mom said to ask you if
I can buy these cds. I've got a whole list," my ten-year-old exhorted
when I finally connected with home. "Want me to read you?"

Absolutely, I did.

"I'm still looking for a partner on the computer who can do
graphic arts," my tech-savvy eldest took the phone. "So I can put
all the stuff that's in my head into actual games."

Hanging up the phone, I felt like a very important person.
And a very fortunate one.

"Are we not the two luckiest sons-of-bitches in the world?"
actor David Schofield asked as we were finishing Sunday lunch at
Eddie's outdoor café in Republic Square, listening to the rhythmic
clopping of one-horse carriages.

It was an afternoon that could certainly make one feel that
way. The city of Valletta on a warm spring day was a cauldron of
kitch in primary colors: tourists in plaid shorts paraded past local
girls in yellow leather minis, laundry hung from balconies like
multi-hued flags and the chromatic neutrality of the sandstone
buildings lent pop-out dimension to red doors and green shutters.

It was further understandable how an unsung stage veteran
might be feeling like a kitten in cream on this day, in this place,
with a role in this movie.

David played Senator Falco, the Emperor's key conspirator.
Despite decades of acting experience, which included the title
role in the world premiere of *Elephant Man*, he was the theatrical equivalent of a mid-list novelist: talented enough to continue
publishing, with earnings that could barely cover the groceries.
Though his part *in Gladiator* was on a lower tier when it came to
screen time, it was still the biggest paycheck he'd ever seen.

"I've maybe been solvent two years in the last twenty," he
said. "But it's not because I haven't been working."

Fortunately, Schofield's wife - a former actress - was that support-ive partner every man dreams of. This was evident from the day they met, when he was at one of the lowest ebbs of his life and career.

"I was marginally employed at menial labor and couldn't get an acting job to save my soul," he recalled. "But acting was still the way I defined myself and I couldn't give it up. So, one night after work I went to this bar where actors hung out, saying to my-self 'I am an actor. I am an actor. I AM an actor.' And I met her. And she understood. And I fell in love."

His wife made the choice to quit her own acting career to raise their children. Then, when financial necessity moved her back into the workforce after their daughter entered school, she felt like a fish out of water.

"You can't change identities like a suit of clothes," he said. "She'd made huge sacrifices for me and for our family and she was feeling very much at a loss for a sense of who she was. One day, she came home from work feeling particularly depressed and de-feated. I just took her in my arms and told her, 'Sweetheart, no matter what else you may be doing, you're just an out-of-work actress.'"

That solidarity had paid off in a twenty-year marriage. Not long ago, he experienced the dividends of being a loving parent as well.

"My teenage son is a musician with a rock band and they re-cently played their first big concert which went over very well," the actor recalled. "After the concert he said to me, 'Dad, all these years I've wondered why you do it. But near the end, when I could feel they'd really liked us and we heard the applause, I understood what you meant about how great it feels.' Hearing him say that justified everything for me. I can die a happy man tomorrow and go to my grave with the knowledge it's all been worthwhile."

On Monday, as Branko had promised, we resumed filming... somewhere.

Cameras were squeezed inside Commodus' Wagon which was supposed to be en route to the German Front but was actually in the car park where we based our catering tent and caravans. The scene was a dialogue between Commodus and Lucilla concerning their father. The crew had a late call - 9:00 a.m. - which was a way of easing us into night work that would begin the next day and continue all week.

Returning to the Phoenicia in late afternoon, I wandered out to see what the pool looked like. It was deserted except for one couple, a woman in her mid-thirties reading a novel beside a white-haired man holding a sun reflector at the sides of his goatee.

"I'm being forced to keep up this Moroccan tan," Oliver Reed explained. "No sacrifice too great for art, you know."

He introduced me to his wife Josephine. A round face that made her look even younger than her 35 years, she had the strong, steady gaze of a champion at cerebral chess with judgmental strangers. They were married in 1985 - he was 46, she was twenty.

Josephine and I exchanged a few empty sentences, which, like both our smiles, were merely a cover that allowed other senses to probe. Most evident was that her pugnacity wasn't the close-to-the-surface sort that could be learned at the elbow of a master like her husband. It was a kindred spirit the rebel Reed had recognized in the body of the sixteen-year-old Irish lass he'd courted to up-raised eyebrows throughout County Cork.

Turning back to Ollie, I mentioned that I'd looked at the curriculum vitae his agent sent me and was surprised to note the absence of theater credits - that subject, of course, being fresh in my mind.

"I've done practically no theater at all, no interest in it," he smiled. "It's hard work and all you end up with is a kick in the ass from the critics. I'm a movie actor. That's all. It's all I've ever wanted to be."

The front desk had a package for me. It was just this morning that I'd given Reed a large selection of photos spanning nearly the entire shoot in Morocco. I thought it would take him days - if not weeks - to look them over, mark his approvals and return them so I could submit his choices to the studio. There, on the envelope, his name was crossed out and mine written in.

Inside the large manila mailer were the unmarked photos and a note:

Dear Rob, I'm sure nothing bad will escape your trained eye.
Love Oliver

By day, the stunt team - coordinator Phil Neilson, sword master Nick Powell, horse master Steve Dent and Maximus's stunt doubles Stuart Clarke, Peter White and Randy Miller - began blocking the Tiger Fight and Battle of Carthage scenes in the arena.

By night, the production team filmed. First in the parking lot where they'd marooned Commodus' Wagon along the German Front, then a bedroom of the Imperial Palace where the sovereign's lust for his sister Lucilla spins out in unsubtle threats.

Inside her candle-lit trailer, Connie Nielsen sat serenely in front of an altar she'd created for her character. There were iconic carvings, tapestries, burning incense and rows of books. The books, she admitted, were mostly unfinished but not unopened. "I'm constantly looking through them, researching. I want to feel enveloped by this time and place. I want to draw energy from the spirits we're bringing back to life here."

The sofa inside Joaquin's trailer was three-dimensional art: random splashes of denim and crumpled cotton accented by CD covers, matchbooks and a carton of Marlboros. The kitchenette table was piled with call sheets and multi-colored script pages. Etta James was blasting from the stereo. The young Emperor paced and avoided eye contact. "Hey, man. I've got those photos for you around here someplace. Where the...? Ah, bummer, maybe I left them at the hotel."

So, how were things going on the movie? "Great. Ridley's great. Connie's great. I just sometimes look around and wonder what I'm doing here. I just hope I don't embarrass myself."

Filming began in the main rooms of the Emperor's Palace the next night.

Night work is always tough on a crew - and Ridley hated it because he believed crews worked slower at night - but there was a noticeable ease, good humor and general lack of tension on set all week. Some were eager to attribute it to the changeover in leading men.

"Easier to do everything without that prick around, idn't it?" one of the grips bluntly summed up sentiments for that faction.

When we were filming in England, I'd wondered if there was a dynamic between our star and the British crew that differed from that of our American crew. The question was crystallizing into a theory: Brits were much more egalitarian. There was one "Guv'ner" – the director – and everyone else was there to serve him. American crews more readily accepted diva-like behavior from stars because... well, they were Stars. I was coming to understand that much of the antagonism toward Russell wasn't a reaction to his behaving badly – British crews are the biggest cut-ups and reprobates in the film world – but more from a sense that he was behaving "above his station."

There are no Stars in the British celluloid cosmos – only actors.

To test this theory, I asked one of the crew if he could name a British movie star.

"Well," came the long deliberated answer, "I s'pose Richard Burton."

I'd arrived early one evening and parked at base camp where John Shrapnel, who played Gaius, Derek's senate colleague and fighter for the republic, was sitting outside the hair and makeup trailer waiting for rehearsal.

Shrap was a direct descendant of Henry Shrapnel, the inventor of the artillery projectiles that revolutionized warfare in the 19th Century. John and his family chose paths as far from the science of manslaughter as they could get. His father, Norman, was a journalist for *The Guardian*, his mother was an artist and his younger brother a composer. His sons all aspired to careers in the film business.

Shrap's own career had been well balanced between film, stage and a good deal of exposure on U.K. television in both contemporary mysteries like *Dennis Potter's Blackeyes* and a series of BBC-produced Shakespearean plays. Veteran though he was, John was among the actors anticipating a record-breaking run on this movie.

"They have us scheduled for, I think seven or eight weeks?" he mused. "It's a long time in terms of the actual size of the part. I spent six weeks on *Nicolas and Alexander*, mainly waiting around to be rain cover - and it was weather like this. Blue skies, not a cloud in sight. So I said to myself, 'might as well dig in.' And that's when I met my wife."

It was John's first major film, at age 28, after nearly a dozen years on stage. It was production assistant Francesca Bartley's first movie job as well. She was taking time off between college semesters and had been hired by producer Sam Spiegel at the request of her mother, the actress Deborah Kerr.

Something like wartime romance erupts in young hearts joined on first-time film locations and it exploded like cannon fire in these two.

After six weeks in breezy sunshine, waiting for his rain-cover scenes to be shot, then waiting at night for her to finish handing out the call sheets at wrap so they could take long walks, have longer talks and partake in the hot-blooded gropings of young lust, the rain that would send him packing finally fell - but by then, so had Francesca. At the end of the movie, she returned to her university studies and Shrapnel returned to the stage. But unlike most location liaisons, this was one time for all time. Nearly thirty years and three children later, the now bald, still physically fit 57-year-old's eyes glistened in the recalling.

A lot can happen in six, seven or eight weeks on location. And for most of us, this one was to continue even longer.

I'd been so transported by Shrap's Russian love story that I was sure my watch was lying when I glanced down to see the little hand on the seven. I was a half-hour late for my appointment with a reporter from the *Times of Malta*.

Sometimes it's easy to forget I have an actual job.

Ariadne Massa was just walking out of the Phoenicia's lounge when I arrived, breathless and at a tactical disadvantage for having mucked up our rendezvous. A slim brunette in her mid-twenties, she had an elegance of the kind that overestimated her beauty.

She only had time for "a quick soda," she said as we returned to the bar. She was meeting some friends for dinner and a night on the town.

She was charming, intelligent and totally transparent in her desire to become my new best friend in order to gain access to the set. But I liked the malleable way in which she made her pitch about wanting to write "anything" about the movie and her Brenda Starr eagerness at being invited to visit the Colosseum set "soon" in order to do a story "all of Malta is interested in reading."

Part of her urgency, she admitted, was to publish a story before "the other paper" and asked me if I'd been in contact with *The Independent*. I told her David Kelleher, from that paper, had stopped by the office the other day - uninvited.

"They are very inaccurate," she spat. "And their circulation is very small."

The U.S. bombing campaign over Kosovo had begun after months of equivocation by President Clinton and obstruction by conservatives in Congress. It was big news in Malta, which had a sizable Albanian community that strongly supported the action.

I'd been talking with *USA Today*'s London-based correspondent Marco della Cava about coming to Malta to do a story on the movie but world events had taken precedence.

"Looks like I might have to push back my visit there," he apologized. "The paper wants me to go cover what's happening in the Balkans."

The postponement of the *USA Today* visit was fine with Ridley who, through Millie, informed me that he didn't want to do "any interviews" during production.

On set, where we were back on a daytime schedule and Russell was back at work, I found my moment between camera setups to press our director on that decision.

"I don't want to talk to anybody."

Talk as in "interview?" Perish the thought. You have your movie to direct, of course. But what if a writer comes all the way here, watches a few takes, you see him standing with me, ya come over to say "hi?" Maybe you tell him about what you just shot. That's it. You go back to your camera; I take him to talk with the actors.

Ridley arched an eyebrow and shifted his cigar. But he didn't say "no."

Joaquin had a bad cold but had gotten all his photo approvals ready for me. He was nervous about the memo I'd sent advising of upcoming press visits.

"I mean, I'll do it. I mean, I know I have to do it. But I never know what to say. I always go off on some tangent and feel like I sound like some jerkoff just spouting meaningless nonsense, y'know?"

Get a couple of comfortable phrases that describe your character and the movie and keep riffing on those whenever you find yourself staring into the void, I advised.

"Could you tell me what to say?"

Connie had no similar qualms about talking to press.

"I have so much to say about this movie, this character, this period in history," she effused as she lit another stick of incense. "The role of women in the times of the ancient Romans is fascinating to me. In obvious ways, they were totally powerless but behind the curtains, they were often the ones who were running things. Look at Nero's mother, Claudius's wife. Of course, Nero eventually had his mother killed and Claudius's wife tried to poison him..."

Matricide and mate-icide aside, there were topics the publicity department preferred the actors avoid in their discussions with the media. She was getting to those.

"But I'm not even sure how to play Lucilla. There have been so many new pages I haven't had time to collate them into my script. And we don't even know what's coming next. How am I supposed to convey the nuances of a scene without knowing what information will come after? Am I supposed to be conspiring with this one who I really don't trust? Is there going to be a scene with Maximus in which we reveal that we had a mad, passionate love affair? You need that information to clarify your actions."

Writers, on your marks...

CHAPTER NINETEEN

NO MAN IS AN ISLAND

In recognition of their wartime bravery, England's King George VI awarded the George Cross to the entire population of Malta. Although Malta officially gained its political independence from Britain on September 21, 1964, it remained part of the British Commonwealth with agreed-upon status as a military protectorate until 1979. March 31st of that year, to be precise.

On this March 31, Malta was celebrating its twentieth Freedom Day. I discovered this as I was driving to the set and came to a dead stop at a square in the town of Cospicua, where I usually turned left (curbside) on my way to Fort Ricasoli. The production had offered me a car. Despite my unfamiliarity with right-hand steering, I eagerly accepted. I was constantly getting lost but it was safer than driving with Reno.

Today, a black and red-uniformed marching band was occupying the street space I was accustomed to dashing through, heedless of pedestrians in the grand Maltese tradition. Perhaps I appeared to be the band member playing the automobile horn but the police officer standing not five feet from my car paid no attention when I shouted "Excuse me," in both English and Italian.

A leathery old man, standing on the fringe of the gathering, did hear me, however, and hobbled over to help. His response to my question about how I might detour around this plaza, to get back on the route to Fort Rinella, was an aborted:

"Go straight, then turn left... I'm going that way. May I get in? I'll show you."

So, I gave Frank a lift and he showed me the way – while telling me a little about his 91 years.

He had fought, not only in World War II in defense of Malta, but in the Spanish Civil War in defense of liberty.

"I wasn't so young, nearly thirty, and I was married with two young children," he began with a lightness that belied the subject. "But I was old enough to know what was right and so I couldn't keep from going. You know, you can't blame a man who is deaf for not hearing the truck that will run him over. But a man with all his senses should get out of the way. There is too much good in the world to allow the bad take over. So, if you see it, you must fight it.

"The war here, *mela*, that was different. In Spain, I never worried for my family. I knew they were safe. But during the bombing I was in the merchant marine. I was at sea for a year before I saw my home and family. I worried all the time what was happening to them."

He asked what brought me to Malta and I told him I was working on the movie *Gladiator*.

"Ahh, the Gloster Gladiators," he smiled. "Maybe you will protect us too, eh?"

I knew about the Gloster Gladiators: three planes, known as Faith, Hope and Charity that fought off German and Italian bombers here during the Second World War.

"Of course, there were more than just the three," Frank corrected. "But those are good words. Just like the planes, the words helped many people live through those times."

As a merchant marine, both before and after the war, he had traveled a lot, he said. "But I only saw America from the boat. I thought maybe someday I would go there but I never did. Maybe one of my children will send me there someday. I would still very much like to see America."

Ninety-one years old and still a bit of wanderlust.

I dropped Frank at a block of row houses, in front of a new model home in which he said one of his daughters lived.

"Now, you just follow this road around until it ends and turn right. Goodbye. I hope you get to know your way around Malta. It is only a little confusing at first."

As he got out of the car, I looked at my odometer: we were ten kilometers from where I'd picked him up. He'd been fully prepared to walk.

I've met presidents and princes, scholars and philosophers, the rich and famous. But no one has embodied the resilience of the human spirit or summed up the sweetness of life better than Frank.

There is too much good in the world to allow the bad to take over.

Hard as I tried to keep my eye on the Big Picture Frank had framed for me, a tedious day of petty complaints and clerical quagmires from studio bureaucrats soon wore me down. Back at the hotel I phoned Margaret. Our conversation sliced into a thicket of out-of-sync needs from which each of us should have taken a mulligan but both failed to think of that before hanging up feeling misunderstood and deserted.

"I'm a single mother," she played the card she never played in response to some thoughtless criticism I was unwilling or unable to retract in time. "I'm doing the best I can."

We'd covered this ground often enough to know our quarrel wasn't about who contributed more to keep the family boat afloat. It was about recognition: yes, darling, you have a tough job sometimes; yes, honey, you do an amazing job with the children. But ennui had already tied my shoelaces together and I fell short of that understanding.

In the Phoenicia lobby, I ran into Connie Nielsen, accompanied by our pixie-blonde key dialect coach, Sandra Butterworth. If these two couldn't put a pitter in one's patter, he was a corpse absent only six feet of dirt. Sandra asked if I'd like to join the two of them and Joaquin for dinner later.

There are times when even the most attractive company can't compete with a need for simple solitude.

I was hungry now, I lied. Thanks just the same.

She cocked her head and with a suit-yourself lift of her lashes, headed off to the bar with Connie.

I went for a walk.

Being a department of one has its advantages and disadvantages. Departments usually hang together after work hours. They're a nuclear family within the extended family. The publicist is an orphan.

Technically, Jaap and I were a department but the photographer is equally a part of the camera crew. He'd been hanging with them more since trading his room at the Phoenicia for a bachelor pad nearer the nightlife in Sliema and Paceville.

Before the reader sheds any tears for the publicist – the medic or script supervisor, who are usually the only other departments of one – I'll let it be known that I quite enjoy this outsider status. I dine with a wider variety of people and can wander off solo without colleagues wondering why I'm being anti-social.

Yet every free-floating organism in nature looks for a place to attach. And what I wanted more than food this night was a grounding outside the realm of lenses. Perhaps a bit of inspiration: Faith, Hope, Charity. At least the expansion of my island to this island.

I turned onto a street no wider than an alley where a solitary light bulb drew me to a doorway on whose faux marble cornice a sign read The Labyrinth.

One entered the Labyrinth through an alabaster portico into a high-ceilinged outer lobby with a 1950s style Rock-Ola jukebox and a red-velvet armchair.

Inside was a coffee shop with a half-dozen patrons sipping warm drinks and eating sprout-stuffed pitas beneath walls packed with original paintings and framed fruit crate labels. This was the kind of atmosphere into which I might happily have settled for a light supper of soup, sandwich and decent reading light. But there was a staircase to the right that drew me in deeper.

Descending, with one eye on the young woman behind the coffee counter, half-expecting her to warn me there was no admittance downstairs, I entered a subterranean hallway lined with eclectic art and potted palms. More paintings, sculptures and multi-media montages filled two adjacent gallery chambers.

A hostess appeared at the end of the hall.

"Are you here for dinner?"

She led me into a candlelit room with a dozen limestone arches, more potted palms, more artwork and Miles Davis' *Kinda Blue* bleating through scratchy speakers. At the far end of the dining room was a stage out of a *Twilight Zone* episode on which rested a drum set, a piano and a portable fan. Behind these hung a gold velvet curtain.

"How close do you want to be to the music?"

With maybe five of a dozen tables occupied, I picked one in the middle – a round one, as they were of various sizes, shapes and wood with mismatched chairs.

Soon, a short, middle-aged man in a dinner jacket emerged from behind the curtain and sat at the piano. He played for the next hour, his repertoire ranging from Monk to Joplin. My peppercorn steak was delicious and the price more than fair.

I strolled through the gallery on the way out. None of the art would ever find its way to the Louvre but it was varied, chosen as much for uniqueness as craft. And the basement walls, thick as pillars of Stonehenge, flawlessly whitewashed, sanded to silken smoothness were a masterwork. Someone had put a lot of heart into this place.

I'd found my Maltese hangout.

I returned to my hotel and phoned Margaret again. Funny how much better the conversation went this time.

CHAPTER TWENTY

SOUND THE TRUMPETS

The 7:00 a.m. crew call on April 5 was proclaimed by assistant director Terry Needham:
"Awright, ya lazy sods, breakfast is over. We're in."

The printed call sheet was equally unceremonious in stating:
EXT. ROME - ARENA - Cassius speech, bread for the people; 'Tiger' enters arena... start: Maximus enters.
Filming was about to begin in the Colosseum.

It was originally called the Flavian Amphitheater, but a 'colossal' statue of Nero, towering 120 feet above the entrance nearest the Emperor's palace, gave the Colosseum its popular name. The arena rose in four tiers, seating 45,000 spectators and beginning high enough off the ground so the front rows were safe from stampeding elephants – a small design flaw of the Circus Maximus where Nero had previously held his games. No expense from the public coffers was spared for the gold inlay bas-reliefs along the marble walls, halls and benches. The complex took over a decade to complete.

Branko Lustig didn't have a decade in which to work or a limitless supply of *denarius* with which to pay for his Colosseum. And Branko's crews, under the direction of construction manager Malcolm Roberts, ran into building problems the Romans never had to worry about: pirating - not on the high seas but on the docks – and island weather - Malta's most severe winter in thirty years, which brought rain with high winds that delayed material deliveries and limited scaffold labor.

They soldiered on toward the newly extended deadline of mid-March – which Malcolm knew they'd never make - with 400 European and Maltese carpenters, welders, mold makers, painters, pipefitters and plasterers, working with 600 tons of plaster and miles of lumber and metal in 'round-the-clock shifts. Finally, Roberts' exhausted workmen stood back and watched set painters apply finishing touches to the architectural jewel of the ancient Empire.

For Branko, it had been almost a year from the time he'd become involved with this project until this moment when the first camera was put in position on the Colosseum floor. For Arthur Max it had been nearly the same span of studying, planning and dreaming; for Ridley, even longer.

So, although no actual fanfare accompanied the start of filming this morning, inside the hearts of these three, a band of trumpeters were blowing their lungs out.

No horn section accompanied the arrival in Malta of *USA Today* reporter Marco della Cava, though he was deserving of at least three cheers. A slightly built, olive skinned thirty-five-year-old with soft, dark eyes that leveled on their subject in disarming earnestness, his recent assignment to Macedonia was his baptism in war coverage. His assignment here was a needed respite from all he'd just witnessed.

Last week, I spoke to him in the city of Skopje, near the Kosovo border. He'd been watching women and children arriving by the truckload, escaping the Serbian siege.

"Maybe twenty percent of the refugees were men. Maybe less," he said. "Most of the women have stories of the men being shot. Husbands, brothers, sons.

"The majority of the people I talked to had had little or nothing to eat for days. One image I can't get out of my head was a little boy, I couldn't tell how old - looked like four or five - clinging to a carrot that he'd been carefully nibbling since he left home, three days ago."

Marco admitted he had reached burnout.

"The news organizations don't want any of their people staying there too long, 'cause that's just what happens. Either you become so numb to it, you can't do a good job, or it just gets to you and you start feeling it too deeply. A part of me doesn't want to leave. It's the most important news event in the world today and it's gonna kill me to walk away from that - and from the people. But the paper's making the choice for me. I've gotta tell you, a big part of me is relieved that they are."

Over breakfast, Marco confessed something he found "interesting" about being here in Malta visiting a movie set: the unreality of his present circumstances didn't feel so different from the scene he'd left on the Kosovo border.

"I'd go visit the camps and ask refugees who'd just lost their homes and husbands and walked for days to escape with their lives, how things were going," he said with a sad smile. "Then I'd say 'thanks' and go back to my clean, warm hotel room, order room service and write the story."

On set, seemingly everyone was anxious to speak with him. His recent posting gave him the inverted identity of being a celebrity to the actors he was here to interview.

None of those actors was more interested than our star.

"I found it fascinating," Marco later recalled, "that Crowe would actually seek me out because he respected where I'd recently been."

CHAPTER TWENTY-ONE

MIDWAY MALAISE

Every movie suffers a midway malaise. It's inevitable: there's a hump to get over. Sometimes it manifests in lethargy, sometimes in costly mistakes; sometimes it resolves by redoubling efforts and pushing through, sometimes just by bearing up and getting on with it. Sometimes it feels the center will not hold. And sometimes it doesn't.

After a day of playing EPK spies because Joaquin had decided he didn't want the documentary team around and we had to steal shots from the rafters, I needed a drink and some diverting company. So, I wandered down to the Phoenicia bar.

At one of the cocktail table islands, David Schofield sat in a chair next to Jacobi, across from Shrapnel who was sitting on a couch delivering what seemed an important bit of information to

Oliver Reed. Reed's tanned skin was nearly lineless in the dim light. His moist eyes caught the reflection of the table candle as he relaxed with both arms draped on the sofa back.

I said "hello" just as David and Derek got up, looking impatiently at Shrap.

It was suddenly obvious John was finishing, not a discussion but a heated reprimand - to which Oliver was responding, not with silken calm but with a teeth-gritting slow burn, evolving into the kind of exaggerated snarl that I've seen on my twelve-year-old when he wants to show that he's in control - shortly before he goes completely out of control.

Derek's voice was imperious in announcing, "We're going to dinner now."

He turned to me and commanded, "You're coming with us."

Shrap rose with a flourish. Derek took my arm and the four of us hurried out.

At my suggestion we went to the Labyrinth. The chef and main waitress had just quit and one of the managers was doing the cooking, so dinner took an hour to arrive and was disappointing when it got there.

In that time, however, there was plenty to talk about: mostly related to Oliver.

Ollie had starting drinking at the Phoenicia long before Sonny the senior barman arrived for his 5:00 shift. According to Sonny, Reed cleared most of the room with loud swearing, then took care of the remaining few by standing up and unzipping his pants, claiming - later verified by third parties - that he had a rose tattoo where the sun didn't shine.

"He was like a car that had lost its clutch and couldn't shift gears," Shrapnel said.

It was no coincidence that the first time Ollie had fallen off the wagon was two days after Josephine left to attend a relative's funeral in Ireland. He'd made it through Morocco under his own direction, then handed over the steering wheel. He kept telling everyone in the bar how much he missed his wife.

Dinner arrived around the same time as a couple more guests: Gilly and Adam, two young British actors just in for a couple of days to play Roman soldiers whom Commodus orders his Praetorian captain to turn into human pincushions in reprisal for the botched assassination of Maximus. The older cast filled the newcomers in on the night's events at the Phoenicia.

Reed remained the topic throughout dinner but gradually with more head shaking than censure.

Derek, who knew Ollie best, sighed that Reed was famous for "always wanting to pick a fight with the biggest man in the room." But his goal was asserting his superior masculinity rather than blackening someone's eye.

"I worked with him in the '70s when he was at his hell-raising worst," Jacobi began a story. "We were sitting in a pub one night and he was regaling a couple of soldiers. With no apparent provocation, Oliver took a handful of peanuts from a bowl on the bar and dropped them on the floor. Then he challenged the soldiers to a race to see which of them could push the peanuts across the floor and out the door with their nose. He said, 'Anyone who can beat me, I'll give him 500 pounds.' Of course, Oliver won."

We walked back to the hotel through the near-deserted streets of the capital city, pausing once to peer in the window of a rare bookstore. The crisp night air mixed well with fermented grape, engendering a comradely esprit as we exited the city gates and saluted the mermen in Triton's Fountain outside the bus terminal.

Entering the lobby of the Phoenicia we saw Sonny the bartender at the front desk, talking to the night manager. He glanced in our direction, raising a single eyebrow.

"I'd like to see if Oliver is still in the bar," I said.

Gilly volunteered to come with me. Sonny wasn't more than ten seconds behind.

As Gilly and I walked down the tile hallway leading to the closed glass doors of the bar, I was aware of the similarity of our sizes: both about 6'2", both in the neighborhood of 200 pounds.

It was no surprise to see Oliver still seated where we'd left him three hours ago. Sonny's younger, pint-pulling partner Pierre unlocked the doors for us, explaining they'd closed the lounge and tried to lure Reed out by having some food sent to his room.

"Ollie, there's dinner waiting for you in your room," I said, perching on the arm of a stuffed chair opposite him. "Why don't we get up there before it gets cold?"

He smiled some foggy recognition and remained slumped against the sofa, spinning his fists like a man punching a workout bag in slow motion.

Gilly plopped down next to him.

"Hey, Ollie, how's it goin'? We're gonna take you upstairs. There's a good lad."

Gilly said something else in this patronizing vein and I cringed. Besides the fact Reed didn't have a clue who this pre-sumptuous upstart was, the biggest man in the room — at least one of two — was now challenging his manhood.

"Oliver, the bar's closed," I coaxed. "Sonny and Pierre want to get home."

He swore at me and I laughed it off.

"We can probably get Sonny to send a bottle up with us. How about it?"

He swore again. But more softly. I almost had him there, I thought.

"Come on, get off your lazy ass Reed and let the gents close up," Gilly said, standing as he grabbed one of Oliver's arms.

Ollie cursed him, shook loose his arm and fell back against the couch, motioning a roundhouse punch with the lightning speed of a mud-caked creeper and delivering an equally sluggish kick whose thirty degree knee-extension didn't get past the cocktail table let alone within three feet of anyone's groin.

"You fat fuck!" Gilly shouted, standing over him with fists clenched. "You wanna fight? I'll fight you, you fuck. I'll kick your fucking fat ass."

Pierre and I each took one of Gilly's arms and led him backwards towards the exit. He offered no resistance.

"Your friend is not very nice," Pierre said to me at the door.

"He's not my friend," I snapped.

In front of the other actors, I lit into Gilly for the stupid way he'd handled himself and cut off his "self-defense" explanation that the others, who didn't see how incapacitated Reed was, might even be inclined to buy.

But Gilly being a jerk wasn't what I was mad about. He was just some third-stringer who'd made a meaningless error after the game had already been lost.

Sonny and Pierre carted Oliver upstairs soon after we left. They used the old school method: persistence and courtesy.

My steps fell heavy up three flights, partly with sadness, partly deliberation and unflatteringly from the distant toll of publicity warning bells: how much headache is an unleashed Oliver Reed going to cause me?

I got a call from Margaret shortly after getting back to my room. She put Sam on to tell me about the "great day" he'd had rehearsing for his fifth grade play and all the compliments he'd gotten from all the girls about "what a great voice" he had when he sang his solo. "It gave me so much confidence about wanting to be an actor."

Go for it, kiddo. It's your dream. Still, forgive my dread that, one day, we'll have to have The Talk: not about sex - about the realities of life on center stage.

Russell was back on center stage as we continued the Tiger sequence. As usual, he put up resistance to his stunt-doubles claiming any of his glory.

The scene had been carefully choreographed and our star knew the moves as well as any of the stuntmen. However, he was not a stuntman. He was an actor. A stuntman is trained to make the action *look* dangerous – not actually *be* dangerous.

There were experienced handlers beside each of the trap doors in which the big cats were penned and Sled Reynolds stood beside a marksman with a tranquilizer-dart gun. The morning had been marked by frustration, as Sled's tamer, American-trained tigers couldn't be motivated to pounce. Russell paced and fumed, as if their reluctance to attack him was a personal affront.

So, as the cameras waited, the wilder French-trained cats were substituted.

Once the new tigers were in place, Russell and actor Sven-Ole Thorsen who played his opponent in this death match were invited to take their places in the arena.

"Cameras ready?" shouted Terry Needham.

"Action," ordered Ridley.

The actors crossed weapons and began their fight. Russell was felled, as scripted, and the signal given for Tiger One to be let out of his trap.

Russell had rolled just a foot or so off his mark.

The tiger took a swipe at our star – millimeters from the short sleeve of his shirt.

"Cut," Ridley jumped out of his chair.

Russell was checked for wounds and summarily removed from the game. So were the French cats. The day proceeded with stunt doubles and the tamer tigers.

A later segment called for Maximus' double to put his arm in a cat's jaws. The arm was wrapped in sheet metal with a tough hide covering. Actor and animal were positioned and the cameras rolled.

As they wrestled in the dirt, the tiger bit into the protected arm – clamping its jaws and *piercing* the metal brace. A trainer rushed in to bop the animal with a baton and the tiger, giving a surprised look, let go.

The stuntman was rushed to the hospital. The teeth had broken skin but not torn. The actor was treated with antibiotics and released later that day.

There were no complaints from Maximus about not doing this one himself.

Sometimes a stunt really *is* dangerous.

Beneath eyebrows like raven's wings, David Hemmings took in a room like a grifter checking the exits.

During London's Swinging Sixties, Hemmings was the poster boy of the partying elite, linked with glitterati from the Beatles to the mobster Kray brothers. He claimed little of it was true. Well, yes, he was "friends with John and Paul" but he "really didn't have the time or stamina" to keep up with all the super-models he was reported to be dating. On the other hand, the tabloids may not have had the staff or ink to keep up with what stamina David did demonstrate during those dizzying days in the Mecca of Mod – or later, in Los Angeles where Hemmings sight-ings at groovy Malibu galas were as ubiquitous as paisley ties. He was an energizing addition to our nightly galas as well.

Having done his big Colosseum scene a few days ago, he was on hold until the filmmakers decided if they were going to write anything more for him. So here he was in Malta on "sort of a paid holiday," as he put it.

Hemmings was alone in this contentment.

Waiting was on the minds of all who joined us that night in the Phoenicia bar. Creative unease over our perpetually in-prog-ress script was now intertwined with an itch to know when one would be freed to go home, at least for a visit.

"It's not fair that I'm weather cover!" Derek moaned moments after joining the conversation. The weather had been just sunny enough to shoot what had been scheduled but too unpredictable for the filmmakers to release him to fly back to England.

Shrap, Schofield, Tomas Arana, Connie and Joaquin came down from their rooms in similar doldrums after a day in which none of them had worked. Waiting was something a film ac-tor had to get used to. But the added strain of waiting without

knowing when – or even if – you were going to work again –
and on what - was making these scriptless actors restless as caged
cats.

Midway malaise and script uncertainties had been getting to
the crew as well. So, to fill the dead air in our programming, they
concocted a little diversion.

Our Colosseum had the irresistible appeal of onlookers and
open spaces. Combine that with a restive, mostly male crew and
some sort of sporting competition will emerge.

This one began when prop man Mickey Woolfson remarked to
one of the cameramen that he looked like he was putting on a few
pounds.

"Yeah, well I can still beat you in a foot race," came the retort.

Melodramatically grasping his "trick knee," Mickey demurred
but nominated second a.d. Adam Somner to carry his colors into
battle.

"Adam looks like he walks without lifting his feet," Mickey
described. "He's a slow starter but he comes on like a Jaguar in
overdrive."

So, the lunch hour match was set, with Mickey and Terry
Needham holding the money and covering the bets on their man
Adam.

Adam won the race handily.

Mickey and Terry set up two more races the next day with a
couple of other challengers who fancied themselves speedsters.
Adam left them in the dust.

There was no way anyone was going to be competing for anything on our set without the Big Dog asserting himself. It was
inevitable that Russell would want to "show you boys how it's
done."

Russell told Terry and Mickey that he had been "a champion
runner" back in his youth and could sprint circles around the
duck-walking a.d. with the Coke-bottle specs.

Mickey talked him down from the $1,000 he initially wanted
to wager to around 100 British pounds. The other bets came in,

with most - including Russell's assistant Bob Long - favoring Adam.

Russell lobbied for a distance of 100 meters because that had been his race, he said. Mickey marched off 72 meters and said, "That's it. That's all our man can go. He's already run two races today."

"Yeah, well I've been fighting tigers all day!"

Those in attendance simply stared.

Russell eventually yielded. He told his dresser, Michael Castellano, he wanted fresh socks and a wooden box to rest his feet on. Michael brought him the socks, the box, massaged his feet and laced up his shoes.

"They're too tight. Looser."

Castellano made the adjustment.

"Too loose. Tighter."

And again. Finally getting the perfect runner's squeeze fit.

Mickey appointed himself the starter.

"Two false starts and you're disqualified," he informed the runners - knowing Adam would lose a second off the line and trying to psych the challenger out of his advantage in that.

"Bullshit," Crowe protested. "Any competition I've ever heard of you get three."

Mickey finally consented - after getting in an extra few minutes of psychological sabotage. With Terry goading the crowd of 2,000 extras to cheer for the unknown, Mickey gave a "Ready. Steady. Go," and they were off.

Russell shut out the crowd, the psych jobs and the shenanigans of the bookies, to burst off the line into the lead.

But Adam quickly overcame a meter-and-a-half deficit, evened up, then started to pull ahead.

Crowe, seeing he'd lost his lead, tried to pour it on from the deepest coal stove in his engine... and tripped.

Adam broke the tape.

Russell catapulted himself up and didn't even take time to dust the dirt off his shorts before grabbing Adam and dragging him back towards the starters' line.

"Here, here, there'll be none of that," Terry ordered.

"The hell there won't," Russell argued. "I tripped. I want a rematch."

Ridley, seeing his star tumble, had risen from his seat, poised to put the kabosh on anything that might endanger his movie. But Terry was steps ahead of him.

"Our man's already run three races. That's it for today. Everybody back to work."

With the crowd still roaring "Aaa-dum, Aaa-dum," Russell made a final, futile effort to force a runoff, insisting that if there were no rematch right away, he wouldn't pay off his bets.

But Terry held his ground and Mickey quickly took off Adam's shoes. The games were over.

Russell cooled down and paid up – everyone but Bob Long.

To prevent a rematch the next day, Mickey and Terry had Nicki Nurse put a bandage around Adam's knee and made him wear shorts to display it.

Sometime later, Djimon told the two bookies that he could beat Russell or Adam and offered to prove it. Terry and Mickey were willing to sign him up but required a £100 fee for their promotional services. Djimon told them to forget it.

As the sporting life took over the Colosseum, other sporting pursuits were gaining popularity outside the *Gladiator* arena.

Crew cavorting was hitting high stride: makeup ladies tumbling with stunt studs, wardrobe personnel fitting production assistants and special effects boys leaving trails of smoke through the set dressing department. The construction crew knew on which corners the local pros built their customer base and pillars of disco dolls were seen supporting leaning towers of gladiators all over Paceville nightly. Nicki Nurse could hardly keep enough penicillin in stock. Jaap innocently offered his spare bedroom to two beautiful Czech makeup girls with whom he'd worked in

Prague and awoke to find one of them naked under his covers. What's a boy to do?

But in my circle, intercourse was mainly verbal.

During dinner with Connie, Joaquin and Tomas one night, la bella Lucilla told tales of her courtship.

One would hardly think of Connie Nielsen needing more than a coy tilt of the head to lure any heterosexual within fifty miles and fifty years of her into any carnal compromise she might have in mind. But when romancing her husband, a full compliment of female combat weapons was required.

After meeting and targeting her intended, she asked a friend to bring him to a dinner party for which she cooked her most irresistible Northern Italian. This may have made him bite but it took more than a primo primavera to reel him in.

"We started dating and went months without him so much as making a pass," one could feel the pent up passion the mere memory revived. "I kept wearing shorter skirts and lower cut blouses, hoping he'd notice. He still wouldn't give me more than a peck on the cheek."

All the men present leaned forward craving details. She leaned back with a smile.

"But when he was ready, he was really ready," she concluded, leaving our imaginations to fill in the blanks.

Joaquin shyly admitted that he'd met a girl he liked here in Malta.

"But she hardly speaks any English," he said with foot-scuffing exasperation.

"I'm sure you can teach her just what to say," encouraged Tomas.

CHAPTER TWENTY-TWO

JUST IGNORE IT

The DreamWorks publicity department would not let go of the notion that if I really *tried* I could talk Russell into waiving his rights of photo approval and permit *Conde Nast* and *Premiere* to send their own photographers to shoot some pictures.

So, I tried again.

"No. That's final. I don't wanna hear about it again."

There would be two more requests from the studio – one an order, the other a plea – a week after I'd sent in his "final" answer. Many studio publicists are under the impression we unit publicists don't work hard enough.

Back at my office, there was another message from the studio publicist in charge of EPKs, copying everyone in the department, reminding me we still had Russell Crowe's interview to do the next time John Pattyson visited Malta.

As if I wasn't going to remember?

A fax came from a writer at the *London Express*. On the cover sheet, he handwrote in the politest tones:

We have a story about the atmosphere on the set of "Gladiator" which I enclose for your attention. I would be very grateful if you had a moment to comment on the matter.

I also wanted to ask if a part was ever found for Vinnie Jones who was auditioning with Ridley Scott last year? If so, what part does he have and if not, why not?

Thanks very much for your help.

Yours,

Edward Black

The attached story read:

Liv Tyler, girlfriend of Joaquin Phoenix for the last few years, recently had an amorous liaison over the course of filming Plunkett & Macleane with her director Jake Scott, son of Ridley.

To get back at Jake, Joaquin held a party in Malta and heavily came onto Ridley's much younger girlfriend. I don't know whether he had any success, but the tension on set sounds so thick, you could cut it with a knife.

On the bottom of the page was a handwritten addendum:

Note: I did send a fax last week but I am not sure if you got it. I would be very grateful if you could get back to me about this as otherwise we shall just run it saying that the production office declined to comment.

Thank you very much,

Edward Black

I didn't get last week's alleged fax but I did get both the implicit message - "we'll run this as fact or we'll run it with your denial" – and the unintended message: all he had was a two paragraph item. He was asking for enough information to turn it into a story.

When I showed the letter to Ridley, he bit into his cigar and squeezed out the words, "Fucking bastard. You tell him he'd better not fuck with my family."

You sure you want me to tell him that?

The truth, I'd learned from some of the crew who had worked on *Plunkett & Macleane*, was that Jake Scott did have a location romance with Liv Tyler - though she claimed to have broken up with Joaquin before that. And no amount of alcohol would make the Kid from Florida confident enough to *seriously* "come on" to Giannina Facio, Costa Rican diplomat's daughter, international B-movie bombshell and Ridley's steadfast girlfriend.

To quell the director's bloodlust, however, I drafted a letter with phrases like, "you drew conclusions that were wildly inaccurate," and "The 'atmosphere on the set' of *Gladiator* is one of enthusiastic commitment to this project..."

I showed the letter to Ridley. He read, nodded and handed it back to me.

"Maybe it's best if we just ignore it," he said.

CHAPTER TWENTY-THREE

EXTRAS

Margaret and the boys arrived in Malta around midnight, turning that darkness to bright new day. Six loving arms encircled me. I was home again. Now I needed to make it feel like we all were.

I hadn't seen my sons since January, Margaret in over a month. This was the reunion we'd all planned the first half of our year around. We were a family again.

When one thinks back on the experience of a film location, the highlight isn't the big battle scene but that special visit from loved ones. Memory, as we've discussed, is editing. In reality, these visits are hard work – on top of your day job.

The Phoenicia had exchanged my small room for a two-room suite and provided a pair of cots for the boys in the living room. My new third-floor accommodations were situated above the bus terminus that encircled Triton's Fountain. Traffic noise was loudest in the boys sleeping area, which was fine for Sam who could sleep through artillery bombardment but not for Casey who claimed the sound of Sam's rolling over was enough to keep him awake.

At about 2:00 a.m., Casey who had slept during most of the long flight - and not eaten - came into our room wide-awake and hungry. I scrounged together a dinner of a pear and two cups of yogurt and stayed up with him for an hour before introducing him to the 15 part audio edition of Peter Jennings' The Century, guaranteed to put any 12-year-old to sleep. He was up to Pearl Harbor by noon the next day.

At around 3:00 a.m., I returned to bed where I had a mosquito buzzing in my ear. It apparently entered through a bedroom window that Margaret, battling the constrictions of hotel air, had opened in a gasping fit.

At around 4:00, Sam crawled into bed to "snuggle." By 4:15, he realized he was too restless and asked me to walk him back to his own bed where we talked (quietly) for a few minutes before he decided he was "maybe getting a little bit sleepy again" - by which time I was wide awake.

The boys had a two-week break from school and, discounting two days of travel plus one day that my spouse had sensibly allocated for recuperation on the back end, I would have them in my life for the next eleven days – the longest I'd seen them all year. It was the longest Margaret had allowed for a location visit since the boys were toddlers.

I knew Sam would be up for spending time with me on set. Casey was fine anywhere, as long as he had an audio book to listen to. The big question was whether their mother would relax and enjoy or just endure so lengthy a visit. Being away from home was hardest on her. So that was where I'd focus my campaign.

Things were off to a good start: Margaret was in love with the hotel. Its lavish lobby, Victorian-style tearoom, acres of gardens and elegant restaurant delighted her senses. The place that had most regularly delighted mine, the Club Bar, didn't quite live up to my advanced billing. Sonny and Pierre were still serving but missing were most of my buddies. The Senatorial trinity, John, David and Derek, had finally been granted leave to go home for a few days.

The next night, we ordered room service for our boys and I took Margaret for a romantic dinner at the Labyrinth. Unfortunately, their lone waitress had called in sick and only the upstairs coffee shop was open. The Labyrinth's owner, creator and curator, Colin Henry, was behind the counter. Pale and thin, sporting a cardigan with an ascot, he was crestfallen that his restaurant wasn't open for us but what could he do? We were his only customers, so he sat with us and told us his story.

Colin was a British exile who came to Malta 14 years ago to escape a bad marriage, debts and a drinking problem.

"At first I was the kind of drunk who'd just be silly, y'know? It was all lots of fun. The longer I kept at it, the more I became an angry drunk."

He'd run a music store in London.

"I'd been a huge Tom Waits fan and I put together a big window display of all his records," Colin recounted. "One of our regular customers was a concert promoter and I told him all about Tom Waits and he got inspired by all that and booked a concert for him, one of Tom's first London concerts.

"The night of the concert, my friend brought me backstage and introduced me as 'the man who was responsible for getting you here.' Tom was very gracious, maybe even a little grateful, and we had a nice conversation. Next time he was in town he invited me to go out drinking with him.

"Well, I got drunk and I got to thinking too much of myself, carried away with being on his level and all, and I guess I became downright insulting. It wasn't too long after that I stopped drinking."

After his move to Malta, he pulled himself together enough to start this restaurant and become a patron of the arts.

His gallery curatorship was far from lucrative and I'd seen him pay musicians for performing when there were only three of us in the room. His waitresses, cook and suppliers were always at least a payment behind. But he was clinging to this little Camelot, his dream, his glory, as if it were his last chance at redemption.

"Do me a favor," he said as we got up to leave. "If ya ever run into Tom Waits, tell him I'm sorry."

It wasn't the candlelight and music I'd planned but Margaret admitted it was an interesting evening. I chalked up a point for the home team.

My jetlagged love and I abandoned all pretense to unconsciousness around 7:30 the next morning and found Ralf and Djimon in the dining room having breakfast before their morning workout. They greeted her like a long-lost sister and filled her in on how everything was going.

"Everything is great," said Ralf. "My part has gotten much bigger. I talked with Ridley about some ideas for the ending."

"Everything is fine," said Djimon. "Only we're still not sure at the end of every day what we're going to be doing the next morning."

We woke the boys for breakfast and introduced them to Djimon and Ralf.

"How'd you guys get so many muscles?" Sam asked, in the seconds it takes a ten-year-old to assume such familiarity.

The former Mr. Universe told the boys about his strict weight training regimen, lifting up to six hours a day when he was preparing for a competition.

Djimon said he never lifted weights or at least rarely used them for much more than warmup. "I got my muscles from swimming and boxing."

The actors invited the boys to come to the gym where they would put them through a workout.

"I'll show you how to lift weights so, by the end of the day, you'll have muscles like mine," enthused Ralf.

"You don't want anything of yours to be like him," Djimon jibed. "You come and I'll get you started hitting the heavy bag. That's how you get strong."

The day's scene, in a cell under the Colosseum, was inaccessible to all but shooting crew, so my sons and I spent the afternoon at the Fort Ricasoli gym. Ralf and Djimon, good to their words, put the boys through a rigorous routine. Margaret stayed at the hotel and swam in the pool.

The next afternoon, I took my family to the set and, during a break in filming, introduced the boys to our star.

"Ya shoulda been here last week when I had to fight a hungry tiger. Come to think of it, the two of yas together woulda made about the right-sized snack," Russell teased the two young strangers. "You guys gonna be around for awhile?"

Both nodded.

"Well, take care of your mum and keep your old man outa trouble. I've gotta go to work now."

To me he added, "They're gonna be here for the Carthage stuff, right?"

Err, the Carthage scenes are scheduled for the day they're supposed to leave.

"Ah c'mon, they don't wanna miss that." The wily little boy in Russell addressed this to Mom.

The boys looked excitedly to their mother. Margaret forced a smile.

With my wife's grudging consent, I phoned the production office to extend their stay an extra day so they could see the Battle of Carthage.

Days later, a white Mercedes sedan slowed in passing as we walked from the catering tent along the dirt road leading into Fort Ricasoli.

"Hey, Rob," Russell stuck his head out the window, "They're not paying you enough on this movie, you've gotta put your family to work?"

Yes, I'd done that most foolish of all foolish things a movie employee can do: I'd signed up my family to be extras for the day.

I somehow got Margaret and the boys out of bed before 5:00 a.m. and delivered to the wardrobe warehouse, which was already manufacturing Roman citizens when we arrived. My family's appreciation of this movie marvel descended in enthusiasm from Sam in reverse order of age. The costume department outfitted Sam in street urchin's sackcloth and the makeup department smudged his face with ash. He had a character. He was ready to show his acting chops.

Casey hated being hand-held by his younger brother. He chose instead to stumble behind, following what he could see of Sam's back, tripping over discarded garments and bumping into the maze of benches in the crowded fitting room. He was nominated to be a Patrician Child and fitted with regal tunic and sandals. His gown itched, he complained.

Margaret had her eye on the fancy frocks put aside for the Senators' wives or even one of the off-the-shoulder slit-up-the-side gowns worn by entertainers and concubines. But those had all been given out by the time she reached the front of the line. She wound up in the brown sackcloth of a serving woman. Her makeup was removed and her hair pulled back in a tight knot.

With her worry lines thus exposed, Margaret was reunited with her sons outside the styling area and loaded onto a bus that would take them the two kilometers to Ft. Ricasoli. Casey sat squirming and scratching beside his mother; Sam had the window seat in front of them. Waiting for the bus to fill up, stripped of her vanity and sleep-deprived, Margaret took out a book and slipped on her reading glasses.

"Hey, Mom," Sam turned in his seat. "You look just like Gandhi."

Margaret later told me she suspected "someone was probably trying to get even with the publicist" through his wife.

The scene today was key for both the film and the EPK crew: it would be the production's only attempt at a large-scale re-creation of life on the streets of Rome.

The scripted drama would occur between Gracchus and Gaius - Jacobi and Shrapnel - conspiring in an outdoor cafe as the carnival of commerce in the Empire's capital performed around them. Acrobats and minstrels joined merchants and beggars where horse drawn chariots shared the boulevard with circus animals and slave wagons. There were 546 extras, including thirty mounted Praetorian Guardsmen, ten Horse Grooms, five Mule Cart Drivers, two Elephant Handlers and an Oxen Handler. Ancient Rome was the star today.

With Margaret and the boys corralled in the extras holding area, I sought out Terry Needham.

"I'd like to put in a shameless request to have my family prominently placed in this scene."

"Done," snapped Terry.

He called forth a chariot and the Serving Woman was summoned aboard with her noble ward while the dirty little Street Urchin scampered up and hid behind them, having stolen a ride.

They were supposed to pull up to the cafe where Gracchus and Gaius plotted, disembark behind a quartet of Sedan Chair Carriers, and walk in past the "A" camera. Instead, they rode back and forth for a few takes until Ridley decided the chariot obscured the depth-of-field and had it removed from the scene - reducing Casey and Margaret to common foot traffic amongst the street crowd.

For Sam, however, this new configuration was liberating and an actor was unleashed. Suddenly, he was alone on the streets of Rome, a surreptitious scoundrel forced, through cruel circumstance, to live by his cunning. With each take, Sam darted and

dodged, zigged and zagged, snatched and grabbed, ran and hid
- too often, unfortunately, from the camera. But no matter, the
play was the thing and he was playing The Urchin of Rome, a role
second in importance to none.

During lunch, one of the elephants was grazing near the catering tent and Casey got close enough to be tickled by its trunk.

"Is it safe to get close to him?" Margaret asked.

"Very safe," his owner assured. "He's very gentle. I raise him
myself from a baby. He only gets upset when he can't see me."

To demonstrate, the trainer walked away and hid behind one of
portable outhouses. In less than a minute the pachyderm started a
mournful trumpeting that made this seem a cruel experiment. The
man reappeared and permitted the elephant to pick him up with its
powerful proboscis and place him on one of its tusks where he balanced, scratching the big baby between the eyes.

"What happens when you have to use the toilet?" Casey asked.

"It's a problem," the trainer replied.

All too soon, the day of the Big Scene was at hand. Margaret
had given up her planned day of recuperation in Ithaca for this.
Sam, well, no sacrifice was too great for his new pal Russell
Crowe. Casey, for whom flexibility was not a defining character-
istic, had given up the comforts of a temperature-controlled hotel
room and wanted it known he was not happy with that privation
on this last day of location adventure.

The fortress in which our film was being shot lay in a straight tra-
jectory across the Mediterranean to the capital of what is now Tunisia.
It was once the Empire of Carthage. There were three great battles
between Rome and Carthage, called by the Romans The Punic Wars.
The second of these occurred between 218 and 201 B.C. and would
determine which of these empires ruled the world.

David Hemmings was wearing a dress, cranapple lipstick and
an orange Shirley Temple wig. He sat on a section of bleachers,

smoking a cigarette, gazing over the whole of Ft. Ricasoli from a rooftop, as veteran assistant director Brian Cook stood by the second unit camera.

"Alright then, camera reloaded? David, if you please, we'll go again."

Hemmings adjusted his wig, put out his cigarette and stepped to his mark in front of a gilded, plaster Roman Eagle perched on a column.

"On this day we reach back to hallowed antiquity," Cassius the Orator boomed, "to bring you a re-creation of the second fall of mighty Carthage."

John Pattyson was contemplating his own mighty fall – from grace with the studio. His mandate was "don't come back 'til you've bagged Our Star" in an interview and there'd been no opportunities thus far. This was his last scheduled EPK day and overages came out of his pocket. I was on roundup duty for Russell today.

Margaret sat with a handful of other visitors in the canopied section of seats reserved for the Senators. These would be out of frame all day.

A chainlink entrance to the arena was shut to prevent runaway horses from exiting - or non-essential personnel from entering. On the outside looking in, Sam was miming the swordplay between 11-year-old Spencer Treat Clark, who played Lucilla's son Lucius, and sword master Nick Powell who was instructing him for an upcoming scene in the Palace. Casey was hiding under a tower of scaffolding, listening to his audio edition of Douglas Adams' *The Hitchhiker's Guide to the Galaxy* for about the 17th time.

"Wouldn't you be more comfortable sitting up with mom?"

No. There were too many people around who might talk to him.

"You don't wanna sit there in the dirt all afternoon?"

No. What he really wanted was to go back to the hotel. But sitting in the dirt was a good way of making that statement.

"You want me to describe what's going on in the arena?"

Admittedly, there was nothing going on at the moment.

"What's bugging you?"

With only a little cajoling, the answer shifted from "nothing" to "it's hot" to "Sam" - a fairly predictable sequence.

"Sam's always trying to be so cool."

Cool and its practitioners were a constant burr in Casey's jockey shorts.

I explained, not for the first time, that what he perceived as Sam "trying to act 'cool'" was like someone trying on costumes to see how he looked in them.

A few minutes later he came out from under the bleachers.

"What's going on?" he asked.

"The Emperor is pleased to bring you the legionnaires of Scipio Africanus," Orator Cassius roared above the imagined cheers of bloodthirsty thousands who would be tracked in later. Three ornate chariots, driven by horse master Steve Dent's charioteers, carried three women athletes from the British television show *Gladiators*. Each Amazon warrior was black, brawny, beautiful and wearing a form-fitted, bronze breast plate.

"There are three chariots racing around the arena. Not really racing. Sort of in formation. They each have a beautiful woman riding behind a chariot driver. Two of the women have bows pulled back, ready to fire arrows at a group of gladiators who are kinda gathered around the middle of the arena."

"Whaddaya mean?"

"Whaddaya mean what do I mean?"

"What are they doing?"

"What's who doing?"

"The guys in the middle."

"Uh, well, standing around."

"What's the other one doing?"

"What other one?"

"The other one in the chariot."

Before I could explain, filming stopped and Terry shouted "moving on."

While cameras re-set in the middle of the arena for a gladiator's point-of-view of the circling chariots, I saw Crowe walk off to have a cigarette with his costumer, Michael Castellano. I had work to do.

"Tell ya later," I told Casey.

He crawled back under the scaffolding.

I hurried over to Russell.

So, you wanna do your EPK interview now?

"You've got twelve minutes."

I'd told him before that they needed twenty.

"I wanna get back here to watch the next set up."

I don't know where "twelve" came from: possibly he'd considered allocating ten to fifteen and compromised on the low side of splitting the difference. He could've said "five" and I would've had to jump on it.

I led him to where Pattyson lazed in the interviewer's chair.

"We've got twelve minutes, guys," I shouted. "Let's go."

Forty minutes later Russell was still talking. It was a great interview.

"The other one has a spear," I returned to Casey. "She's gonna get cut in half by a spinning sword that's attached to the chariot wheels. Not right now. That'll be second unit. With a wax dummy. Now they're all just riding around the arena."

Casey sighed heavily and asked if he could go back under the scaffolding to start his 11th reading of *The Hitchhiker's Guide sequel: Life, the Universe and Everything*.

By late afternoon, Casey was finishing his 11th reading of *Life, the Universe and Everything*, Sam had seen enough chariots circling around cameras and Margaret had turned the last page of her novel. I turned to the last chapter in my playbook.

At a separate compound a short walk from where we exited the fort's main gate, I dropped my name into an intercom and double doors opened to the animal holding area.

Inside we found Thierry Le Portier, the French cat trainer, who had invited us to see a tigress that had given birth to six cubs only nine days ago. The mother tiger had lost two previous litters. Thierry was hoping her third time would be lucky.

"It feels just like a kitten," Margaret said about the one Thierry put in her arms. "Except it's solid muscle."

Thierry offered to let the boys hold two others but they contented themselves with petting the one Margaret was cradling while the cat master shocked and amazed them by sticking his arm inside the cages of various lions and tigers and scratching the beasts behind their ears.

"I wouldn't recommend any of you try this. Especially not the children. For some reason, they do not like children."

Nothing like the threat of a mauling to end the day on a lively note.

Lions and tigers and elephants and chariots. Workouts with muscle men and acting in a movie. The boys would have some stories to tell back home - where they'd be by this time tomorrow.

A week later, I would have to report that all the tiger cubs had died. Sam cried. Casey pondered the meaning of a tiger's fate in the big stew that is life, the universe and everything.

CHAPTER TWENTY-FOUR

SO MANY LITTLE DYINGS

There are so many little dyings that it doesn't matter which of them is death.

-Kenneth Patchen

Roger Lowe had moved to Marsascala. I drove to visit him one Sunday.

"I'm always around. Give a call. We'll have a beer and look out at the bay." I called, on and off, for about four hours. By then, I'd walked the wineglass-waisted harbor where the Eye of Osiris winked from the prows of red-yellow-blue-green striped fishing boats in a scramble of sizes. I'd visited three cozy cafes along the main street, hiked to Zonqor Point overlooking the Mediterranean and strode the shore of St. Thomas Bay, a bowl-shaped broth of turquoise.

I'd found my Maltese heaven.

After seeing five newly furnished apartments with more space than I needed, I looked at a small two-bedroom, third floor walk-up with a monastic master bedroom, army surplus kitchen, second bedroom with peeling paneling and near-complete lack of water pressure in the bathroom... and ignored all that.

The living room had a 180-degree, unobstructed view of Marsascala Bay, from the narrow inner harbor to where it opened into the sea.

"I'll take it," I told the agent.

My final days at the Phoenicia were almost enough to make me regret leaving. However, hotel living wasn't something I could put up with for more than a short time and I was entering my sixth week of what could be a 12-week stay.

I resent mini-bars and I don't make much use of room service because, to me, dining is an excuse to get *out* of my room. The heat's always too high, the cooler too cool and the air recycled to the consistency of collar starch. I concoct conspiracy theories about laundry prices that make it more practical to *buy* new under-wear. I don't like hollering through the door at the maid to come back later. I don't like having to call a bellman for my car. I find it strange that there are people in the lobby whose *job* it is to open the door for me. I don't like having to dial "9" to get an outside line. I like having a kitchen. I don't mind making my own bed.

But I sure was going to miss my nights at the Actors' Hotel.

The night before my move, I wandered down to the lounge at around 8:00 to find Sonny behind the counter and no one else from our little group.

"An old Chinese woman come into the bar one time," Sonny began a story. "She look at me like she know me from somewhere, you know? Like she's trying to figure out from where. She don't speak English but she's got a lady with her who's a translator. She says something to the translator and the translator ask me, can she touch my moustache?

"Touch my...? 'Sure,' I tell her. She's a old lady, wha's she gonna do? So, she reach out, and, like this," he demonstrated, lightly stroking his bushy upper lip. "Then she says, through the translator, 'look happy but sad underneath.' She sees that. Nobody ever sees that. She don't know I lost my grocery store, I fight with my wife, nothing. She just sees that.

"Then, she reach into her purse and she give me a coin with a little squeeze 'a my hand," he took my hand, closing my fingers. "She squeeze, it feels warm, you know? I tell you the truth, you believe me. I take that coin the next day and buy a lottery ticket. You know what happens? I win 700 pounds!"

I don't even care if it's true. It's a terrific tale of affirmation, mysticism, fate - until he adds the tag:

"I get every one of the numbers except one! I get that last stinking number I get 100,000 pounds! I'm kicking myself, to this day I'm kicking myself because I missed that last lousy number! *Mela*. I pick a 17 instead of a 19!"

I finished my drink and was about to leave when a voice resounded from the rear. "Ah, there you are!" I turned to see David Hemmings standing like St. Peter, beckoning me through the door to the patio overlooking the garden.

Outside, three wicker tables had hand-printed signs reading "Reserved for '*Gladiator*.'" Seated in fan chairs around them were Shrapnel, Schofield, Tomas, Connie, Joaquin, assistant costume designer Sammy Howarth, Lucy Hemmings, Derek and actor Tommy Flanagan, newly arrived from Glasgow.

Sonny brought out champagne; we popped corks and lifted glasses to Shrap's 57th birthday. Glass two was in praise of Hemmings being "a born producer" for orchestrating this social symphony. He rose to the moment like a huckster selling time-shares. He'd suggest to management a plaque above the bar's back door proclaiming the exclusivity of the patio for the

"Gladiator Club" and a wall of plants dividing the Club from the dining room veranda. He even offered an alternative to Russell's "macho" stadium matches.

"A bit of mini-golf, some backgammon. For those who are a bit more sporting, a table for blackjack, another for craps," Cassius appealed to the gathering. "For the more athletic types, we'll string a net across the pool and splash around with some volleyball."

Actors live in the moment. At this moment, we were colonials in exile — not a group of short-timers celebrating a birthday in the waning weeks of a temporary assignment.

I drove to the Fort late in the morning to watch the setup for the "chariot overturning" scene.

The scene called for Maximus to cut loose the fallen horses, jump on one, then gallop past a barricade erected by his gladiators from where Djimon would toss him a sword. A stunt rider was supposed to make the actual one-handed catch but Russell argued it would look better if he did it. Terry Needham argued back but Ridley decided it was worth letting his star give it a try.

After only a couple of takes, Our Man made a clean grab and the crew broke out in applause.

Was there a shift in the breeze?

The production's momentum would pick up again from here. Russell was the driving force - though it wasn't because our tiger had changed his stripes.

On set the next day, the Carthage Battle continued and Russell, angry over a botched take, kicked over a trashcan.

"I'll clean it up. I'm always cleaning up everything around here anyway. Anyone else have any garbage for me to clean up?"

We're none of us so far from our inner child.

The Senators were sitting like cardboard cutouts in the bleachers. They had no lines but were needed for continuity and reaction shots.

"We've been here all morning making silly faces," Jacobi demonstrated, Gaius and Falco following in pantomime chorus.

Shrapnel asked if I'd read the new script pages we'd gotten last night. I said I hadn't. He proceeded to describe, in dramatic detail, the final scene in the film: a touching eulogy that Proximo delivers over the body of his greatest gladiator who had finally won in death the freedom that life had denied him. It would be an outstanding moment for Oliver Reed. Maybe even the kind that's remembered at Oscar time.

I awoke Sunday morning to the blastings of bird hunters as sunrise glared through my curtainless bedroom windows. Then I walked to my living room, stepped onto the balcony, looked out over the unobstructed view of the Mediterranean, breathed deeply and smiled.

Besides the absence of bedroom curtains - which wasn't a huge privacy concern since the only building within sight of the bedrooms was a weed-covered goat shed - there were other items and repairs for which I would be asking the entire month I stayed here: the shower water was only a trickle, an electric socket in the kitchen had a blackened cover plate above a burn-marked toaster, the refrigerator had no coolant and the toilet ring broke the first time I pulled it to flush. Needless to say, the peeling paneling in the guest room was still peeling.

But walking into my living room and seeing that view, well, they couldn't have gotten me out of there if the shag carpet had caught fire.

Crispian, our set decorator, had fallen from some scaffolding just outside the Colosseum dungeon. He'd backed against a wall, forgetting it was made of Styrofoam, and taken a dive that broke his pelvis. Carted off to the hospital unconscious, he awoke in a room with seven other patients - all speaking Maltese. Branko was working on getting him a private room. Meanwhile, he was desperate for English-speaking company.

I'd agreed to be part of a small assemblage visiting him this Sunday.

Around mid-afternoon, I got a call from Nicki Nurse saying Crispian was in particularly poor spirits and wasn't up for socializing. That freed me to idle away my day off. I went to a couple of flea markets, walked my new neighborhood and had coffee at a beachside food stand overlooking St. Thomas Bay.

My stroll had taken me past several interesting restaurants, one of which I thought I'd try that evening. At around 5:30, I was deliberating whether I should make the effort to invite Roger, who never answered his phone... when my mobile rang.

Oliver Reed had found a new drinking place. It was a little dive off Valletta's main street, populated largely by unemployed boatyard workers. A plastic sign extended over the sidewalk with the bar's name, The Pub, printed in gold script above a foaming mug.

Inside the rough-hewn walls, Ollie had gotten a celebrity's welcome and unquestioned service - constant service - even license for self-service. Josephine was a pillar at his side. Guarding? Maybe. Indulging? Certainly. Tilting her nose in the same skyward slant at the supercilious snots who'd banned him from the Phoenicia? No doubt.

Her husband had been expelled from 14 schools as a boy. He'd worn out his welcome in many times that number of high-hatted cocktail lounges. The cause of Robert Oliver Reed's classroom misbehavior could later be traced to undiagnosed dyslexia. The cause of his barroom misbehavior would never be traced.

The call came from Aminta Townshend. She was the daughter of guitarist Pete Townshend and Branko's assistant on this movie.

"Josephine Reed has been trying to get hold of Ridley, Branko or you," she said. "I've been trying to find Branko and Millie's been trying to track down Ridley. I'm glad you're there. It sounds fairly urgent."

My first thought was "who died and left me third in charge?"

My next thought was what kind of havoc did Oliver cause that would make getting hold of the publicist so high on Jo's priority list? I hoped she didn't expect me to get bail money at nearly six o'clock on a Sunday night. Did he hurt anyone?

"She sounded a little drunk," Aminta added.

I called Josephine and she didn't sound drunk at all. She sounded like a woman whose bad boy husband had gotten into trouble that she couldn't deal with on her own. She asked if I could come to the Phoenicia, saying she'd "rather not discuss the reason on the phone."

I drove the twenty minutes to Valletta wondering how much press, how much damage and what kind of charges were going to be involved. I couldn't imagine him killing anybody. But accidents do happen:

He used to have head-butting matches with rock musician John Entwistle but that was a game played by mutual consent and stopped after the third time Reed rendered The Who's bass player unconscious.

He'd once been accused of tossing his stunt double over a balustrade but he'd been cleared of those charges. And anyone he threw over a balcony these days would have to help him with the lifting.

Of course, it could be something other than mayhem, I thought, as I drove listening to Jesse Winchester's *Evil Angel*.

Evil angel, on my shoulder, oh you sure do know your stuff
First you tempt me with a little, 'til I just can't get enough.

Ollie was known for challenging groups of men to "tests of strength." There was a famous drinking contest with 36 rugby players that ended with a nude sunrise run through Surrey.

He once claimed to have drunk 141 pints of beer in two days. Might he have caused a row after being cut off trying to break his own record?

That first sip of whiskey burned your tongue, (didn't it?)
That first sip of whiskey burned your tongue
But you had to go and have another (didn't you?)

Maybe he made an unwanted play for a lady? He'd been quoted saying his only regret was that he "hadn't drunk dry every pub and made love to every woman on earth." There were certainly enough pretty Maltese girls in tight shirts and short skirts with whom a man of reasonable impulse control - let alone a besotted, late-middle-aged movie star obsessed with proving his virility - could get in trouble. And there was that indecent exposure charge filed by one of his young female co-stars some years ago.

That first cheating love, it made you ashamed, (didn't it?)
That first cheating love, it made you ashamed
But you had to go and find another (didn't you?)

Of course, whipping out his penis in public places was practically a Reed cliché. The only controversy over that anymore was whether the tattoo on the tip was a bird's claw or a rosebud.

So, what could he have done this time?

Marion the hotel manager, offered a gloomy greeting.

"I haven't told anyone." She was a dour woman anyway, so this seemed only a minor modulation.

"Was he in the Club Bar?"

"Thank God, no. It didn't happen here."

Too bad, I thought, since that would've made for the least exposure.

Climbing the stairs to the third floor, I started to imagine how much wreckage there had been in the bar where it did happen. But I couldn't extract a picture of Hurricane Ollie from the nearly immobile drunk I'd seen a couple of weeks ago.

The door was open six inches in anticipation of my arrival. I knocked and pushed through, calling for Josephine.

Her eyes were red but she forced a smile and asked straight away, "Have you heard?"

Playing dumb, which wasn't too hard, I said that Marion, downstairs, had hinted at some sort of problem but nothing specific.

"He's dead," she said bluntly.

The sequence of phone calls in the hours that followed blurs no more in memory than it did at the moment. Was it after Jo broke down from the first one or the second that I started answering her phone?

One call was from the British High Commissioner, another from "friends" she didn't want to see who were waiting downstairs, then, of course, all the local media - followed almost instantaneously by all the British tabloids. A call from the front desk informed me that Ridley and Branko were waiting for me downstairs.

I told Josephine I was going to meet them and they'd probably want to come up.

"They really don't have to. I don't need to see them," she said with sincere neutrality and a constitutional resistance toward forcing anyone to stand on ceremony.

The producer and director were seated in the lobby. Almost as they rose, Branko declared, "We should tell everyone his part in the movie was almost finished. There was only one small scene he didn't do."

Joaquin and Connie spotted us and Joaquin rushed over to give Ridley a big, tearful hug. Connie looked somber behind dark glasses.

I saw the Hemmings, whom I'd been trying to call, heading to the Club Bar, excused myself from some other nonessential instructions Branko was giving me, and rushed to tell them the news. They were stunned. They hurried to Josephine's room.

Branko and Ridley were not so quick to follow. They asked if she wanted to see them. Based on nothing but my own bourgeois sensibilities, I assured them she did.

"I really didn't know him that well," Ridley reminded as we got in the elevator.

Did any of us?

We are comrades in arms but battlefield bonding isn't like the bonds cemented by time. There is shock, maybe even sadness but we close ranks around our fallen comrade and march on. We come together in unifying purpose. When that ends, the slenderness of our attachment is exposed. We are intimate strangers.

Oliver was lucky enough to die in the arms of his beloved. Should this have happened to any of the rest of us, there might've only been a last word with a colleague, then a phone call from a producer - or maybe the publicist.

The meeting of Jo and the filmmakers was awkward. My fault for romanticizing the connection: they *really* didn't know him very well.

The following day's *Malta Times* featured a self-serving interview with the bar owners, Paul and Kathleen Cremona and their son Warren. Headlined "The Pub Owners Recall Close Friendship with Oliver Reed," their recollections reeked of sentiment.

In their account, the Reeds entered The Pub and joined them for a morning drink at around 10 a.m. By 1:30, Reed had fallen asleep "sitting in his favorite corner" near the jukebox. A Hallmark moment if ever there was one.

"He was snoring loudly and we were teasing him," noted Cremona senior. "But then his wife saw him change colour and go blue... and we immediately called the ambulance."

The final paragraph quoted Mrs. Cremona saying, "The Pub was like his second home. We will miss him terribly."

These were the *friends* Josephine had turned away when they came to the Phoenicia. Tomorrow they'd be plastering their storefront with "Oliver Reed Died Here" news clippings. Business would boom.

The Times' piece was written with unctuous sympathy for *their* loss by Ariadne Massa – who had tried to buttonhole Branko at his hotel in hopes of seducing him into an interview and permission to visit the set under his escort.

Nurse Nicki was already on set when I arrived a half-hour before call time. She'd visited Josephine the previous night and administered a sedative to help her sleep.

Many of the crew had heard the news before arriving at work. Some had their first glimpse of it in the morning papers. Others didn't hear until they'd reported to location and some of the women were still crying.

While it was true Reed had just a couple of scenes left, his sudden death had blown an emotional hole in our production. Most of the crew had known only the cooperative professional who showed up prepared for work everyday. Most of them also knew that a movie legend had left the screen and a great performance in this picture was cut short – possibly in danger of being cut out altogether.

Some acknowledgement was needed.

Ridley had asked Millie to send flowers to the widow. Branko had told Aminta to "find out what religion he was and we should hold a service on Sunday." Nice thought but he was a devout atheist and Sunday was a week away.

Something had to be said this morning.

At official call time, with the crew gathered in the arena, Terry Needham announced over the bullhorn, "We will now have a moment of silence for what happened yesterday."

What happened yesterday?!?!

Elegiac, considering the source.

But we all awaited words from Ridley – which never came.

"Alright, back to work," Terry broke the silence.

Would it have meant anything for our Guv'ner to make a speech? Maybe. Maybe not. But what he didn't say sent a lonely chill through the ranks, as the brief ceremony ended without even mentioning Oliver's name.

Into the Valley of Death... Forward march.

Oliver's adult children, Mark and Sara, along with a family friend, had arrived on the afternoon plane from Heathrow. Also on that flight was DreamWorks UK publicity chief Peter Dunne, bringing with him - not intentionally - writers and photographers from *The Sun, Express, Daily Mail and Mirror*, all hoping to get surprise snaps and off-guard comments from the widow. The lobby of the Phoenicia looked like a press junket.

Time was needed to overcome Josephine's initial opposition to an autopsy but after a day's delay, one was conducted. It would reveal that Oliver Reed didn't die of drink but from a congenital heart disease more commonly exacerbated by cigarettes. He was a non-smoker. Completion of the procedure meant the Reeds could fly home with the body the next night. The Phoenicia had become a tabloid-infested prison from which they were now desperate to escape.

I had made a dinner reservation a week earlier for a dozen international journalists we'd planned to have on set this day. These and all other scheduled press activities were cancelled because of the obvious entertainment-inappropriate circumstances. With Peter Dunne getting permission from DreamWorks to pick up the tab, we kept the table and just changed the crowd.

On this evening, Oliver Reed's last in Malta, Josephine and his family were secreted out of the hotel for a small celebration with some of his *Gladiator* cohorts. It was an impromptu affair that was intentionally kept small: in addition to the five in the Reed party (Oliver's brother had flown in to join the four already here), those in attendance included Joaquin, Connie, Tomas, David Schofield, Sammy Howarth, Ralf, Tommy Flanagan, David and Lucy Hemmings.

Based on past performance, The Labyrinth could have been a disastrous choice.

Colin closed his doors for our little party, turning away some of his few regular customers to keep our function private. The entertainment he hired for the night was an enchanting vocalist named Ira Losco, a teenager who was on her way to becoming Malta's top pop artist. All lauded the food and service. No one knew he had to borrow money to buy our steaks from the butcher.

At the end of the evening, Josephine would say this was exactly what she needed: a little closure, a little comfort, a small acknowledgment of the man she'd loved for more than half her life by those in the community that had given his life purpose.

CHAPTER TWENTY-FIVE

CROSSING THE LINE

I'd thought about telling Margaret that Jacqueline was coming for a visit. By the time I'd finished thinking about it, it was too late. I should've mentioned it weeks earlier, as something in the far off future: *friend might be coming from North Carolina... scuba diving... separate bedroom, etc.*

What was the big deal? I'd told her about my gorgeous former-assistant Dondi's visits to New York where she slept on my couch. My own sleep on those occasions wasn't easy but the full disclosure kept me faithful.

I'd let it go way past the point where I could slip it into casual conversation now. *Oh hey, forgot to tell you... she'll be here tomorrow.* There'd be a lot of questions for which I didn't have good answers.

227

We'd met in the most innocent way possible, in a Unitarian Church reception hall after a service in Charlotte, North Carolina where I was working. She was tall and tan - having just returned from a scuba diving trip in Aruba - with light auburn hair that fell past the shoulders of a white summer dress. I was going to a matinee of a play in which an old friend was performing. I had an extra ticket.

My wedding ring was always visible but she claimed later she didn't see it. I made my marital status clear about mid-way through dinner that night. I blurted it without equivocation: I need to tell you, I'm married.

Her mouth formed a confused half-smile. Then her eyes welled, all sound suspended. She appreciated my honesty, she said after a century of awkward silence.

We walked to her car in the parking lot. I took her hand and spouted some hope-I-didn't-upset-you-wish-you-all-the-best mumbo-jumbo. She moved my hand to her waist just above the hipbone where my thumb could feel the flatness of her stomach. With her arms at her sides, she leaned forward and pressed her lips on mine. It was the saddest, softest, sweetest kiss I'd ever known.

Jacqueline was not her real name. It was the name she gave herself after fleeing her husband. Leaving him wasn't easy. Moving to North Carolina stopped the beatings but not his obsession with her. He hired detectives, phoned her friends, put traces on her credit cards, found her in one place so she had to move to another, got her fired from one job so she had to seek work under a name for which she had no traceable employment history. A restraining order only further enraged him and physical threats continued in letters sent through her mother, as well as phone calls to unlisted numbers she thought were secure.

She borrowed money from friends who were helping her hide and completed a course in massage therapy. She found a position with a health club, worked hard enough to rent her own apartment and hooked up with a boyfriend – seven years younger – who was no threat physically or emotionally.

There was a survivor's strength and calm about Jacqueline. Her initial suspicions of men, including me, were overcome by pure resolve: she would not allow *him* to represent the entire gender. She would not be a prisoner.

Among the lessons she learned from her escape was that the world was full of hiding places. Over the next state line, in a new identity, there was shelter.

But nowhere did she find a greater peace or surer sanctuary than under the sea. No phones could ring, no familiar-looking cars could pass, no banks could report inquiries into her credit. Only weightlessness in a color-filled world where the inhabitants could care less who or what she was.

Jacqueline's greeting card had ended:
"Thinking of you."

I'd received it in a package of business mail that Margaret periodically forwarded to me on location. The postmark was impossible to read but it must have been at least a month old. I returned her note by phone.

Her voice was bright and our conversation easy. She had been working long hours and needed a break. She'd been looking through travel brochures, was considering Barbados or maybe the Virgin Islands, and just couldn't decide where to go. I had an apartment with a spare bed, I teased.

There was a pause. "Well, I hear Malta's one of the best wreck diving places in the world. I'll think about it."

Twenty minutes later she called back.

"I just think we should make it clear," she began, "You might not get lucky."

When I hung up the phone, it started to become clear that I might.

A string quartet played Chopin and Jaap was flirting madly with a black-eyed beauty in the sheerest of silk matador pants. Jaap knew she was Russell Crowe's Maltese girlfriend but he could afford to throw caution to the wind even though our star was standing maybe a hundred feet away.

Russell, cricket bat in hand, stepped away from an errant spinner, then smacked the next toss through the infield. His two cousins, both former captains of New Zealand's national cricket team, cheered him from the sidelines.

Crowe had organized this tournament between a *Gladiator* squad and the Maltese national team, as a gift to his visiting family. He had paid for both teams' uniforms, provided barbeque catering and a full bar, hired the string quartet and the obnoxious DJ who followed them.

It was Seurat's *Sunday Afternoon* sans parasols, with the cricket pitch standing in for the Seine. The foreground featured Tomas playing backgammon, Joaquin and Tommy toasting until toasted, David Schofield lying on a bench waving his fingers to the music, and a group of stuntmen lying shirtless on the grass stretching their bellies for the next assault on the barbeque.

I was sitting at a picnic table, scanning the sky for incoming planes.

Jacqueline wore a brown dress suit that did nothing to augment her figure. She had cut her hair so it now came only to the nape of her slender neck. Even her application of makeup seemed designed with severity as its purpose. Then she spotted me and smiled. And she was beautiful.

We embraced but didn't kiss.

The drive from the airport was full of pleasantries without connection: looking forward to the diving and how's the movie going? She had no interest in movies, I knew.

"He called me," she said when we were halfway through our first glass of wine at La Spigola, a cozy bistro that was walking distance from my apartment. "He threatened to kill me if I didn't 'come home.'"

What did you do?

"I changed phone companies," she laughed. "If you'd called a week later you would've gotten a disconnected number."

She had dropped the younger boyfriend several months ago.

"He just wanted too much," she said without further explanation.

Our third glass of wine, second bottle, came during dinner. I had a poached grouper, she a grilled bass. Neither of us, by then, was paying any attention to the food. I was mostly paying attention to her laughter, a soft Southern laugh that swells at the throat but finds only the tiniest of outlets.

We had our waitress cork the remains of the second bottle and walked, arms around each other's waists, four short blocks to where I'd parked the car outside my apartment. I dragged her heavy suitcase up the three flights of stairs to my door.

I put her suitcase in the guest bedroom while she took off her jacket in the front room and looked the place over. I came back, walked to the balcony doors and opened them. The air was warm, the night smelled of sea spray and the moon shone on the bay.

Leaning over the balcony, she threw her arms open to the night, to the stars, to the feeling of escape. Then she stepped back inside, barely inside, standing inches before the doorframe, and made a single, slow pirouette with fingers sliding down buttons like they were dipping into water. She shrugged off her blouse, waved it like a flag above her head and let out a yelp. Her small, perfect breasts bared to the world.

I cupped one breast and kissed her mouth. Her mouth wanted more.

We awoke in the master bedroom to the sound of shotgun blasts and braying goats. She looked lovely in the morning light. After a few lazy kisses, she retreated to the bathroom.

I could have warned her the shower had all the water pressure of an old man urinating but I didn't. Instead, I lay in bed assessing my own feelings about events of the last twelve hours.

I'd broken a vow, deceived a woman I truly loved, mother of my children. How aggressively had I pursued this involvement with Jacqueline whose intentions may have been slightly ambiguous but not really provocative – at least not until she took off her blouse? Did this officially make me a womanizer? How much wine did we drink?

Those were the things I should have been thinking. Instead, I was thinking about Jacqueline's generous nipples, her flat belly, trimmed pubic triangle...

"Leave some cold water for me," I shouted towards the bathroom.

I drove to the set with a little more bounce in my accelerator foot.

But that night, something started feeling wrong.

Not with me: I had the shamelessly clear conscience of an adolescent who knows masturbation doesn't cause pimples. Jacqueline, however, was talking to me from behind a curtain. It could've been jetlag or the fact that she had blown up the coffee-maker she'd brought from America - not realizing that 110 into 220 doesn't go.

Whatever the reason, she was somewhere beyond the horizon when I came home, found her on the balcony of our apartment staring out on the bay and wrapped my arms around her waist, spooning gently against her shapely bottom.

I may as well have been pressed against a couch cushion.

Might it have been the obvious: regret over starting a pointless affair with a married man? She never gave a hint she wanted anything more than that. Did she? Did I miss a cue? Did this qualify as an affair?

That night, I satisfied her as she lay impassively on her stomach.

The next night, she satisfied me as I lay impassively on my back.

On the fourth night, I moved the guest bedroom mattress into the living room in front of the balcony doors where the sun would wake me before the sounds of goats or gunshots. That was where I would sleep for the next week while Jacqueline lived with me.

Jacqueline found a diving school that kept her occupied while I was at work.

I began spending a lot of time on set. This was partly to avoid going home and partly because, one by one, my actor pals were leaving Malta.

John Shrapnel had flown out last week. Back to Francesca and the boys and a starring role in a TV movie.

The Hemmings were homeward bound, David en route to do battle with legal issues he'd been dodging and to preside over a gallery opening of his watercolors.

David Schofield would be leaving the next day, reuniting with his sorely missed wife and children, joining the cast of a new play that would pay him crumbs but provide creative grist more nourishing than any fancy meal he'd bought with his per diem.

As production approached its penultimate week, Jacqueline and I entered into a routine of unhurried breakfasts on the patio of Summer Nights restaurant, me reading the local papers and British dailies, her staring out at the fishing boats in the harbor. We'd wait out the worst of rush hour traffic, then drive to the docks in Sliema where she took her diving lesson and I'd go to the set or the office.

In the late afternoon, I would call Margaret.

My double life with Jacqueline continued as early evenings found us barefoot at low tide on St. Thomas Bay watching men washing their plow horses greeting other men hauling in fishing boats, carrying them in tandem to the community of shacks above the waterfront dirt track. There she spoke of happier days, her first love.

"I was thirteen. I know that sounds young but it was so beautiful. He was three years older than me. Mexican. His family worked the fields. We lived just outside Salinas. A lotta people talk about their first time being awful. That wasn't the way it was for me. He was so gentle. And we were really in love."

Then, inevitably, after dinner - having no television, incompatible music tastes and limited local cinema - the what-am-I-doing-here blues would lull us to bed. Separately.

In one night I sealed the deals on my next two jobs: another six months of work. The toughest part of the negotiations had been with Margaret.

The Perfect Storm had pushed back it's start-of-production date until late July. Meanwhile, Larry Landsman, publicity director at Showtime, had called to see if I could work on a five-week picture in Toronto that Emilio Estevez was directing, starring him and his brother Charlie Sheen. It would begin the week I got home and wrap the day before I flew to Los Angeles to start *Perfect Storm*.

I first sought Margaret's consent.

Then maybe I coaxed a little.

I reminded her that Toronto was weekend driving distance from Ithaca and, if *Perfect Storm* was pushed again, we'd be broke by August. Home every weekend with cash in hand, I crooned.

Why was I trying to talk my wife into letting me take this small movie to fill a relatively short gap in my working schedule that would've been a welcome respite, a revitalizing transfusion of family and even a chance to do some of my own writing?

Let me list my excuses:

1. We could use the money
2. I'd worked with Charlie Sheen twice before and really liked him
3. It was an interesting – if deeply dark – subject

4. I owed a debt to Showtime for employing me after I quit my executive job three years ago and couldn't find work with any of the major studios.

5. We could use the money

I omitted the main reason: this is an addiction.

While one realizes one can't be on every interesting movie that's made, one still wants to be. You forget about the long hours, the long separations from family and friends, the very short periods in which it's *actually* interesting to be hanging around. Like a movie itself, which requires an average 60 days of 12-hour labor producing approximately two useable minutes of film per day, memory splices experience into only the best takes.

A year later when the picture is released, the hours of boredom, the moments of angst or pure panic, the days in broiling sun/freezing rain/scummy neighborhoods come back in a postcard of palm trees and sunny beaches. And when your name speeds by in the credit roll, a little slice of immortality is indelibly stamped as yours.

Margaret finally conceded we could use the money.

Though I'd become quite capable over the years of bouncing from one film to another, I was proving completely inept at bouncing to another woman.

I'd invited Jacqueline to the film set twice and twice she'd repeated she had no interest in movies. On the third try, I finally succeeded – only to find myself stuck with the studio execs who'd flown to Malta to discuss the ramifications of Oliver Reed's death. Hours later, I located Jacqueline in a remote part of the compound talking with a couple of set painters.

She seemed neither happy nor annoyed to see me.

"I had a good time," she responded to my apology for leaving her unattended. But she said it in a way that ended all conversation about it.

The next day, Saturday, Jacqueline tried to open her world to me: she bought me a diving lesson. I'm more cat than fish in the water but I figured even a rescue from drowning would give us something to talk about.

Kevin, the instructor, drove the group of us to a diving point across the bay from one of Malta's most famous attractions: Popeye's Village, a theme park of the movie sets from Robert Altman's *Popeye*, which filmed here in 1979.

Kevin took the advanced students – which included everyone in the class but me - on a 45-minute dive, while I sat on the rocks staring at the outline of the amusement park on the opposite shore.

When it finally came my turn I was grateful for his undivided attention since, even with the weight of the tank, my body rejected sinking on a primal level. But the experience was mostly positive - especially the part where we came to a cliff and I got the wobbly feeling that I shouldn't get too close or I'd fall off the edge.

I had a good time, I told her.

But relations at dinner that night were worse than ever.

O.K., I'd gotten a little crabby at Kevin for making me wait so long before taking me out. I wouldn't have minded so much if someone had given me advance warning that I'd be sitting alone and idle for nearly an hour.

"What difference would that have made?"

What diff...? Well, I might've at least brought along a book! That was when I learned Jacqueline couldn't read.

She wasn't illiterate but she was "never good at it in school." Sure, she'd read "some" books. She just couldn't recall if she'd actually ever finished one. In her life.

"So shoot me. I thought the day was supposed to be about diving, not reading."

"Why didn't you tell me I'd be waiting there for 45 minutes?"

"It wasn't 45 minutes. More like 30 or 35."

It was at least 40.

Geezus, we were like an old married couple. Right down to not having any sex.

The scene in which Proximo walks a corridor to open the gladiator cell doors before the Praetorian Guard attack was filmed over-the-shoulder with Oliver Reed's body double. Dialogue could be inserted later by splicing voice samplings from previously recorded scenes – the way you make a ransom note out of newsprint.

Tonight, Jacqueline was going night diving in Sliema, which left me free to attend a final dinner with some of my old Phoenicia friends.

The grand lobby was just closing its tea service and my dinner partners were at least an hour away from showing up in the bar, so I joined Spencer Treat Clark's tutor, Marjorie, who was lingering over a late afternoon Earl Grey.

English-born and educated, now living in Florida and close to retirement, Marjorie may have looked like a late middle-aged school marm but she'd seen a lot of world in her working life. She had a few stories from her years traveling with the Barnum and Bailey Circus.

"The scandals there made the movie company seem mild by comparison," she began. "Everyone was always changing partners and emotions were wild. These were highly passionate people. I remember once a couple got into a fight and he lifted her up and threw her off a moving train. They got back together but I think he slept with one eye open for quite a long time."

Sexual liaisons seemed to be proliferating throughout the crew and I wondered how much Marjorie knew when she made the comparison: wardrobe women had been working overtime suiting some of the camera boys; more of the make-up ladies were learning tricks of the stunt trade; our gay office p.a. had discovered a lively drag queen scene; lit-up gladiators were becoming as ubiquitous as neon in the nightclub district; Jaap had split with his long-distance girlfriend and there was a long line of applicants for the vacancy. It felt like everyone was getting some but me.

Among the celibate single males was our shy Emperor. And it appeared to be affecting his emotional balance. This brilliant talent who was delivering a seamless performance for our cameras was unraveling in his un-scripted life.

The party in Joaquin's suite was in celebration of the news that Tommy Flanagan's movie *Rat Catcher* had been named a finalist in the Palme d'Or competition at Cannes. Joaquin was already a little tipsy when I arrived. The music got louder and so did our host before Derek and Connie proclaimed it was time to go to dinner and escorted him downstairs to a waiting taxi.

At the restaurant, Connie made an effort to engage us in adult conversation, introducing a controversy over Germaine Greer's new book. But highbrow discourse was having a hard time competing with Joaquin shoving spaghetti up his nostrils.

Inevitably, Joaq's attentions turned to Connie – the only woman in our midst. He played lascivious Commodus and she exercised sisterly compassion in rejecting his more-silly-than-salacious advances. He reverted to his I-can't-get-a-girl-to-look-at-me-unless-she's-checking-her-makeup-in-my-sunglasses routine. Now he was playing the fool.

Twice, the restaurant manager came over and asked us to keep the noise down. Finally, with all but one other table in the restaurant evacuated, Joaquin stood up and started to unzip. He was playing Ollie. We were asked to pay the bill and leave.

On the way down the stairs, I was walking in front of him when he "slipped" and fell into my arms. I must have been gripping him pretty tightly because he suddenly pulled himself up, reassuring me, "no, no. That's just part of my act."

The next day, our young emperor turned in another stellar performance, menacing his sister into revealing the plot against him. All present felt they were watching a rising star. Only a few of us feared the potential freefall in that.

The mountaintop city of Taormina in northeastern Sicily had been a source of inspiration for writers from Ovid to Goethe to D.H. Lawrence, who was supposed to have begun *Lady Chatterley's Lover* during his two-year stay there.

Jacqueline had never read any Lawrence – or Ovid, for that matter – but I thought, with her time in Malta drawing to a close, doing a little traveling together might be just the thing we needed to salvage a few good memories, if not a friendship, from her visit. So, I signed us up for a day trip – as a surprise. A nice thing. A gesture of peace.

"I booked us on the morning ferry to Sicily tomorrow," I told her. "Just for the day but it'll give us a chance to see another part of the world."

"O.K." *Nothing.*

"I thought you might enjoy it."

"I might. I just need to think about it." *Hmm, would I rather wash my hair?*

"I thought you might even be a little excited about it."

"Well, I don't even know what it is."

"It's a tour. To one of the most beautiful places on the planet!"

"Are you going to be that way the whole time?"

"What way?" I shouted.

We didn't speak for the rest of the day.

Despite high wind warnings, the boat set out across a choppy sea at 7:00 a.m. Ninety minutes later, half its passengers stumbled onto Sicilian shores green with seasickness. Jacqueline seemed o.k., though sullen as she'd been all week, I might not have noticed a difference.

Our tour group boarded the bus on instruction from a petite twenty-year-old named Adella who spoke to us in broken English like we were a Sunday school class. The first major stop was Mount Etna, the biggest active volcano in Europe. Much of the jagged black rock was still smoldering, though the last eruption had been seven years ago. Ash paths led to towering vistas from which the legendary Cyclops might have overlooked the valley before its neighborhood was overrun by souvenir kiosks.

We had lunch on the patio of the main store where a strong wind kept knocking over our drink bottles. It made us both laugh for the first time that day.

There were two elderly Englishwomen at a nearby table sorting the lava samples they'd collected and one smiled in such a pleasant way we struck up a conversation.

"Forgive my staring, my dear. But you and your wife remind me very much of my husband and I when we used to travel together."

Her name was Eleanor, her friend was Sally and we did not correct her about our marital status.

"I've only recently developed the travel bug, I'm afraid. He traveled for business and he was constantly begging me to come with him. But the children, after all, and who was going to tend the garden… well, I'm afraid I missed out on a lot. Now he doesn't want to go anywhere. Sally's husband used to be her constant travel companion until he passed just two years ago. Since then, she and I have been to Greece and Turkey, Mexico twice, Jamaica, all over Italy…"

As I listened, I watched her transform into Margaret, twenty years from now.

The bus brought us into Taormina at around 1:30. All travelers were to meet back at the dropoff spot by 4:00.

Jacqueline's mood seemed to brighten as we walked cobblestone streets that bundled gingerbread villas with a flower shop bursting from every balcony.

"Oh, wait, I just want to listen to him," she touched my arm, letting her hand linger as we paused along a steep road to take in the sound of a wistful one-stringed instrument played by an old man in a doorway.

We sat on the steps of a church in the town square, huddled against a chill sea breeze that invaded the warm afternoon.

Couples passed.

Children passed.

Handsome men.

Beautiful women.

Old men.

Old women.

Does it say something about a person, who they watch in a city square?

"She loves all the flowers, you can tell," Jacqueline's eyes followed the measured gait of a woman who might have been in her eighties, print dress and flat-brimmed hat, walking by herself. "I'll bet she's got her own little garden somewhere."

The old woman was met by a middle-aged woman and a teen-aged boy in front of a café. Jacqueline's eyes drifted away.

As we continued our tour, I was beginning to learn how to have a pleasant time in Jacqueline's company: don't make any suggestions, don't give her any choices, just tell her what I intended doing and leave her free to do what she wanted. Liberating for both of us.

This approach worked on our hike up to the ancient amphitheatre (she sat while I explored and explored while I sat); it eliminated controversy from a stroll around the botanical gardens (I started to go there, she said she'd rather see more of the town. We saw more of the town); it got me a cup of coffee (she went along passively and didn't order anything).

The bus was a welcome shelter as the sun dipped to the edge of the cliffs around 4:00 p.m. We'd all dressed for a balmy spring day and few of us had brought coats. The link Jacqueline and I had forged in Taormina draped us like a treadbare shawl, warming ever-so-slightly.

Our bus crossed the second of two bridges – the second and third highest bridges in Europe, according to tour guide Adella – and made its next-to-last stop at a petrol station/pizza parlor outside Modica, the southernmost city in Sicily, around dinnertime.

I made a beeline to the men's bathroom and Jacqueline queued for a slice of pizza. I came back, got a glass of wine and joined her at her table. She'd barely finished her pizza slice when someone lit a cigarette at a neighboring table. She sprang up like the guy had put a match to her pants.

"I've gotta get outa here."

I saw her walk into the ladies bathroom. I saw her walk out. I saw her walk over to the bus and start chatting with the driver inside. I crossed the road to a pasture where I would be clearly visible so she knew where to find me when she was done talking to the driver. Ten-minutes-or-so later, she got off the bus and walked in the opposite direction from where I was communing with a couple of cows. She disappeared around the far side of the restaurant and I didn't chase after her.

She found me flipping through a cd rack in the adjacent convenience store just before we were about to reboard the bus.

I asked if she was feeling alright.

"I'm fine."

I asked if she was angry with me for some unintended slight.

"No."

Then why, I asked, did you walk away without the simple courtesy of a nod in my direction, clearly seeing me standing across the street, not even come by to let me introduce you to the cows, then disappear without so much as a wave *tah-tah* and avoid my company completely until it was time to board the bus?

"I'm sorry you feel like that."

Sorry. I. Feel like...

That was it. I pulled up my drawbridge and vowed not to lower it until she was on a plane back to North Carolina - which fortunately was the following night.

This night, however, was far from over.

The bus drove us to the dock in Pozzallo where other busses were also unloading their day-trippers and we all funneled onto the ferry. The wind whipped against the windows of the boat and an announcement was made that we would remain docked until the gale died down.

Meanwhile, Jacqueline's half-assed attempts at making nice with her pissed-off partner were too-little-too-late. I settled into my seat, popped a Dramamine I'd had the foresight to buy at our last pitstop, opened my copy of <u>The Milagro Beanfield War</u> and hung out a shingle: Not Open for Conversation. Ever the gentleman, I did offer her a Dramamine.

"I don't like pills."

Right.

We began our voyage across the Mediterranean around 11:00 pm. With the ferry bobbing like a bathtub toy, she distracted herself by examining her fingernails in great detail. Every bored sigh from my seatmate prompted my evil twin to pantomime The Joys of Book Reading: turn a page (*can't wait to see what happens next*); flip back (*was that really his Uncle who did that amazing thing back there?*); soft laugh (*how very witty, that clever writer*). She curled up on her seat to get a closer look at her cuticles. My twin reveled: meanness can be it's own reward.

Jacqueline finally succeeded in getting my attention by turning white and retching. I was able to get wet paper towels from the bathroom – stumbling over bodies that had been dragged to the toilets by stewards - to apply to her neck as she filled a motion sickness bag with half-digested pizza dough.

The ferry returned to dock in Pozzallo around midnight.

We disembarked and were ushered into another pizza restaurant near the terminal. There, we were told, pizza and beer were on the house for the rest of the night until the boat captain deemed it safe to chauffeur us across the channel the next morning.

There was no logic to feeding and watering a boatful of nausea victims with unlimited quantities of pasta and alcohol. It was an emergency measure because our particular tour company – unlike some of the higher priced others - had no resources with which to make sleeping arrangements for 80 people. However, the sickest among us were secretly being driven to one of Pozallo's cheap hotels and the sickest of those were quietly being given plane tickets back to Malta.

Jacqueline tried to get back on the bus but was told no one was allowed to sleep there. She stumbled in the direction of my table and slumped down across from me.

Meanness is no fun with the semi-comatose.

Seeing her in such misery, head on the table - facing away from a couple smoking at one end but stuck next to a 300-pound guy inhaling an anchovy and garlic with extra cheese - I sought out Adella.

"My friend is sick," I told our guide. "She needs to lie down."

"Is o.k. lie down here," our head cheerleader grinned.

"Is not o.k. here. She needs a hotel room. She is not sleeping on a bench in a pizza restaurant tonight. And neither am I. I also need a hotel room."

I think this stipulation of our need for separate beds confused her. Adella gave assurances she would "find out" and went to call her supervisor, Babs.

Babs was a trim efficient woman with a fine grasp of both the Sicilian in which Adella spoke to her and the agitated American that I used. She made a phone call and asked me to get my friend. There were rooms for us at a nearby hotel and a van ready to convey us and a half-dozen other travelers who weren't up for a pizza marathon.

Having pounded the forces of indifference in defense of the weak, I went to my incapacitated companion - now face down on the table, breathing into the air pocket between her elbows - and told her the good news.

"I'm fine here."

It's o.k., they're not charging us anything and we have separate rooms.

"You go ahead. I'll be o.k. here."

"I'm not leaving you here!" I screamed.

Babs approached.

"Is anything wrong?"

I explained that now my "friend" was reluctant to accept the company's offer of a bed for the night. Babs sat down next to Jacqueline.

"Your friend, he worry about you. Come. Get a few hours sleep in the hotel. Come now."

Weak as a kitten, Jacqueline got up. Babs helped her into the van. I later helped her off. That was more contact than I wanted.

In the morning, she was feeling better. But we didn't exchange a word on the van ride to the ferry or the entire ferry ride back to Valletta – though, quite without intention, she fell asleep on my shoulder about halfway across the sea.

We landed in Grand Harbor around 8:00 a.m. Three hours sleep at the Pozallo Inn and another hour on the ferry didn't help our sour attitudes towards one another. And we still had the whole day together before I could dump her at the airport.

I made one final stab at conversation.

"I want some breakfast. You coming?"

She lowered her head and started walking – more like creeping - in the general direction I was heading, maybe five feet behind.

I don't know why this bothered me as much as it did but I wheeled around and exploded at her.

"You're taking up space on the planet that somebody with a pulse could be using! What the hell is wrong with you?!?!"

Her face reddened.

"I hate that you used me to get a hotel room last night!"

What?

"I hate that. You. Telling me what to do, where to go. Ordering me around," suddenly the floodgates opened. "I don't belong to you. I'm not yours. I'm my own person. Nobody owns me!"

If this had been a movie, I would have taken her in my arms, pressed her to me and told her everything was going to be fine now, it all made sense now, I was blind but now I see: she was a

whole, independent, fabulous person. A strong, brave, worthy –
did I say 'independent?' - person...

But all I could do was reach out and stroke her shoulder once.
She continued sobbing. I continued understanding. Both came
in great waves.

Later we talked about it over eggs and bacon.

Following a few hours nap at the apartment - me on the living
room mattress - I drove her to the airport where we sat watching
children play in the lobby until she could check in at 6:00. A
half-hour later, we hugged goodbye.

Jacqueline sent me a postcard from Jamaica about a year later.
But I couldn't read the return address and her old phone number
had been disconnected.

The last few days' filming included a new ending in which
Juba stood alone in the Colosseum, burying the totems carved by
his friend Maximus. It was the scene that would've gone to Oliver
but most of us agreed Djimon elevated it. His patience had been
rewarded with one of the most poignant moments in the film.

With themes of death, fictional, real and metaphorical, playing out around and within me, I wasn't prepared for that afternoon's phone call from Margaret.

She'd had a routine medical checkup and the doctor found a
lump in her breast. He told her she should have a biopsy. There
was "only about a 25 percent chance of cancer," he'd reassured.
Still, she said, she was "freaking out."

"When are you coming home?"

I said I'd try to fly out tomorrow, two days early.

After visiting the production office to rearrange my flight,
I got back in my car and started driving – with no idea where I
wanted to go.

Popeye's Village was a monument to whimsy. It was ram-
shackle. It was sappy. It was a theme park built from a film set,

standing twenty years, trampled upon by only slightly fewer visitors than had seen the box-office-bomb of a movie.

I bought my ticket at an unmarked kiosk with peeling paint and entered past the children's playground, where no children were playing, down a steep path cut from the cliff to the cockeyed village of Sweethaven. There were roofs built to look misshapen, doors and windows set in off-kilter frames, slanted supports, jagged joists and a teetering outhouse. The Cinema offered clips from the Robert Altman film on a loop.

So, why was I there?

I just needed to spend an hour someplace more ridiculous than my own life.

Sometime later, I was at a sidewalk café with Judi Dickerson, rehashing the paradox that most regularly plagues us: how when you're lucky enough to have both work you love and someone you love, you have to accept that you can't always have both at the same time. Life is full of such paradoxes.

As we sat sipping coffee, we saw Bob Long standing outside a nearby toy store. He joined us for a minute but declined an offer of a drink.

"Can't stay long. I'm waiting for Russell."

Where was Russell?

"He's inside the toy store buying model airplanes for a sick friend," Bob reported. "When I asked him if his friend even liked model airplanes, he said 'I don't know.' I think the child in Russell would've liked someone to bring him model airplanes when he was sick. So, he assumes everybody else would like them as well."

Bob got up to help Russell carry three bags of toy planes to their waiting car.

Paradox personified. Bless him.

I went back to the Phoenicia for one last drink and maybe a final dinner with whomever was there.

I saw Tomas and Sandra hovering in the lobby.

"Hang out here with us for a minute," Tomas said in a conspiratorial whisper.

A moment later, Ralf appeared with a German filmmaker named Gunter with whom he was having dinner.

"We're meeting Ridley at his favorite restaurant. Then tomorrow morning we fly back to L.A. in the private jet."

Gunter's private jet?

"No," laughed the genial giant.

And before further explanation was needed, Arnold Schwarzenegger entered the lobby.

Ralf beamed as he introduced us to his ride home.

PART VI
INTERLUDE

Rated X – Showtime Networks

CHAPTER TWENTY-SIX

ARCHAEOLOGY

The doctor who'd first sounded the alarm about the lump in Margaret's breast had advised her to get a biopsy. But her sister, who lived next door to us and used to work for Planned Parenthood, advised her to get a second opinion before submitting to that painful procedure. With a week to wait until her next doctor's appointment – and a week of prep on my new movie, which I could do from home - Margaret decided to accompany her sis to a conference in Orlando where their younger brother Robert lived. She would leave the day after I got back from Malta.

Thank God you're home. YOU take the kids. I'm outa here!

I had a production meeting in Toronto the Friday before filming started on *The Mitchell Brothers Project*. Showtime Networks was putting me up at the Skydome Hotel where the city's Major League baseball team played. So, the boys and I set off on a little weekend outing.

Driving past the dog park along the lake, I pointed out a stone mansion that was The Paleontological Research Institute (PRI), reminding them they'd once seen a Mastodon skeleton there.

"Dad, we're not really into dinosaurs anymore."

I had some catching up to do.

So we'd start with the more recent past: yesterday's Little League baseball game. Sam had pitched for the first time.

"Your team won and you struck out the side in the last inning," I reassured my youngest.

"Yeah, Dad, but I walked eight batters."

"Your team was ahead by 10 runs. The umpire wasn't giving you the calls."

Casey was listening to a recording of *The Golden Compass* through one earphone so he could keep his other ear free in case his brother and father said anything interesting.

"Why?"

"Why what?"

"Why didn't the umpire like Sam?"

Oh, how I'd missed this intimate father-son banter.

The farmland along the Upstate New York lake country sparkled in the summer sun, camouflaging the economic depression that had hit towns like Geneva, Waterloo and Seneca Falls when manufacturing migrated and military bases closed. Kodak Corporation had recently laid off thousands. Buffalo still hadn't recovered from the loss of Bethlehem Steel in the mid-1980s. Factory life in this part of the world was on its way to becoming extinct and people were moving on.

Our car hit the New York Turnpike at Syracuse, headed towards Rochester, and a light rain lulled both boys to sleep.

I always thought of Margaret when I approached Rochester. She was born and raised there. But my thoughts now went beyond that – to pre-history.

Married people get to know the depth of each other's fears. But they don't always know the root of them. Margaret was afraid. The reason was obvious. I was afraid too.

Ann Sue Pomerantz-Harris couldn't understand why I needed time away. Not just a physical separation but for a while at least, a separate existence. *Firestarter*, shooting in North Carolina, would provide both. This would be my first movie location.

The three of us – me, her and breast cancer – had been living together for nearly three years, which was about the full length of our marriage. I'd been in therapy for a year re-learning how to breathe. Ann had been cancer free for six months before I got the phone call.

"Hi, this is Frank Capra," *Isn't he dead?* It was producer Frank Capra, Junior. Still… "Wonder if you'd like to work on a picture with Drew Barrymore, David Keith, George C. Scott, Burt Lancaster, Art Carney and Louise Fletcher."

Lancaster had to drop out and was replaced by Martin Sheen.

Ann was healthy again. The only lingering trace of her illness was an occasional lapse into morbidity over the baby that had to be aborted before she began chemotherapy. But she was alive, we'd made the right decision and now, now after three years of trying to do what was best for her, I had a chance to do something for me. I didn't want a divorce – just a release, in hopes it would lead me back to my right mind. Back to her.

I debauched my way through Wilmington and Hendersonville: no party too late to stay up for, no bottle of whiskey that would keep overnight, no pretty southern belle who wasn't fair game. I was having a grand old time. And I'd been able to drown out thoughts of Ann with a torrent of booze, sex and work. Thinking about her meant worrying about her. She was well. We were *separated*.

I can't tell you why I stopped at that phone booth. All I remember was the sound of relief in Ann's voice – even as she was telling me the cancer had returned, this time in ribbons around her lungs.

I remember the rain that started almost the moment I stepped back into the car. I remember how tough visibility was, even after the rain had stopped.

A million years ago it was.

The Canadian border guard at the customs booth asked who the young men in my backseat might be. I told him.

"May I see their birth certificates?"

Uhhh.

"Any documentation to prove you're the father?"

Uhhh.

"Boys," he leaned into the car, "is this man your father?"

Sam answered in the affirmative and the guard repeated the question for Casey, once he removed his earphone.

"Do you know where your mother is?" he inquired of Casey.

"Well, I'm not sure."

Sam, for whom this high-pressure interrogation was extremely stressful, came to our rescue.

"She's in Florida with our Aunt Annie visiting our Uncle Robert."

This, to our border guard, didn't sound like a rehearsed response. He let us pass.

Thankfully, he didn't ask details about the project for which I was crossing the border with two minors to work on.

It was around noon when I pulled into the Skydome Hotel. Casey, Sam and I swam in the pool and I bought us all sodas from the bar. Then I had to go to my production meeting.

"Dad, how come we can't go with you to the set this time?" Sam asked.

Well, they're not filming anything today and we go home tomorrow. So, another set another time, ok? I'll be back in time for us to go to the baseball game.

I left out the part about 'Dad's working on a porn movie.'

"It's finally happened, he's finally gone too far," publicist Jeff Ballard remembered thinking when he heard the radio report that his longtime friend and client Charlie Sheen was dead of a drug overdose. That was a little over a year ago. Reports of his demise were exaggerated. Just.

The Mitchell Brothers Project was the working title of Charlie Sheen's first acting job since his return from the dead. He would play Artie "Party" Mitchell. His brother Jim Mitchell would be played by Sheen's real-life brother and the film's director, Emilio Estevez. This was a biography of the filmmakers who helped make pornography a genre and whose high life through the psychotropic seventies came down with a crash.

I'd last worked with Charlie in the summer of '88, on *Major League* – when he was thrown out of the crew hotel after a maid discovered a loaded pistol under his pillow.

A year or so later, his girlfriend Kelly Preston dumped him when he accidentally shot her in the arm. Sometime after that, his father had him arrested on drug charges – an intervention that was an attempt to turn his life around. He spent thirty days in rehab and stayed clean for a year – then went to Nicolas Cage's house on day 366 and got drunk.

Between that relapse and his recent drug overdose, there were two charges of alleged battery, a small scandal involving $50,000 worth of hookers rented from Hollywood Madam Heidi Fleiss, a divorce, a few porn-star girlfriends and a lengthy estrangement from his brother Emilio.

Now the two brothers were making a movie together – about two brothers who slept with porn-stars, took drugs, got into trouble with guns, became estranged and ended their relationship in fratricide.

What the hell was Charlie doing?

Martin Sheen had tried to talk his eldest son out of casting Charlie in this film.

"He's coming off a relapse," Sheen senior advised Emilio. "It's just too dangerous for him to get back in that mindset."

Martin had gone through his own troubles with alcohol abuse, contributing to a heart attack that delayed filming of *Apocalypse Now*. He understood Charlie in ways no one else in their family was able. He knew what a hard fight addiction was.

I'd gotten to know Martin on *Firestarter* and he did me the favor of calling Ann, who was a longtime fan, telling her to get healthy so she could visit him on his next movie. I could always get a smile by reminding her she didn't want to piss off Marty.

But I had no idea how to return the favor with Charlie. He was his own worst enemy and the similarities between him and Artie Mitchell were uncomfortably close. Showtime's publicity department wasn't about to ignore the exploitable parallels between fact and film – and neither were the brothers who were banking on those to help this cable television feature get a theatrical release.

Spitting into the wind, leaning into a punch, playing on the freeway, you name the self-mutilating metaphor. Were we all simply aiding Charlie Sheen in an act of public mortification? Or might there be a restorative subtext buried in this project?

The Tivoli Theatre in Hamilton, Ontario is haunted by the ghost of its former owner, a wealthy philanderer named Ambrose Small who vanished one December night in 1919, leaving a trail of disgruntled gambling associates and seduced showgirls. Forty years after the largest manhunt in Canadian history, the case was closed, unsolved. His wife was always the main suspect.

On this first night of filming, in the 80th year since Ambrose Small's disappearance, ghosts and showgirls once again populated the Tivoli as it stood in for the San Francisco-based Mitchell Brothers O'Farrell Theatre, featuring *The Tenderest Loins in the Tenderloin.*

In the holding area across the street, a bevy of background beauties waited in bathrobes and parkas for their pass in front of the camera. This space was also where our catered crew meal was served at around 5:30 p.m.

I was eating with producer Dick Berg, talking about his overachieving sons – Jeff, the head of ICM, Scott, a Pulitzer Prize-winning biographer, Tony, a music biz executive and Rick, a lawyer and literary agent – when I couldn't avoid noticing the blonde in a low cut, spaghetti strap blue dress seated on the other side of me. As Dick's attention was diverted to a business conversation, my attention turned to the blonde. Her name was Gwenne. She was a figure skater, she told me.

I spent the next few hours on set watching the scene in which Artie's wife leaves him and only two – maybe four - times visited the holding area where Gwenne awaited her scene as one of "three beautiful women" who dance in the Mitchell Brothers' office while the guys snort cocaine. Eventually, I ran out of even the slimmest work excuses to stay. When I told her I was leaving, she grabbed my hand, locked eyes with mine and said, "You're a really special person."

O.K., then.

I said I'd hang around if she wanted to have a drink after her scene. She said "yes" with so little hesitation, I wondered for a minute if, in really bad light, I might look like Charlie Sheen's obscure, much older brother.

She wrapped filming at midnight and we found a dungeon-esque bar called Manhattan 69, conveniently located around the corner from the Howard Johnson's where I was staying. We were the only customers in the place, so the DJ asked what music we wanted to hear. Gwenne said she didn't care. I asked for Sinatra.

With figure skater's legs revealed to mid-thigh and breasts bulging from a scooped-neck nylon chemise, I really didn't care that she didn't care about music... movies, literature or current events.

I listened to her talk about herself.

She didn't want to be "caught" in any kind of "regimented" job, she said. Her mother was a harsh disciplinarian. She remembered her father giving her piggyback rides but never talking to her. She had a boyfriend whom she was about to dump. He called twice before we got to the bar and texted twice more while we were sitting there.

We stayed until closing time and I suggested we continue our discussion around the corner at the Howard Johnson's. But somewhere between *Fly Me to the Moon* and *Anything Goes*, she'd assessed my special personhood to merit no more than a peck in the parking lot. As I held open her car door, her phone rang again. She laid it on the passenger seat, fastened her seatbelt and drove away.

I walked to my hotel more pensive than disappointed.

Yes, I was willing to cross that line again so soon after my last disaster. Slightly drunk but totally willing.

What was *I* doing?

Had I learned nothing from the past – the *recent* past?

Back at the Howard Johnson's, I fell asleep concluding only that Sinatra may have been too big a gap. (*Hey, Nineteen...*)

The next night's big scene was the premiere of *Behind the Green Door*. Billed as the first porn film with a plot, it starred a former photography model for "baby-soft" Ivory Snow soap, Marilyn Chambers, who would become the genre's first real Superstar.

I arrived around shooting call to learn production had been delayed while the hair department addressed the problem of unsightly seams on the fringes around the Mitchell brothers' monk-like baldcaps.

While we waited for the reupholstered wigs, I had a chance to chat with Charlie.

"Uh, Charles. I prefer Charles these days."

New beginnings.

He was much more subdued than I remembered him. The mischievous twinkle that had always made him more than merely cool seemed to have flat-lined.

I wanted to ask him how he was feeling. I wanted to ask if he worried about backsliding. I wanted to reassure him that his father adored him – from a father who knows what it is to have sons.

But we wound up talking about his sports memorabilia collection.

"Yeah, I had it at the All Star Café," he folded his arms against the night chill. "I think they're going bankrupt and I didn't want my stuff to become part of their assets."

Sheen, an ardent baseball fan, owned some of the most important historical pieces of the game. There were the boyhood memories of a lot of boys in that collection.

"I've just gotta find someplace to store it that's not a warehouse."

It would have been most logical if the filmmakers had decided that this set would be closed to press. Writers would have time enough to write about the movie later - once all concerned had figured out how to position it. But Emilio had told Showtime that he wanted all the publicity his film could get. It was my job to prove they'd heard him.

So, standing under the marquee reading "Totally Nude, Live Sex," I felt some ambivalence that Jefferson Graham of *USA Today* wanted to do a story on this movie.

Emilio quickly approved Graham's request for a set visit – with one proviso.

"Just check with Charlie first."

"I don't know why Charlie picked this project," Jeff Ballard moaned. "I advised against it, so did his manager. But he wanted to work with his brother. And ultimately, Charlie's gonna do what Charlie wants to do."

This was before I started explaining the reason for my call, which was to convey Jefferson Graham's response to Ballard's demands of narrowing the parameters of Charlie's *USA Today* interview.

"I mean, c'mon, they're making a movie about the porn industry," Graham had groaned. "Everybody knows his name showed up in Heidi Fleiss' black book a coupla years ago. All he has to do is address it. He can say, 'What's past is past. I just wanna move on' or 'I don't wanna talk about it.' But my editors expect me to ask the question."

Sounded reasonable to me. But Ballard's counterpoint was also well taken.

"He's just looking for a quote they can put in a box under the banner. I say, forget it. I'll talk to Charlie about it. But I think he's gonna say the same thing."

I was having these conversations while the cameras rolled on Charles, as Artie, stumbling, stoned, through the Tenderloin District, past hookers and drug dealers.

I called Emilio's publicist, Lisa Kasteler, and asked what she thought of the USA idea. She didn't trust Graham any more than Ballard had.

"I don't blame Charlie for turning it down."

But he hadn't yet.

On my drive back to Ithaca for the weekend, I tried calling Jeff Ballard again to find out if Charlie had killed this Frankenstein or invited it to dinner - but the roaming service on my mobile phone wasn't working. It was a relaxing drive. I got back in time to see Sam's baseball game. That night I stayed up late listening to music with Casey.

Margaret was asleep by the time I came to bed. When she slept alone, she slept on her back. I rolled her into spoons and held her breast.

I worked from home that Monday and drove my boys to school. Sam was excited about his class trip to the Corning Glass factory. Casey... well, nothing about school excited Casey. He was twelve years old and already craving independence.

"Dad, can I get sailing lessons?" my blind son asked.

"Well sure, I guess. Why?"

"'Cuz I think I might want to live on a boat. Away from people. Where I don't have to pay taxes."

Had my eldest befriended a Libertarian yachtsman's son at the hippie charter school he attended?

At 10:00 a.m., Margaret called me.

In the short spaces between wrenching sobs, she reported the death of one of Casey's schoolmates, Patricio "Pato" Gonzalez.

Menequita Gonzalez had moved to Ithaca with her husband Ruben in 1988, after fleeing their native Argentina in 1982. They were both political activists in a time when the ruling dictatorship was murdering dissidents by the busload.

Menequita was a lawyer in Argentina but could only find work as a teacher's aide in Ithaca. Pato was born with Down syndrome in 1985. Four years later, they had a daughter, Michelle, who was in Sam's class. She was strong and beautiful and normal, like her mother. At least her mother appeared normal – until yesterday.

Michelle was spending the night at a friend's when Ruben Gonzalez came home from work at 8:30 p.m. to discover the bodies of his wife and handicapped son on the floor of their living room, their heads wrapped in plastic bags. Meniquita had left notes around the house indicating deepening depression had led her to choose suicide. In the dementia of such despair, she reasoned the disabled child she so loved couldn't survive without her. Now, he was dead; she was in a coma.

Margaret couldn't stop crying.

The next morning, I followed Margaret to the clinic in Rochester where she was to have a final, conclusive test on the lump in her breast. The results of her "needle biopsy" wouldn't be in until the following morning.

After the test, I continued on to Toronto to begin another week's work. She drove back to Ithaca, sobbing most of the way.

The *sturm und drang* of the proposed *USA Today* visit was a little difficult to wrap my head around that morning. Fortunately, within the first twenty minutes of arriving on set, I had a chance to end the silliness with a definitive "no" from Charlie.

"Sure, I'll do it," he said.

You sure?

"Unless the questions get to be too much about me and not enough about the movie."

Jeff Ballard wasn't happy about my talking to his client "behind (his) back." Or maybe he just wasn't happy with Charlie's decision.

"There are gonna be some ground rules," Ballard declared. "Graham can only do this thing if he agrees to take a written, one sentence statement from Charlie about his personal life. That's it. No other questions about his personal history."

Lisa Kasteler, apparently having talked to her client, Emilio, was now eager to make this story happen and thought Ballard was at risk of sabotaging the visit with this new, impossible demand.

"I (meaning *me*) would (*should*) just tell Graham, 'Fine, you can talk to him' and then let Charlie stonewall the questions as they come up."

Instead, I went back to the source and told him my dilemma.

"I know, I just talked with Jeff," Charlie said.

Then he got called away to work.

I stayed to watch part of the scene: the Mitchell brothers filming a movie in a mad scientist's laboratory. The two main characters were the scientist and a gorilla in whom he'd implanted his own overactive libido – or vice versa, it was not a major plot point. The scientist was screwing a nurse on a lab table while the ape was chasing other nurses around the room.

The action called for Artie Mitchell to interrupt the filming, yell "cut" and tell his brother the scene was all wrong: no one would be turned on by girls in nurses uniforms.

"Then what would you suggest?" Jim Mitchell asked.

Artie displayed two scanty costumes hidden behind his back.

"Cheerleaders!" Artie grins.

One of the things that came out during the Heidi Fleiss trial was that Charlie had a thing for... come to think of it, if you don't already know, it doesn't bear repeating.

A number of the male Canadian crew thought it was pretty funny.

Laugh and the world laughs with you?

"O.K., that was good. Let's do one more," Emilio instructed.

Charlie returned to his starting position with somber professionalism – as if they were shooting a scene from *Wall Street*.

I wondered if Jeff Ballard had read this part of the script.

I phoned Margaret as soon as I got back to the hotel that night.

"It hurts," she said about the needle puncture in her breast. "And for the first time during all this, I couldn't stop thinking, 'what if I have cancer? What if I died? What would it do to the boys to lose their mother?' I thought about Michelle without Menequita. I thought about my mother."

Clara Gebhardt had earned a liberal arts degree from Smith College before marrying a handsome Air Force pilot on his way to England to fight in The War. Her husband was killed before he'd served six months of duty - also before he'd learned of the birth of his son, Aldon Taylor.

Friends from the Fingerlakes town of Levanna, introduced Clara to Frank Wakeley, a junior executive at Kodak Corporation in Rochester, New York. The pair courted on Cayuga Lake and married within a year. Frank adopted the baby, whom they called Tad, and they had three more children – the youngest, they called Margaret.

When Margaret was nine years old, the family learned it was going to have a new addition. The usual excitement attended the two girls. The usual preoccupation with high school sports continued to occupy the two boys. Everyone's eagerness grew as months progressed and, on February 28, 1960, the expectant mother went into labor.

Then something went terribly wrong.

Less than an hour into the delivery process, a bubble formed around the release of amniotic fluid and began a rapid ascent through a small tear in Clara's uterus. It traveled along an artery into the left ventricle of her heart. It was difficult for the attending nurse to distinguish her distressed breathing from the normal rapid respiration of a difficult birth. The doctor would be in shortly, she assured. Meanwhile, try to relax. By the time Clara's breathing had become alarmingly irregular, most of the damage had been done.

The toxic bubble had burst, releasing amniotic material into the vasculature. The left side of her heart began going into failure as the process of anaphylaxis turned the flowing liquid of her ventricular blood into a gooey gelatin.

The panicked nurse ran to the waiting room where she found Clara's husband.

"We need the doctor," she screamed.

Frank sprinted down the hall, pushing open doors, resisting the urgings of hospital staff to "calm down" as his wife gasped her last before her heart imploded from an unbearable pressure. The doctor finally arrived and performed a Caesarian section to deliver Margaret's brother.

Like the fossil remains of an animal, time preserves events in muscle memory. Encased in Margaret were the secrets of a girl passing through adolescence without a mother. Feelings about birth, sex and death forever entangled, sealed in amber.

Margaret would get her test results tomorrow. They would be negative. She would spend the night sleepless, uncomfortable. The physical pain could be numbed by medication. The fright of shaking hands with mortality was less easily dispatched.

Jeff Ballard called to tell me he'd just gotten off the phone with Charlie and they'd come up with a one-sentence statement that should apply to any and all questions about his personal history.

What's past is past. It's time to move on.

"Charlie is too candid," Ballard proceeded to explain. "He wants too much to be liked. He also has a deadpan sense of humor that doesn't always come across in print."

He then chatted amiably about Charlie, the business of publicity and the difficulties of it all. A personal publicist has to be part traffic cop, part power broker, part pitbull, part whipping boy and hopefully not forget he's also a human being. Jeff's humanity was what Charlie trusted. Jeff guarded that trust.

Ballard recently had to deflect a suggestion from Charlie's manager that Daily Variety columnist Army Archerd be given an item about how Charlie had been clean and sober for a full year. This would run in contrast with an item about Robert Downey, Jr. having been committed to rehab again.

"I had to remind him that if it was his client who'd slipped, he wouldn't appreciate some other actor showing him up like that. Charlie looking like he's turned a corner is great but not if he's gotta be a dick to somebody else going through a bad time."

Jeff had also represented Johnny Depp for five years – including the well-documented time when he trashed a hotel room.

"That was no picnic," he sighed.

In terms of dollars spent, Toronto was the third biggest center for filmmaking in North America – after Los Angeles and New York. But they didn't have much studio space. We'd been shooting the last few days in a former beer factory, Gooderham & Worts. The building that housed our set looked like it could crumble from a loud sneeze.

"Let's get the *fluffers* in," called Estevez, in character as Jim Mitchell directing *Behind the Green Door*. At Jim Mitchell's command, two semi-naked women rushed in to attend a Black actor with a strategic hole cut in the top half of his white jump suit.

At "cut!" – was that the director or the director playing the director? - Marilyn Chambers (played by Tracy Hutson – future host of *Extreme Makeover: Home Edition*) and her toga-clad captors returned to first position.

Real naked women engaged in pretend porn should have been amusing to watch - at least from a technical standpoint: how would the cameras *cheat* the large rubber dong hanging out of the white jump suit? What kind of lighting would be required so the five men Marilyn services simultaneously didn't throw shadows on the star?

But I had something better to do than stand around watching simulated sex.

I started my four-hour drive home around noon, arriving just in time to join Margaret and Casey for Sam's graduation from elementary school.

Rueben Gonzales was also there to watch his daughter Michelle graduate. He looked like any other proud parent in the audience.

The next day, while Sam went to his friend Noah's house, I took Casey rollerblading at Buttermilk Park. He skated, I jogged. Gershwin ran alongside us.

"What's Gershwin doing now?"

Sniffing another tree.

"Let's go faster."

Sweetheart, I can't run as fast as you can skate.

"What's he doing now?"

Peeing on the fence.

The thought of Gershwin peeing always cracked Casey up.

While Casey and I were at the park and Sam was visiting his friend Noah, Margaret was attending Pato Gonzales' funeral.

That night, we all sat around the television watching a rented mini-series called *The 60s*. We got to a scene where a naïve Catholic schoolgirl accepts an invitation to "go upstairs" with a member of a rock band.

Margaret became inexplicably angry – at Sam!

"You know that's not right. I don't ever want you to do anything like that."

Our bewildered 10-year-old wasn't quite sure if she meant casual sex, sex in general or sex with groupies in particular.

So, I tried to interpret – in my own inept, male way.

"What your mom means is, sex is better with somebody you know and like."

"That's not at all what I mean!" she exploded. "I mean he should have more respect for himself and for women."

Alright, so much for movie night. We sent the boys to bed and stayed up arguing. To Margaret it was a matter of teaching sexual ethics. To me it was about not sexually traumatizing our son before he'd reached puberty.

Margaret finally calmed down and, while still angry at me for "making that scene seem o.k.," told me, "If you think Sam will be scarred by my reaction, then you should go up and talk to him."

Sam was almost asleep. I lay down beside him.

"I heard from Stevie and Carter that *South Park, The Movie* is going to be illegal for people under 17 to see," he said. "Even with a parent."

Do you want to talk about sex?

"I dunno. Can I have somebody sleep over tomorrow?"

You've got a baseball game tomorrow.

"What about somebody from the baseball game?"

We said goodnight. I went into Casey's room but he was already sleeping.

I went downstairs and told Margaret it didn't seem either boy was deeply scarred.

She still wasn't happy with me.

The next morning, Sam and I did our Sunday rounds, driving downtown to pick up bagels and the New York Times.

"Dad, would you someday show me how to put on a condom?" he asked on the drive home.

I said I would. Someday.

Margaret was talking to me again when we got back with the bagels. But there was a cloud around her most of the day.

"Did I tell you, Menequita has come out of her coma?" she mentioned after coming in from gardening that afternoon.

I drove to Toronto Monday morning feeling much had been left unsaid.

Jefferson Graham was a delightful guy. We both had sons named Sam, about the same age, who both liked to draw. We got acquainted over lunch, a quick trip to get fresh batteries for his tape recorders and a drive to the location, having as good a time as two people can while anticipating a potentially tense afternoon at the job site.

The company was filming outside a municipal building that stood in for the Marin County Courthouse, site of the brothers' first obscenity trial in 1971.

I brought Graham to Emilio for introductions and the director said he'd talk to him when the camera turned around for the next setup.

Charlie came right up the moment he saw us.

"I've got a few minutes, if ya wanna…?" Charlie motioned for them to sit down.

I sat nearby. The interview went without controversy – except for the parts that the subject introduced.

"It's been a cathartic experience," said Charlie. "There's a lot I can relate to."

I could picture the veins popping out on Jeff Ballard's temples as he read the headline of Jefferson Graham's story:

Recovering Alcoholic, Sex-Addicted, Trigger-Happy, Ex-Druggie

Movie Star

Finds "A Lot To Relate To" in Story of Porn King Brothers.

Hey, in the end, Charlie was going to do what Charlie wanted to do.

After his interview with Emilio, Graham said "thanks" to both his subjects and caught a cab to the airport.

I stayed around until filming wrapped and said my goodbyes to Dick Berg, Emilio and some of the crew.

I found Charles outside his trailer.

"It was great working with you again."

"Yeah, see ya on the next one," he said, shaking my hand.

That wicked little twinkle was back in his eyes.

The sun was low and the traffic thick for my final return drive to Ithaca. I left the highway and took a northern route to watch the dusk settle over Lake Ontario.

In the still summer air, the small towns between Buffalo and Rochester slid by in deepening silhouette, a Rustbelt diorama of tidy clapboard homes where lawn ornaments were still a decorating mania and shopping malls consisted of a convenience store and a gas station. One imagined a carrousel in the town center of a purer, healthier America.

Then Route 104 snaked inland, and if you turned onto one of the narrow two-lanes south towards the interstate you might pass a factory as defunct as a dinosaur. Old bones of what the families here used to feed on.

There was a time when all the porch lights were on all summer. You'd notice most of the porch lights were off now.

There was only the moon and the high beams of someone passing through.

PART VII
CLIMATE CHANGE

The Perfect Storm – Warner Bros.

CHAPTER TWENTY-SEVEN

ALL THAT GLITTERS

A warm hug from Karen Allen outside Stage 16 on the Warner Bros. lot was a fine welcome to L.A. We'd exchanged emails in celebration of her getting this part. This was a sweet, unexpected reunion with a new/old friend - any imaginings beyond had blown away in the Moroccan wind.

Karen was a little nervous, not just because *The Perfect Storm* was her first big movie in awhile but because of the trials that awaited her behind the giant stage doors.

"I was standing in the middle of the stage when they opened up virtually everything they could open up, water cannons, wave-makers, the gimbal spinning every which way," she said, laughing. "And all I'm thinking is, 'I'm gonna have to go out in *that?*'"

That included water cannons shooting spray that could send an elephant flying, wind machines turned up to 80 miles per hour, a giant gimbal cranking the boat nearly perpendicular to the water, dump tanks and the wave maker combining to create 10 foot swells. The real boats had confronted waves ten times that size but no performance was going to suffer for lack of verisimilitude.

"I love physical challenges," Karen flashed a game smile. "And you know, for an actor, there's nothing like getting hit in the face with cold water to put you right in the present moment."

"We're not making *My Dinner with Andre* here, folks," director Wolfgang Petersen told anybody who asked how rough it was going to get.

This movie had seemed impossible to make – from both a technical and creative standpoint - and even more impossible to get green lit by a studio.

It had half-a-dozen bright red lights from conception:

1) the book contained enough meteorological jargon to cross your eyes and followed multiple storylines about people who were unconnected by anything except the storm: an air and sea rescue team, a Canadian fisheries agent on a Japanese factory boat, three civilians in a sailboat, an official at the national weather service and six fishermen who die at sea.

2) the main characters DIE at sea.

3) name a movie that took place on water that didn't go over budget? *Titanic? Jaws? Mutiny on the Bounty? The Bounty? Waterworld? Raise the Titanic? Jaws: the Revenge?* The good, the bad and the very ugly.

4) creating a realistic storm required more than flashing lights and two guys with buckets off stage: practical effects on this movie would be expensive and unprecedented.

5) visual effects geniuses at ILM would be attempting the single hardest thing to do in vfx: making realistic water. You could

shoot a great film but if the water didn't look real, you were dead in it.

6) did we mention, all the lead characters die at the end? For a load of fish?

First-time author Sebastian Junger had a few Hollywood meetings before his book was published and got the brush-off at every one. Then his tale of a Massachusetts swordfish trawler became a New York Times best-seller and everybody wanted it. From the ensuing frenzy, Junger picked the bidder he "instinctively trusted" and asked his agent to sell the rights to Paula Weinstein and her Spring Creek Productions, regardless of highest bid.

Weinstein got a brilliant script from William Wittliff (*Lonesome Dove*) and sent it to the director who made *Das Boat*, the most critically and financially successful foreign language import ever filmed on land or sea.

The movie had two casting delays: first when Mel Gibson dropped out, then when they couldn't sign their first choice replacement, Nicolas Cage.

Petersen liked working with big stars. The studio wanted a big star, of course, but the movie already had a big budget. So they compromised on a reasonably priced, still unproven leading man who referred to himself as "the actor who destroyed the *Batman* franchise."

George Clooney had starred in big movies before but following five years of being the biggest star on television's biggest hit show, *ER*, he had yet to score big on the big screen. This time, he was neither the romantic lead (*One Fine Day*) nor an action hero (*The Peacemaker*). In fact, he was less a lead than part of a talented ensemble.

As fishing boat captain Billy Tyne, he'd be onboard the ill-fated swordboat Andrea Gail with Mark Wahlberg playing Bobby Shatford, the character who was more the centerpiece of Junger's book. The two had recently worked together on *Three Kings* and Clooney had recommended Wahlberg for this role. The rest of the Captain's crew were William Fichtner as David "Sully" Sullivan,

John C. Reilly as Dale Murphy, John Hawkes as Mike "Bugsy" Moran and Allen Payne as Alfred Pierre.

These accomplished actors would be complimented by a strong female cast, including Diane Lane as Bobby's girlfriend Chris Cotter, Mary Elizabeth Mastrantonio playing rival fishing boat captain Linda Greenlaw, and Karen Allen and stage star Cherry Jones as hired hands on a pleasure boat piloted by versatile acting veteran Bob Gunton.

Wolfgang was setting sail with an exceptional group of performers. Now, if only the mechanical part of the production held together.

Location manager Michael Meehan had been on duty for 36 hours straight, supervising filling the tank on Stage 16, which had been excavated to a depth of 22 feet in order to submerge the huge gyroscope on which the boats were to be mounted.

"I'm seeing three of you right now, so I'll just talk to the one in the middle," he told executive producer Duncan Henderson on the first morning of filming. "We almost didn't get this done in time."

After weeks of digging, re-cementing and sealing the stage floor, special effects guru John Frazier began building The Gimbal That Ate Cincinnati.

"If it's not the biggest, I'm pretty sure it's the most complicated rig ever built for a movie," said Frazier, a hulking man with thinning grey hair. "It's motion control on a grand scale. There's never been anything outside of maybe a military flight simulator with this range of motion."

Frazier would construct half-a-dozen gimbals for this movie but the one on Stage 16 was the Big Kahuna. It featured a six-axis hydraulic motion base, 25' across and 15' high, that would support a 150,000-pound fishing boat.

It was the O-rings on this monster that had kept Meehan sleepless for a day-and-a-half. The tank would start filling and an O-ring would begin to leak oil. The tank would have to be emptied and refilled until the rings held against the water pressure. Nearly once a week, over 11 weeks of filming on this stage, leaky O-rings would cause Meehan to have to refill the tank.

"That's a 350,000 gallon tank at approximately a dollar a gallon," the exhausted location manager estimated.

Budgeted at $138 million, this was the most expensive movie Warner Bros. had ever approved. Legendary cheapskate Jack Warner was kicking at his coffin lid.

It was fitting that Stage 16 should be host to such extravagance.

In 1936, Marion Davies, actress and paramour of newspaper tycoon William Randolph Hearst, was set to star in the musical comedy *Cain and Mabel.* Her singing voice, never the strongest, had gotten thinner now, towards the end of her career.

The director showed the mogul some tests in an attempt to dissuade him from insisting on Davies for the role.

"What's wrong with her voice?" Hearst predictably asked.

Trying to be diplomatic, or to save his sound mixer's job, the director offered, "Perhaps the ceiling on the stage isn't as high as it might be in a concert hall."

So Hearst paid for it to be raised thirty feet.

It's still the tallest sound stage anywhere in the world. And now, the deepest.

Every boutique window along Sunset Strip glittered like Tiffany's on this postcard perfect L.A. day. Every third car was a Mercedes, every third woman was a covergirl and every other guy looked like he could buy the restaurant where he just had lunch. This was my new neighborhood.

I'd had a mixed relationship with Los Angeles. It was the place I grew up yet never quite felt at home. It was the center of the movie world, which I loved. It was a universe that revolved around Show Business in a solipsist configuration I found vapid and valueless. The times I'd returned here always felt less like visits than gravitational pull. I had stopped fighting gravity but still floated between attachment and antipathy.

The Sunset Strip was my barometer: sometimes it leered, sometimes it winked. This time it seemed to be saying, "Lighten up Kid and I'll show you a good time."

I winked back. It felt good to be back.

My apartment was on Holloway, a slip of a street immediately south of Sunset. My landlord Howard told me that the person who sold his father the building had told him Marilyn Monroe and Shelley Winters once shared one of the front apartments.

"It might even be yours!" said Howard in a fey imitation of a game-show host.

The apartment was so... Howard – it was hard to imagine Marilyn and Shelley or anyone else living in this environment. The décor might be described as Ayahuasca Amazon, via Davy Crockett Tennessee on the way to Never Neverland. Thank God he sawed the silk canopy off the four-poster bed.

As you entered the living room there was a hanging fountain shaped like a wadded-up piece of paper. On it was a green frog with a motion detector that made it croak every time someone walked by. Beneath a variegated ceiling fan, a coffee table in the shape of a grinning alligator lay atop a fake leopard-skin rug. A large, gray huggy-toy dog and a ceramic mask of a woman's face with a green lizard's tail draped across her nose sat on an antique oriental bookshelf opposite a gunbelt and powderhorn that dangled from a blond bamboo hat rack beside the hickory-branch frame of a floral sofa. It was the design equivalent of experimental theatre. But the motion-detector frog was always happy to see me.

On set the next day, Wolfgang joked about there being "too much in the newspapers already" about this picture. There was a mention of our movie in an L.A. Times story speculating about Warner Bros.' executive reorganization after the imminent departure of Bob Daly and Terry Semel, the popular team that had been running the studio for the past twenty years but had lost a power struggle with Time-Warner chairman Gerald Levin and major shareholder Ted Turner.

Unmentioned in the article was producer Gail Katz's power struggle with the studio's publicity department: they wouldn't let her have the behind-the-scenes crew she wanted.

Two women who called themselves Elan had shot the EPK for *Air Force One*, and Gail wanted them back on this one. It's rare that a studio doesn't yield to a filmmaker's choice of documentary team – all costs being equal.

"I'm going to insist on them," the producer insisted, dragging me into her trailer to watch sample reels the studio had sent over from other EPK companies.

By the time I got out of Gail's trailer, it was lunchtime. I made a sandwich on the craft service truck and took it around the corner to where Cherry Jones and Karen Allen were sunning themselves outside their adjoining dressing rooms.

Karen showed me the black and blue patch under the ace bandage around her arm. She'd smashed it against the side of the sailboat on the first shot of the day and was keeping secret how badly she'd hurt it because she didn't want to lose this job.

I stayed to watch the next scene in which Karen's sailboat, The Mistral, tipped completely on its side. If not for the boom of the water cannons you might've heard her boney arm crack against the edge of the boat again.

I stood next to Wolfgang's assistant, Barbara Huber, from Munich, who taught me how to say *"sehr eindrucksvoll,"* which means "very impressive."

"That's it," shouted Wolfgang. "Realism. I want realism. Fantastic."

The most important part of a studio executive's job is cultivating relationships with creative talent - actors, directors, writers and producers - who have proven track records. The studio is usually prepared to do whatever it takes – sometimes even green light a pet project with no obvious financial prospects - to keep someone with a history of making money in their corporate orbit.

Still, mighty struggles persist over the pettiest issues.

Sweet-as-candy-hard-as-nails publicity chief Charlotte Kandel and her lugubrious lieutenant, project vice president John Dartigue, stopped by the set to talk to Gail about the prospects of hiring Elan to document this movie: slim and none.

They came with the names of three more companies that were acceptable to the studio. They expected this would demonstrate their reasonableness: surely among the five bidders now submitted, there would be one, not named *Elan*, on which Gail could settle.

The fact was, they'd had a bad experience with Elan and had sworn never to hire them again. Quite bravely, from one perspective, the Warner Bros. publicity department appeared willing to bruise a filmmaker relationship to impose the severest discipline.

Looking at the list of alternate vendors, there was one company I knew to be headed by a talented cameraman named Scott McVeigh. I hadn't worked with him since he'd started his own company but recommended him to Gail as "Wolfgang's kinda guy," i.e., positive and easygoing, with a sense of humor.

"Alright, I'll look at their reel," she grudgingly conceded.

I'm sure Dartigue didn't intend his smile to betray so much smugness.

A few days later, Scott McVeigh and his younger brother Dave were darting around the set with two cameras like they'd won a contest to see how many groceries they could pile in a cart in five minutes. Dave nearly followed a crane shot off the camera platform, into the tank.

As I stood with Gail outside the stage, listening to her complain about the studio "forcing" her into accepting what she believed was inferior behind-the-scenes coverage, Clint Eastwood drove by in a golf cart.

"Hey, Clint!" Gail waved. They had worked together on Wolfgang's *In the Line of Fire*. Clint was on the lot directing *Space Cowboys*.

Eastwood backed up the cart. Gail gave him a hug, "How nice to see you!"

"Ah, you'd say anything to get a tee time, wouldn't you?" Eastwood had just bought Pebble Beach golf course. Gail was a golfing fanatic. They chatted awhile before Clint continued on to his own set on Stage 21.

"Sounded like he's had a lot of practice with that line," Gail said as he drove away. She took an imaginary swipe at a golf ball. All complaints about the EPK crew were forgotten.

There would be more pressing issues to occupy her over the course of filming.

That afternoon, a crane tore a piece off the rescue ship Tamaroa, causing a filming delay. It would be the first in a series of behind-the-scenes near-disasters. Later, there was another crane mishap in which the operator's arm smashed through the windshield. He came away with only minor cuts and bruises.

We hadn't gotten to the really challenging stuff yet.

As challenges go, there aren't many tougher than getting toddlers on a plane. It's a horror of managing baggage, strollers, car seats, earaches and tantrums. When the kids get older, it's a different set of problems: studies, sports, music performances.

When does a family ever find time to travel together?

I always thought that was why someone invented summer vacation.

Margaret was a big believer in summer camps. I was a big believer in summer at Camp Daddy. Margaret would only enroll them all here for two weeks in August.

The boys spent their first week in L.A. at a Pacific Palisades day camp and Margaret's days were free. She visited the set, said "hi" to Wolfgang and Karen and hung out for an afternoon. She found a favorite café to read in on Sunset. The weather wasn't too hot to take walks and she could use our rental car while I was at work. She spent a good bit of time with my sister Cynthia and her newly adopted infant daughter and had friends, along with pleasant memories to revisit from the seven years she lived here. Except now, she didn't live here.

The difficult life of a location wife is something with which every movie couple copes differently. Most choose to live in Los Angeles where work can keep them home for at least part of the year. But when they venture on the road together, spouses have to find their own footing. Twelve-hour days, sometimes six-day weeks, make many decide it isn't worth the effort: see you when the job's over – until the next job starts.

There are couples, however, who make it work. Our cinematographer John Seale and his wife Louise were only one example on this film.

They'd met and married in their early twenties when he was a camera assistant for the Australian Broadcasting Company and she was launching her career as a unit production manager. Children came: first a girl, then a boy. John's career got a boost from his stellar camera work on Peter Weir's *Gallipoli*. Increasingly, he was gone. They both saw the crossroads ahead.

When Weir asked him to come to the U.S. to shoot *Witness* in 1984, the couple talked about what they should do. Moving from Australia wasn't an option for either of them. He went off to America to earn an Oscar nomination and offers for more U.S. films. She stayed home. There followed periods of strain and even estrangement. But they decided they wanted to be together. So, Louise and the kids would have to travel.

"Louise was an adventurer," said Seale, with admiration. "And we knew each other well."

John was an avid sailor; he and his family would often go on long boat trips. Louise decided to look at location life like extended boat trips with the sails down.

"We lived like gypsies, you know, like film people do," she explained over dinner one night at Rob and Karen Cowan's house in Hancock Park. "Your home is in a bag."

She laughed as though sacrificing her career and a stable home life was no more complicated than choosing a holiday destination.

As for the impact on their children: "They don't know how to spell but they aren't afraid of people."

There are movie stars who are idolized; there are directors who are lionized. But ask any married man or woman who works in the film industry and they'll tell you their heroes are couples like the Seales, the Cowans and our executive producer Duncan Henderson and his wife Michelle.

The Hendersons met in a geography class at UCLA. After college, she became a school guidance counselor, he a stockbroker. Then an acquaintance told Duncan about the Directors Guild trainee program. He took and passed the test, quit his high-paying job and began his movie career at the lowest level. When he became a second assistant director and work started taking him out of town, Michelle gave up her job at Santa Monica High School and became a location wife.

"My family has always traveled with me," Duncan said, flipping burgers on the grill he manned every Friday at wrap outside the *Perfect Storm* production office. "It wasn't possible all the time but whenever I was going to be in one place for awhile, Michelle would come and live there with me."

They raised four children that way.

"We'd do various things with the kids' schooling. Public schools, private schools, tutoring. Michelle would get the curriculum and make sure they kept up. By the time they got back home they would invariably be a few weeks ahead of the other kids.

Plus, quite the opposite of being ostracized, there was always a little bit of celebration to their return. Like, 'oh, the circus kids are back.'"

The circus kids. That's what they were, alright. But the wife of the guy on the flying trapeze, what's her identity?

No, it's not easy being a location wife. So for most movie couples the baling wire of occasional visits of a few days or a couple of weeks is all that hold marriages together. That and the desire to be together.

Casey made his first visit to the set and he'd "forgotten" to bring his cane. While Sam went off to watch the monitors at video village, I took Casey to where soundman Keith Wester had his mixing board set up.

Keith was a bit of a geek and he and Casey bonded instantly. He fitted Casey with a pair of headphones and let him play with the soundboard. As soon as he learned they shared an affinity for aviation, Keith invited him to climb aboard the helicopter, which was grounded nearby. He showed Casey the panel, gearshift and all the other gadgets in the pilot's reach. Then it dawned on Keith that Casey was blind.

"My first clue was when he asked 'does this thing have wings?'" he would later tell me. "Then I had a hunch something was up."

Sam got to meet Mark Wahlberg who had stopped by to say a few "hellos" before starting work next week.

"I've heard some of your songs," Sam reassured him.

On the way out, Sam confided he wasn't much of a fan of Marky Mark's music.

"But he seemed like a really nice guy."

When Sam and I came back to find Casey, Keith was teaching him Morse Code.

"I think I'd like to get into ham radio," Casey said, taking off his headphones. With this skill, he reasoned, he could live on his boat in the middle of the ocean and not have to pay for a telephone.

My birthday was the reason Margaret had agreed to stay in L.A. as long as she did. I decided I wanted to go to Disneyland. We invited Karen and her son Nick. The highlight was the *Raiders of the Lost Ark* ride – which we almost didn't get on.

Waiting on the lengthy line, Karen became the object of some stares and whispers – most from parents who couldn't quite place her from the family photo album but knew they knew her from somewhere. A few did make the connection and she graciously signed ticket stubs and notepads. When one man looked at her signature and asked, "what were some of your movies?" she thought it might be o.k. to pull rank to get some privacy.

"The line moves pretty fast," was the most helpful response she got from Disney's helpers.

Karen had been one of the most popular actresses of her generation. She'd made her film debut in *Animal House* at age 26, then starred in a dozen pictures over the next decade. But by her late thirties, her youthful glow had gained a maturity that no longer fit the parts Hollywood was offering. So, at an age when her male counterparts were at the height of their careers, hers was on the wane.

"I didn't really master my craft until I was nearly forty," she'd said. "And by then I was too old for any of the good roles."

The movie business is full of ironies but few are crueler than this one: the best years of an actress' life come before the peak of her skills. Male actors are allowed to mature on screen. Most actresses transit directly from ingénue to oblivion - or the stage, which is the Hollywood equivalent.

It required my going to the ride-minders' supervisor's supervisor before we found someone working there who even knew who Karen was. We ultimately did get access through the door they used for movie stars and the handicapped. Our time in line, however, had made me feel more than just a year older.

Still, Sam, Casey and Nick all thought it had been a great birthday celebration. And that was the point, wasn't it? Welcome to Camp Daddy. Come back again soon.

A day later, the ephemera of my domestic life were on a plane to New York.

I walked to The Strip for dinner at Mel's Diner, passing sidewalk cafes packed with pretty people all hoping to be noticed by the right people, Le Dome restaurant where dealmakers had their favorite tables on permanent standby and *Schadenfreude* was everyone's favorite dish, the Spy Store where suspicious spouses could buy something called Checkmate to get the goods on unfaithful partners. For all its glitter, this was still the Boulevard of Broken Dreams.

I was flying to Massachusetts in a few days. I would keep my apartment and leave most of my clothes, books and belongings behind. L.A. still felt a bit like home. Except there was only a motion-sensor frog and a grinning coffee table to come home to.

Margaret and the boys would meet me in Boston for Labor Day weekend. I'd see them once again in New York for Sam's birthday at the end of our East Coast filming – then, not until Thanksgiving.

Dinner for one at Mel's felt about right.

CHAPTER TWENTY-EIGHT

PREPARATIONS

Mark Wahlberg wasn't quite a movie star but he had an entourage – a group of friends he'd known since boyhood. His manager Stephen Levinson, who answered only to "Lev," cautioned me - after a twenty minute lecture on the nature, history, dubious value and various hazards of publicity - "Any press that comes to the set, I don't want 'em to see the entourage. You give him a heads-up. Get rid of the entourage before anybody comes." No journalist I ever invited to the set would write about the fact that Mark had an entourage.

Week three was the start of work for Wahlberg and Diane Lane. Their first scene together was in bed.

"Mark, this is Diane. Diane, this is Mark. O.K., now I want you to lie down next to her like this. Then maybe you start to get aroused."

The two actors shook hands and lay down on their marks. First a.d. Alan Curtiss asked non-essential crew to leave the stage.

"It wasn't the first time this had happened to me," Lane said later. "There must be some special movie god up there who giggles and says, 'Look, I put the love scene on the first day – just like I did on the last show.' But I made a lot of *Boogie Nights* jokes to break the ice and Mark was a total sweetheart."

I'd heard from some of our crew members that radio shock jock Howard Stern had announced on his top-rated morning show how much his wife "would love to be an extra in *The Perfect Storm.*"

In terms of raising a movie's hipness profile, it didn't get much better than that. It would be easy to get Mrs. Stern a walk-on role and the presumption was her husband would talk up the movie around release time, encouraging his millions of listeners to go see her. Sounded great. Like a good soldier, I took the message to my studio boss. I asked John Dartigue if we might be able to get a transcript of the show in order to verify what Stern said and how he said it before I started getting film-maker approvals...

"No," Dartigue interrupted.

Pardon?

"I will not spend a penny to get a transcript of that disgusting man's disgusting show. And I don't want us to have anything to do with him."

Alright, then. Moving on.

"But don't worry, we'll find plenty of other ways to keep you busy."

He let slip a sadistic chuckle.

The New England media were already starting to hound me about gaining access to the set once we got to Gloucester.

Jeanne Blake from the Perfect Storm Foundation was calling daily, as was Robin Dawson from the Massachusetts Film Commission, each asking if certain visits and activities would be possible during our filming in Gloucester. Most of them weren't – unless we were going to turn the production into a regional charity fundraiser.

I got a call from the assistant coordinator at our Gloucester office asking what to do about a TV news crew that had showed up at our main construction site.

"Tell them to go away."

"But they're saying, 'it's public property, we have a right to be here.'"

"Tell them they only have the right to shoot from the public sidewalks."

Five minutes later, I got a call from a guy named Steve who said he was taping for New England Public Access and wanted permission "to go where you're working and take a few pictures." I said, "no." He asked "why?" I said because I'd have to be there with him and I'm not there. He asked, couldn't I make an exception? Swear. He did.

There were arrangements to be made with invited press, as well. My friend Peter Richmond, with whom I'd been conspiring on a *GQ* cover story for Mark Wahlberg, called to tip me off that his editor was playing hardball with the studio in negotiating the cover. The only way I'd gotten Wahlberg's manager to agree to the story was the promise of a cover. I told Peter he'd best make sure his editor sees God.

The most pressing event though, was a press conference that could only take place on the day we arrived, before we started filming. This would be the one opportunity for Boston area media to question the stars and the director.

Everyone had signed off on it. The main hitch was Wolfgang: he needed an extra day in L.A. and a commercial flight would get him in too late for reporters to meet their filing deadlines. So, once again, Gail was arguing with Charlotte Kandel - this time about getting Warner Bros.' corporate jet to fly them to Gloucester. How much did the studio want this thing to happen – this thing that would save the unit publicist from being torn to pieces by an angry mob of regional journalists who, rightfully, would be enraged at being shut out of reporting on an important local story?

Charlotte assured Gail she was looking into it. Privately, she asked me if a press conference was really worth the fuss and bother. I told her my safety was at stake.

I went ahead with plans for a press event, working through Robin Dawson and Jeanne Blake to make sure all key media were invited. I still didn't know if I'd have to call it off as I boarded a plane to Boston – two days before the conference was scheduled.

CHAPTER TWENTY-NINE

THE WORLD'S MOST DANGEROUS OCCUPATION

"Listen to that," Mark Wahlberg cupped an ear to the skies over Cape Ann harbor. "Even the seagulls are going *'George, George.'*"

It did indeed seem like every living thing in this small town had had a Clooney encounter - or a beer with Wahlberg.

We'd come here for a eulogy. Might some mourners be a tad concerned about it turning into a Hollywood party?

The Bureau of Labor Statistics listed commercial fishing as the world's most dangerous occupation. In its long history as a fishing port, Gloucester had lost over 10,000 men at sea. Most of its current population of about 30,000 still depended on the ocean for economic survival.

Unexposed Film:

Our story wasn't just about fishermen, it was about Gloucestermen — the toughest of the tough guys on the foamy brine. Might they object to their portrayers having to go through hair and makeup?

The town was changing. Sebastian Junger's book had turned it into a tourist attraction and local merchants were using this notoriety to stoke the fires of progress. How much more unwanted attention would be created by this movie? How would the production cope with residents who resented being thrust into the spotlight? And what if the movie were to dishonor the dead? These weren't *characters*. They were friends, family, colleagues and neighbors who had perished on the Andrea Gail. How do you show sensitivity to something you're exploiting?

"We realized that we could never come to Gloucester unless the town embraced us," said executive producer Duncan Henderson as we stood watching our trucks unload. "There was one person's cooperation we needed more than the Mayor. That was Ethel."

Ethel Shatford Preston was more than the mother of Bobby Shatford, the ill-fated fisherman played by Wahlberg. She was godmother to half the fisherman in Gloucester and bartender at the beer joint that was the heart of the town and of our story, The Crow's Nest.

Ethel's kindness and generosity were legend: every Christmas the regulars at her bar would get gifts. No fisherman on hard times ever went hungry or thirsty on her shift. Anyone with a sad story would tell it to Ethel and find her arms around them when tears began to fall. In Gloucester, the patron of fishermen wasn't Saint Andrew but Saint Ethel.

Ethel had never read Junger's book.

"It woulda been too painful," she said. "But I thought it was a good thing for the town because it focused on what it was like to be a fisherman."

On the wall of photos as one entered The Crow's Nest was one of Ethel posed with Steven Spielberg and Tom Selleck.

"One day Spielberg came in here with a bunch of people, 'cuz he was interested in doing the movie," explained Greg Souza, The Crow's Nest proprietor. "Ethel didn't have any idea who Spielberg was and when I read about it in the paper, found out he was here, I told her, 'If you ever see him in here again, lemme know.' So, one day she calls me and says, 'the skinny guy with the beard is heah again.' I come down and he's with Tom Selleck. Ethel said, 'I thought the other one looked familiah.' To her they weren't anybody special, just customers."

Ethel told Wolfgang that she probably wouldn't see this movie for the same reasons she didn't read the book.

"But if it's good for Gloucester, then I would be in favor of it," she said.

And that sealed the deal. The company scouted other seafront towns but there was no longer a doubt: they'd film the movie where the story happened and count on the rest of Gloucester to be as accepting of a Hollywood invasion as Ethel.

Our production offices were adjacent to the offices of Greenpeace, which had issues with the number of fish the movie planned to kill.

"None," I assured them, stopping by their cluttered headquarters to establish détente.

"We read the script," one angry environmentalist insisted. "You've got five or six scenes that call for either dead fish or live fish being caught."

"How long do fish last, unrefrigerated, in the sun, without stinking so badly you can't stand to be around them?"

He didn't know. Frankly, neither did I.

"Not long enough to make it through a 12 hour filming day. We're using artificial fish on the docks and mechanical fish for the boat scenes."

"Well, don't think we won't be checking that out."

I settled into my desk next door, in a small room I shared with Michael Meehan and the locations department, and began going through the stack of messages on my desk.

There was one from *The Today Show* asking to film Mary Elizabeth Mastrantonio working as boat captain Linda Greenlaw who was going to be a guest on their program, promoting her own book. We were going to extraordinary lengths to simulate reality in this movie. The televised image of a beautiful actress juxtaposed with that of a woman who looked like, well, a fishing boat captain did us no favors. And why exactly were we helping Linda Greenlaw sell her book?

No. Next.

A woman named Lisa Poole had stopped by the office and told one of our production assistants that she was from Associated Press and I'd said she could come by to photograph George Clooney. I couldn't imagine what I must have been smoking at the time we had that conversation. I said she could come to the press conference.

Next.

Beth Carrey of the Boston Globe wanted to know when the cast members would be arriving at the Boston Airport. Rory Barrow of Fox News wanted to visit the set for "exclusive coverage" on either September 13 or 14. Why then? The owner of the Star Market wanted to know when our stars might be available for a book signing.

Next. Next. Next.

I accepted an invitation to dinner at Jeanne Blake's water-front home that evening. I met her golden retriever, Brewster, and the woman she had appointed chairman of the Perfect Storm Foundation, Dierdre. Shortly after salad was served, Dierdre pitched a plan to get us "great publicity" by allowing the Gloucester Middle School's seventh grade class to shoot a "making of" video they could sell as a field trip fundraiser.

Next.

Back at my hotel, there were multiple messages from a couple of guys who had heard we were "using fake fish" and wanted to "come down and film the fake fish."

I had to think about that one.

Jeanne Blake, co-founder of the Perfect Storm Foundation, waited with me on the dock to meet Massachusetts Film Commissioner Robin Dawson, a couple of representatives from the governor's office and a Public Works official for a walk-through of the press conference. Every major and minor media outlet from Boston to Concord was expected to attend. The Governor himself was insisting on being there.

Everything was in place for the arrival of Wolfgang and our stars via Warners' private jet on Tuesday - as long as Hurricane Dennis turned right instead of left off the coast of Virginia.

A day before actors and filmmakers were to arrive, there were storms brewing on multiple fronts.

Location manager Michael Meehan was negotiating with a truculent attorney for the Catholic Church who wanted a pirate's ransom for permission to film their Gloucester parish houses. Out on the high seas, a fishing boat had tried to play a game of Chicken with our newly arriving Andrea Gail. And Jeanne Blake was furious with the Film Commission because they'd neglected to mention The Perfect Storm Foundation in their press release.

The good news was, about 800 miles to the south, Hurricane Dennis was dissipating over the Atlantic – though it would probably bring rain to coincide with our first couple of days filming.

The bad news was, Hurricane Floyd was coming up right behind it, looking to be a monster that might make it all the way up the coast, threatening lives, property and our production. The irony wasn't amusing. (*Realism! I want realism! O.K., maybe not so much realism.*)

My conversation with Margaret that night was a bit stormy as well.

We'd been battling lately over my prohibiting Sam from bringing any violent video games into the house. It was my rule but she was stuck being the enforcer.

"All of his friends' parents allow their kids to play them," my surrendering spouse suggested. "None of them seem any the worse for it. Noah's dad even plays with him."

Ouch, that hurt.

I changed the subject, talking about preparations for the press conference, my planned move from the crew hotel to a local bed and breakfast and my dinner with Jeanne and Dierdre at Jeanne's beautiful beachfront house.

She asked me about Jeanne and I described her, talking mostly about her dedication to various youth education programs and her background as a journalist.

"She sounds like a very... admirable woman."

Was there a blip in her delivery?

Gathered on the dock the following cloudy afternoon were 15 television news cameras, a couple dozen print press and a pack of photographers.

I'd discouraged relatives of the real Andrea Gail crew from attending because I didn't want to blur the line but some of them came anyway. Among the other unexpected guests were the head of the local Teamsters Union, the executive director of the State Fisheries Department and a couple of state senators – all of whom wanted to sit on the podium with our celebrity panel.

Wolfgang arrived a few minutes late, the Governor arrived 15 minutes late and Wahlberg arrived 10 minutes late and had to use the bathroom.

Clooney had arrived nearly an hour early, mingled with the crowd, signed autographs, posed for photos and helped arrange chairs. I feared I'd have to sequester him to keep the news conference from starting without the rest of the panel but George had no intention of usurping the spotlight and deferred answering any questions until we were officially underway. In an idle moment, I commented on the level of familiarity everyone seemed to assume with him.

"I was walking through an airport once," he recalled. "Mel Gibson had also been on the plane. We got off around the same time. People were coming up to me, patting me on the back, saying 'hey George, looks like you've put on a little weight.' When they saw him, they just stood there nudging each other, 'look, there's Mel Gibson.' They were in awe. It's the difference between a television star and a movie star. I'd been in their living rooms every Thursday night."

An hour-and-a-half after it began, I brought the conference to an end. The Governor made an early exit but Wolfgang and the others on our panel lingered for photos. Our Captain Billy Tyne was the last to leave. At one point I saw him button-holed by a female reporter and came over to rescue him.

"I can handle this," he waved me away.

Later, he told me the woman had worked with his dad when he was a news anchor in Kentucky – and George had been asking most of the questions.

The morning of the first day's filming began under cloud cover with Mary Elizabeth aboard the fishing boat Hannah Boden. I said hellos to some of the crew I hadn't seen in a week and waved goodbye as the boat sailed off into the harbor. There was no reason or room for me to be aboard.

I took a call from *The Boston Globe* asking if we'd been delayed by weather, as downgraded tropical storm Dennis was drenching them 100 miles south. But we'd anticipated showers and rescheduled the afternoon's work for an interior set. The headline *"Perfect Storm* Rained Out" would have to be revised.

It was too cold to walk, too early to drink and after the cacophony of yesterday's conference, followed by a dinner for twenty hosted by Wolfgang, I was too talked-out to face the pile of messages undoubtedly waiting for me in the office. I went to a couple of art galleries, then sat on a cement bench in Fitz Hugh Lane Park, overlooking the harbor.

Fitz Hugh Lane was a painter whose seascapes and ships at sea stand among the finest early examples of *luminism*. Crippled at age two, the studio in his granite house of seven gables, atop the knoll above my bench, was his window to the world.

After his death in 1865, this hill began to fill with tenement buildings, eyesores that blotted out the Lane House. Harbor Loop, which cradles this sloping promontory, evolved into "Drunken Street," a stretch of bars, pubs and ale houses stumbling distance from the docks.

The Park was reclaimed during the urban renewal of the 1960s and '70s. All the buildings except Fitz Hugh Lane's house were torn down. Today the hill is a solitary pocket of beauty in a town that has been built for function on a budget.

Peaceful here. But not for long.

This was where the curious would gather to glimpse a movie star, since the actors had to cross Harbor Loop Road to get to their trailers. There would be t-shirt vendors roaming the park and equipment trucks blocking the view.

So, would this movie bring the change some residents of Gloucester feared? Or, like the blight of row houses and their removal, the Winslow Homers and Edward Hoppers who followed Fitz Hugh Lane here, all the boats that had gone out and come back, was it simply another event in the eventful history of this town?

"We knew from the book she was an eastern rig, a long-liner built in Florida," our maritime coordinator Doug Merrifield described the Andrea Gail as we stood on the dock watching her sister ship, Hannah Boden, pull away on another cold morning. "So, in March of this year, we purchased the Lady Grace, which was a long-liner out of Ocean City, Maryland, for our picture vessel."

At that point in planning, the production was going to film most of the water sequences on the Pacific. So, Merrifield sent the boat through the Panama Canal, up towards California. But by the time it got there, plans had changed: the production was searching for a new lead actor and the schedule was scrambled. The art department painted and detailed Lady Grace for her starring role, then sent her back east - a roundtrip of about 10,000 miles. She would make another roundtrip before the movie was over.

The Lady Grace had been unveiled as our Andrea Gail this morning but cloudy skies wouldn't allow us to film the scheduled scene. So, as the Hanna Boden set off to sea, some of the boat hands and I stood in the fog, taking a few minutes to marvel at our ghost ship in its moorings.

Below the name on its lime green hull was its port of origin, Gloucester, Massachusetts. Like the town, it wasn't a thing of beauty but sturdy, ready for work, a monument to a way of life older than the nation it helped create. It felt as though the spirits of 10,000 dead Gloucestermen hung over it on this morning, welcoming it home, wishing it one more bountiful voyage.

Over dinner at Café Beaujolais, a bistro on Main Street that regularly featured live jazz, Jeanne Blake told me more about her life, career and friendship with Sebastian Junger, whom she had introduced around town while he was still working as a tree trimmer and just beginning research on the book that would make him famous.

Following the writer's fortune he made after publication, he turned to Jeanne for ideas of how to give back to the community that spawned the story. Together, they founded The Perfect Storm Foundation to provide educational opportunities for children of parents making their living in the fishing industry.

Jeanne had begun her journalism career as a crime beat reporter in Atlanta, where she covered the trial of Wayne Williams, accused of 29 homicides of African-American children, known as The Atlanta Child Murders.

"He was guilty of most of them," she said.

Though that kind of reporting can become lucrative, even obsessive for many journalists, Jeanne took the first opportunity to get out of it. She found work as a medical reporter for Boston's ABC affiliate in 1984. In 1991, the year The Perfect Storm hit her adopted hometown of Gloucester, she quit her broadcast job, wrote a book on AIDS aimed at at-risk youth and re-dedicated her professional life to adolescent education, particularly in the area of teenage sexuality and substance abuse.

Jeanne was not unattractive, with long shapely legs, chiseled features and eyes that were both compassionate and lively. She had a sense of humor and a leftist perspective, both of which I enjoyed. But she was also a hardcore moralist. Benefits to the Perfect Storm Foundation aside, she did not leave the press conference with a particularly good feeling about the impact of our stars on the youth of Gloucester.

Of Clooney, she said: "All he kept doing was making jokes about drinking. It made me sick."

Of Wahlberg: "I think he was drunk when he got there. He put on a good performance but he behaved like he didn't care."

The thing that really irritated her about Mark, though, wasn't anything he had any control over. A young girl who apparently knew that Jeanne was involved with the movie approached her with a note for the actor.

"She must have been about 14," Jeanne's tone suggested slight exaggeration. "Of course I opened it. She wrote she'd be willing to do 'anything and I mean *anything*... because you've always been there for me in my life.' My heart just sank."

It wasn't that she blamed *all* of Hollywood or its denizens. Her stepson was an A-list movie star who shall go unnamed here. "He's a great kid," she said of him. "I just hope he doesn't fall victim to Hollywood values."

The merging of Ms Blake and the movies was a marriage of convenience at best. Jeanne was a crusader, warning kids and parents in books, videos, television appearances and lectures about the dangers of sex, drugs and alcohol. She was, as Margaret had assessed, an admirable woman.

But if Margaret was at all concerned about Jeanne as a romantic rival, she could rest easy: I had my own admirable woman and one was difficult enough.

CHAPTER THIRTY

BREWING STORMS

"I spoke to someone at the Hospice Center today," my wife slipped this into a conversation between bills and the weather. "I'm thinking of going through the training and volunteering there one day a week."

What about the job you were thinking about getting at the new Barnes and Noble when it opens?

"I decided not to do that. I think it would be much more gratifying volunteering for hospice."

You're already volunteering for the school's special needs programs two days a week. How are we ever going to put away money for retirement?

"I need to do something that fulfills me. You have a job that you love. I need to have that too."

We had virtually no savings. Whatever money we were able to save while I was working went towards keeping us afloat when I wasn't working. Margaret bringing in some earnings might allow me to stay home a few extra months a year.

But I'd sent up the white flag on this battle years ago. Her casual mention of the bookstore job had only raised false hopes.

"I don't want to talk about this again. This is something I need to do."

O.K., I conceded, we'll retire in poverty.

"Look at it this way: we'll both have library cards," I could hear her warm smile through the phone line. "And we'll be together."

I did adore this woman.

George Clooney didn't go to The Crow's Nest. He wasn't on the wagon. He had drinks in restaurants with friends and sometimes he'd visit one of the other pubs along Main Street. But he stayed away from The Nest. Maybe it was because he knew all the New England media were looking for Clooney drinking stories and that was the first place they'd look. Maybe he just didn't want to be part of the scene there.

But it became the habitual after-hours hangout for some of our other actors and whatever crew didn't mind making the 45-minute drive back to the production's hotel in remote Danvers. Most of them didn't bother, which was great for those of us who did because the Hollywood Crowd didn't have an overwhelming presence. The Nest had entertained bigger boat crews at any given time.

Wahlberg was there almost nightly, surrounded by his entourage and a passel of competing twenty-year-old girls. The tough kid from working-class Dorchester had lived in one of the small upstairs rooms for three weeks before filming began, gone out on some boats and was part of the family now. Gail Katz played pool there so often, the table regulars knew. Even Diane Lane came in to have a beer now and then – but only one or two. She was also aware of the media risks.

"I went the other night and I was showing someone my work boots," she said. "And I slipped and fell flat on the floor. A couple of drunks had to help me up. I hadn't touched a drop but I must have looked like I was falling down loaded. I was sure someone was going to take a photo and it was going to come out in the morning papers, 'Alkie Actress, on Her Ass.'"

But no tawdry tales of our cavorting cast ever came out of the Crow's Nest.

Both the town's Catholic churches, Our Lady of Good Voyage and Saint Ann's Church, were vital to filming – one for the exterior, one for interior. The archbishop and his attorney were obviously not movie fans.

"Most unpleasant negotiations I've ever been through," said Michael Meehan on return to our shared office one day. Saint Ann's was where the real funeral had happened. It would not only be unrealistic but a sacrilege to shoot our funeral scene anywhere else. Still, the filmmakers were looking at the Portuguese Presbyterian Church as backup, just in case.

In addition to "a boatload of money," the archdiocese's attorney was negotiating for content approval and the right to withdraw filming permission *after* the scene had been shot. Wolfgang would sooner film in a mosque.

The contentious clergy, however, didn't represent the attitudes of parishioners in this predominantly Catholic town.

I'd moved from the crew hotel in distant Danvers to the Juliette House, a large Victorian bed and breakfast in downtown Gloucester. Walking to work that morning, I was slowed by a crowd lined up along Main Street to watch the opening event of Gloucester's annual Fish Fair – the Fish Box Derby.

In front of a video store were two pot-bellied men with handmade signs taped to their t-shirts. The signs read: "I saw George

Clooney! Want my autograph?" Hardly a soul passed without
an excited "me too" or thumbs up. An old man teased a shy little
girl, "You a movie star?" The town had embraced us.

Around mid-morning, Ethel, her daughter Mary Anne and
sons Russell, Ricky and Brian visited the set. Wolfgang gave
Ethel a warm hug, as did Clooney. There was a special squeeze
from Wahlberg. Diane kept returning to Ethel's side after almost
every take. Ethel looked frail. She had cancer.

Over dinner that night, at the candlelit Seaward Inn where
she was staying in Rockport, Mary Elizabeth Mastrantonio confessed a romantic dilemma.

"The question was, did Linda Greenlaw and Billy Tyne have an
affair?" the still-lovely, former Maid Marion explained. "Both the
book and the script are a bit vague about it. I just decided to play it
with more irritation than flirtation between them – even though a
guy named Mugsy personally told me 'he did her in the wheelhouse.'"

Mastraontonio had a classic throw-your-head-back laugh. She
also had a classically trained voice, as sonorous when she spoke
as when she sang. I'd last worked with her on John Sayles' enig-
matic *Limbo* in which she'd played a contemporary saloon singer
- like Margaret used to be. Mary Elizabeth had also had a cabaret
career – between starring roles on Broadway – at which she'd been
relatively successful. She expressed both empathy and skepticism
about my wife's former professional life.

"Nobody can really do that for a living," she leaned forward.
"It's like the old joke about the musician who wins the lottery.
His friend asks, 'whattaya gonna do now that you're rich?' Guy
says, 'keep giggin' 'til the money runs out.'"

Her head flew back and laughter sprang out like music.

Her two children and husband, Pat O'Connor, a twinkly
Irishman whom she met when he directed her in *The January
Man*, couldn't come along on this trip like they did in Juno,
Alaska where we filmed *Limbo*.

"*You* know how hard it is," she commiserated. "I'm at the point where all I want to do is stay home and occasionally sing for a few friends in the parlor. Jack just started school and Dak's two-and-a-half, so something new is happening with him everyday. I don't know how you can stand being away from your wife and kids for so long a time. It must be rough."

Right then, in this rustic resort with the pounding surf outside our window, savory seafood on the table and one of the world's most desirable women all to myself, I just couldn't be hypocritical enough to agree.

Premiere Magazine had sent young, attractive, suspicious Christine Spines to Gloucester to write a major production story on the film.

"Why does everything seem too easy on this movie?" she inquired. "Everyone seems too nice."

Christine had been on set all day and gotten interviews with Wolfgang, Gail, Diane, Mary Elizabeth and production designer Bill Sandell.

"I didn't really have time to watch any of the filming," she complained.

Ms Spines was going through some relationship difficulties and conflicts about her job. She was ready to bury herself in this assignment and was determined to tunnel through any publicity b.s. to get the *real* story. The first step was to figure out why none of the movie personnel acted like they had anything to hide from her.

"There have to be some people who aren't getting along here, come on," she chided.

Jeanne Blake joined Christine and me for dinner at Beaujolais. It was a relief to have her as a buffer. What had begun as slightly overzealous fact-gathering on the part of our first sanctioned reporter had coagulated into slightly annoying digging for dirt.

"C'mon, every production has some problems. Challenges. Every film has challenges. Are you guys over-schedule?"

I understood her wanting to uncover holes in our hull – if only to see some bailing action. I'd told her about some of the mechanical difficulties on stage back in Burbank. But the story, she rightly surmised, was here in Gloucester.

"I heard that some of the locals aren't happy about you filming here."

Just then, one of the locals spotted Jeanne and joined us at our table. His name was Joe Kaknes, a former fisherman who'd become a successful fine art painter.

A fireplug with a handlebar moustache, Joe was a talker. Christine mentally licked her lips and asked him about the town's reaction to their recent fame.

"They were all afraid it would change things and for a while it did," he said. "But then everybody just settled back into doing what they've been doing here for the last 300 years, fishing and drinking - not necessarily in that order."

For the next half-hour he regaled us with stories about his adventures at sea, the storms he'd been caught in, the time he went overboard, the fishermen who didn't make it home. Like everyone here, he remembered where he was the day of the "Halloween Storm" of 1991, the Perfect Storm.

"There's another one coming," he said with the kind of relish a man in a bar fight uses to bring on the next pug who thinks he can land a punch. "I hear it's about three times the size of Andrew."

Hurricane Andrew, in 1992, had been the last Category Five hurricane to hit U.S. soil and the most devastating storm in the past 65 years.

Christine's eyes brightened.

Next stop was the Crow's Nest. It was packed, as usual. Surely here, Ms Spines hoped, she'd at least see a resentful seafarer smash a barstool over the head of a snitty set dresser.

A woman named Brenda, who called herself Short Stuff, bought us drinks for no reason other than she recognized me from the film crew. Another regular, Kathy, cornered us and pulled out a stack of crew shots she'd taken from her boyfriend's helicopter. Her boyfriend poured us shots of scotch in a tuna's eye socket.

Gail Katz played pool with Mark Wahlberg. *"Gloucester* rules," Wahlberg declared, which meant that anytime Gail scratched it didn't count and every time he shot he had to make the hardest one he could find. Gail pocketed all but the 13 ball before it was Mark's turn. He re-racked and ran the table. Dave McVeigh couldn't stop gushing to Christine about how great Gail was. Wahlberg paused for friendly exchanges with patrons as he made his way back from the pool table to the table where his entourage was seated.

Then someone noticed a news story on the television and, with a few "hey, shuddups," the entire packed place stood hushed as the bartender turned up the volume on a reporter interviewing Gloucester locals, including several relatives of the Andrea Gail fishermen, about what it was like having the film crew here. Each of the family members had something nice to say about the way the movie was portraying their relatives. At the end of the news feature, the whole bar cheered.

Christine must have thought I'd set this up.

The crowd around base camp next morning included a guy in a mask, cape and red tights, whom I didn't notice until he sprang out and stuck a mobile phone in George Clooney's hand the moment the actor exited his trailer: 108 KISS-FM was on the line.

George had been on his way to set for the day's first shot but spent five minutes answering questions for the ambushing radio station while their emissary in the Robin costume stood holding his breath.

"Gotta go to work now," Clooney signed off and handed the phone back to Batman's sidekick.

I walked with him towards the dock.

You know, now everyone I've told you're not doing interviews is gonna think all they need to do is show up here and you'll talk to them.

"I know," he admitted. "But some of those radio stations can get pretty nasty. I just felt like it was easier to play along with them."

The fact was, anyone within shouting distance of Harbor Loop could get a word or two from Clooney at least three times a day: when he crossed the street to report to set, at lunch time after his daily basketball game, and at the end of the work day when he stood around for an hour signing autographs.

Nick Clooney had raised his son to know the difference between humility - which was nice but still inner directed - and humanity: the extension of oneself into the world. George's father had grown into fame as a television personality in a small market - Ohio and Kentucky - over a long period of time. It had also taken George a long time to achieve a similar status in a larger sphere.

While no actor gets famous by accident, most are ill-prepared to handle the invasions that come with getting what you've wished for. Clooney had benefited from a good role model and a lengthy gestation to fame. Passing off a good-humored exchange with a shock-jock as "playing along" may have been the truth. But it was reflex, not strategy.

"George, George," the seagulls kept shouting.

The families and girlfriends of the Andrea Gail and Hannah Boden crews rushed to the end of the pier to greet their men coming back from The Grand Banks after weeks at sea. Mastrantonio and Clooney steered their boats to port with the agility of practiced captains. Dockworkers helped the fishermen unload and weigh their catch.

Christine Spines stood by taking notes. Dave McVeigh and his cameraman scrambled to capture every angle and every conversation between Wolfgang and his actors – Dave pausing only to confer with Gail Katz now and then.

Gloucestermen, hired as extras, operated forklifts, marked and iced down the fish, pulled in rope lines and helped unload the body of Old Ben who had "passed away onboard" the Hannah Boden, while Michael Ironside, playing the unsympathetic owner of the two boats, asked each captain for tallies of their haul.

All day, the cameras rolled on the Andrea Gail crew, happy to be on land under azure skies and on their way to The Crow's Nest to celebrate.

Approximately 1400 miles to the south, two million people were evacuating the coast of Florida in anticipation of Hurricane Floyd, now a Category Four disaster with "a 600-mile swirl of deadly wind," heading towards the Carolinas.

That afternoon, assistant director Alan Curtiss revised the week's shooting schedule to adjust for rain. We had few remaining rain cover interiors for him to juggle.

Meanwhile, Michael Meehan had still not sealed his deal with the archdiocese. The funeral scene was scheduled for next week, so he pressed forward, informing people living around the church that we hoped to be filming there.

"I was going door to door, across the street from St. Ann's, and this lovely Italian grandmother who lived in one of the row houses invited me inside. By the end of our conversation, she insisted that I bring people over to her house the day we filmed there so she could feed them. That just put all the unpleasantness with the church's attorney in perspective for me."

Not every door he knocked on had residents so welcoming. But the main concern of people with whom Meehan spoke wasn't about how the filming might inconvenience them or how it would change Gloucester.

"I seldom knocked on a door where someone hadn't taught, drunk with or gone to school with one of the fisherman in our story," he said. "I sensed some were skeptical but most knew the stone was coming down the mountain no matter what they did. The main thing they all wanted was for us to 'get it right.' That's what I heard most, 'Just get it right.'"

Local press continued to drop by all day in hopes of gaining access to the set but managed little other than glimpses of Clooney shooting baskets at lunchtime. Dierdre brought the middle school film class to watch from the sidelines and I talked with them for about 15 minutes - while keeping an eye on Christine so she didn't walk into a shot and Dave McVeigh, in his boundless enthusiasm, so he didn't fall off the dock. Robin Dawson and a group of state officials showed up and I stuck them with Gail.

Requests from local charities were mounting back in the office. All I could do was make a list of these and promise to address them later. Unemployment in Gloucester was four to five times the national average and the working poor swelled the ranks of the needy. But with a group of international press arriving the next day and another pack of invited media coming on their heels, charity requests would have to be sorted in L.A.

At the Crow's Nest that night, all eyes were on the weather channel. In anticipation of the coming deluge, local officials had cancelled the Sea Fair. Production manager Todd Arnow sent word to our craft services provider that he might want to move his truck to a garage, lest it blow away.

Rain forced us inside on Wednesday, September 15. We shot the interior scene in which the crew collects their pay. This was the last of our cover sets, not counting the funeral. On the same day, Hurricane Floyd bit into South Carolina.

The storm was a "coast hugger" and would continue to gain strength as long as it stayed near the ocean. Florida and Georgia had escaped a bashing but only after the largest civilian evacuation in U.S. history.

The Boston Globe printed a "Predicted Path" timeline: tomorrow morning it would attack North Carolina with 110 mph winds and forty foot waves. That evening, it would move up to Virginia and Maryland with winds diminishing to 90 mph. It would hit Delaware, New Jersey and, if it stayed on course, New York with gusts up to 80 mph sometime on Friday and smack Boston and Gloucester that night.

During the next few days, John Seale's grips and electricians set lights, flags and tarps so he could shoot through mild drizzle. But some exteriors, like Scene A20 in which Tyne oversees his crew loading groceries onto the boat, stayed on the call sheet for the remainder of the week with a "weather permitting" notation.

We hoped for the best and planned for the worst.

Sebastian Junger arrived on Friday, having driven his beat-up Mazda pickup just ahead of the rain approaching New York. He had agreed to come for an interview with the international press and would likely stay in Gloucester until the storm passed.

Lean and of medium height, Junger wore a teal t-shirt with sleeves to the elbows, old jeans and a functional pair of boots. This unassuming look stopped at his collar where he led with a lumberjack's jaw and met you with pale blue eyes that demanded your best game. It wasn't an aggressive gaze, nor was it fearless - as one might expect from a man who sought the most dangerous jobs, people and places to report on and from. It was a little shy, a little wary and totally engaged.

He suffered questions by the gathered journalists from Japan, Italy, Australia and France as if he hadn't already answered them a thousand times. I ended the interview when it started becoming redundant even to those asking the questions.

Warner Bros.' rep Mary Hunter walked the correspondents to a van packed with their travel luggage. They were anxious to get on planes before the storm hit.

I walked Sebastian to the edge of the dock, where the last shot of the day was being lined up for the cameras – a continuation of Tyne overseeing his crew unloading the supply truck and stacking bait while John Hawkes, as Bugsy, repaired the ice machine that was to fail one final, crucial time at sea. John Seale was shooting dusk for dawn and hurrying to finish while the light held through gathering clouds.

"That's the first time I've ever seen a boat with the name Andrea Gail on it," Junger said softly. "It's so strange to see all this come alive."

I went to Jeanne's house to watch the approaching storm. Jeanne cooked pasta, we drank her pinot noir and I helped Dierdre do some work on the Foundation website. After dinner, the three of us went out on her balcony to feel the tempest's prelude. It was a warm wind. Brewster seemed to like it.

Jeanne invited me to stay the night in her guest room but I declined. I drove back to the Juliette House where I sat alone in the parlor for awhile, listening to the gale before going to bed.

CHAPTER THIRTY-ONE

MAN DENIES WIFE BEATING

Wolfgang looked out at the swelling sea from his hotel window. Whatever was left of Floyd's full force would hit Gloucester around 2:00 a.m. The production had a late call tomorrow and he would stay up to see the climax of this tonight.

As a boy in Emden, a German seaport about twice the size of Gloucester, he'd experienced this drama many times. The ocean still thrilled him. Now, as he watched the torrent whipping up the Inner Harbor, the idea of utilizing nature's own dump tank made him smile.

The storm had begun to rattle windowpanes as Wolfgang walked to his desk and sat down with his script to figure out how to make the most of this opportunity.

Second unit manager R.J. Mino would receive a call around dawn, informing him their schedule had changed. Instead of beauty shots downtown, R.J.'s crew would be taking the Andrea Gail out on the rough seas of the storm's wake.

Battling crashing waves under brooding skies, the result was brilliant – though most of the photo doubles, including experienced fishermen, got seasick. Dave McVeigh went out with the steadier camera boat and managed to keep his lunch down. But he was in no condition to go barhopping that night.

That Monday, the sun gleamed on Our Lady of Good Voyage Church, lighting it for the second unit exterior shots of our funeral scene.

A few blocks away, inside St. Ann's, a thousand Gloucestermen and women filled the pews. A thousand isn't such an impressive number if you think of it in terms of protestors at a rally or fans at a football game. But a thousand was one out of every thirty citizens in Gloucester.

Many had been here for the real event eight years earlier – only on that fall day they didn't have to sit listening to Mary Elizabeth's eulogy over and over again. Sometime during the next 10 hours it would stop being a movie. The initial excitement would've long drained away. They would reflect again on the loss of these men, the fear in the hearts of all fishermen, the courage of wives and girlfriends who send them out knowing there's a fair chance they won't come back.

Bobby Shatford's girlfriend, Chris Cotter, was there. Grey and unsteady, she went outside for a cigarette during a filming break.

"This is probably the last thing I'm gonna do for Bobby," she told me. "The first three hours were pretty rough but..." She took a deep inhale.

This was also a last tribute to her brother by Cathy Sullivan and to friends and relations of other fishermen aboard the Andrea

Gail. Ethel, even if she'd been well enough, could not have sat through this a second time.

At lunch, Michael Meehan dragged Duncan and "whoever else I could find" across the street to the Italian grandma's house where homemade pasta was steaming and ready for them.

Michael Conte from Canal Plus Television arrived around lunchtime in need of an interview with Mary Elizabeth. This was her last day of work on the movie and she was high priority for European TV. We watched from the rear of the church as, all afternoon, she repeated her lines in this wrenching, emotional scene.

There are times a publicist feels like reminding a star that interviews are part of the job: they're not being paid their outrageous salaries for being good actors but for being famous, i.e., letting the press inconvenience them once in a while. This was one of the other times: when a publicist feels like an insensitive drone for even asking. But since she was leaving the next day, there wasn't another time to do it.

"When it's over, it's over," she said. Her eyes were still red and watery. "Just give me a minute to pull myself together."

She gave a fine interview that Conte kept mercifully brief. But it was evident the transition back to her old self was on a dimmer, not a switch.

The next day was press-packed, with L.A. Times freelancer John Clark, Michael Conte, Peter Richmond and, later, Chris Nashawaty from *Entertainment Weekly*, all wanting the same interviews.

With winds still whipping up waves and skies periodically changing to drizzle, Wolfgang had taken the Hannah Boden out early in the morning for some shots at sea. The director came off the boat beaming about the footage he'd just gotten. Gail Katz, boom operator Tim Salmon, video assist operator Dean Striepeke and others came off the boat wan and wobbly. Lunch would be lightly attended since all – except Katz – would be going back out on the hero vessel later.

In the afternoon, I managed to get Peter Richmond aboard the Andrea Gail to spend time with Wahlberg. The other writers waited with me on the dock so I could put them together with Wolfgang, Clooney and some of the supporting cast when the swordboat returned. At dusk, the Andrea Gail docked and Wolfgang disembarked. He came straight over to me and took me aside.

"George told me he'd seen something in *The New York Post* about our budget being $40 million over?" he said calmly. "This is wrong. We are actually under budget. You need to tell them."

Not that I didn't believe him but sometimes directors' egos get in the way of the facts. Wolfgang was very proud of his reputation as one who always brought a picture in on the money. So, I confirmed it with Duncan.

Duncan told me we'd released the figure of the movie costing "around $100 million" but that they'd held back admitting to visual effects and some "above the line" costs – i.e., stars and others whose names come in the front movie credits – of approximately another $40 million. This must have been where the confusion lay.

"We're about $200,000 over," he said when I pressed him. "If we were anywhere near what they say, me and the three producers who followed me would be long gone."

So where did *The Post* get this preposterous tidbit?

"I remember talking about it with somebody while we were on the lot," Duncan strained to recall. "I think one or two of the actors were around but I can't remember who else."

No real need to remember because the same column that claimed we were disastrously over-budget also ran a cutesy little item about how some of the locals had mistaken actor X X for a real fisherman. Gee, I wonder how they'd come to print that nugget?

Duncan asked me not to say anything to X, who would be needed back in L.A. to film a scene inside the Crow's Nest on stage. Wouldn't have gained me anything to argue. I did call *The Post* but the columnist only laughed and said he stood by his story – having gotten the information "from one of your actors." What could I do? Open Warner Bros. financial records to him? He asked me if I would go on record with a comment. Tomorrow's headline: *Man Denies Wife Beating.*

Meanwhile, Deborah Norville of the television magazine *Inside Edition* was rumored to be on her way to Gloucester with a camera crew from New York to do an exposé on how all the fishermen in town were angry at the production for not casting real fishermen and townspeople were boiling tar and plucking feathers because they felt we should let the dead rest in peace.

Jeanne Blake knew Norville from her television news days and offered to contact the tabloid TV hostess to give her the real story – that there was no story. That afternoon, a group of real fishermen we'd cast in the movie – albeit, not in starring roles – presented Wolfgang with a mounted swordfish in "thanks" for the experience. We sent a photo of that to *The Gloucester Times* and I spent most of the afternoon on the phone with Norville's producers – citing the local paper's story from the previous day, which described the funeral scene as a love fest between citizens and crew.

The next day at lunch, Jeanne let me listen to a phone message from Norville saying – after, "Wow! What a blast from my past!" – that they'd only been "sniffing around" for a story but were "surprised at how strongly the Warner Bros. publicity machine responded" with calls to counter it.

I later got a call from an *Inside Edition* producer asking for a Warner's rep to go on camera to "respond to the story about the movie being $40 million over budget." (*Man Persists in Denying Wife Beating*).

On our last day of filming in Gloucester, I went out on the camera boat with *Us Magazine* reporter Laura Maurice.

Skies cleared as the Andrea Gail set off toward its demise. In chops of only two-to-three feet, Tyne and Bobby lowered the outriggers, Bugsy painted the net floats and Alfred Pierre inflated the polyballs that fisherman use as spotters.

At the end of the day, I confirmed my flight to New York – coordinating times with Jeanne who was also going there that weekend for business.

In my phone call to Margaret, I mentioned this.

"You're not getting too close to Jeanne, are you?"

The threat of an Admirable Woman – not a sexy one – had aroused a rare spark of jealousy in my wife. I assured her nothing could be farther from the truth.

That night however, I had a dinner date with a lovely lawyer named Nicki. We'd met at Beaujolais and had a couple of barstool flirtations there. She did child welfare work and told me about the rampant cynicism affecting most attorneys in that field. She talked a mile a minute. But she was very sexy. Outside the restaurant, we loitered awhile in the street. She asked if I wanted to "come over." I said I couldn't. We parted with a goodnight kiss that lingered long enough to make me think twice. But we parted.

No, Margaret, I had no interest in falling in love. I was apparently unable at this point even to fall in lust. I had a woman at home who was my joy and my ballast. I just needed to get back to her.

I phoned home when I got back to my room. Although it was late, Sam was still up. Way up. He'd gone to his first Middle School dance and was "brave enough" to ask a girl out on the floor. In fact, he'd asked several.

"I danced about 12 dances – including three slow ones," he told me. "It's the first time I've ever been that close to a girl. It made me feel so alive!"

Sam said goodnight and Margaret got back on the phone.

"I want you to come home," she used a tone I'd not heard in a long time.

I can't. Why don't you take the boys out of school and come to L.A.

"I can't. I have a life here. And Sam has his play. It's the most important thing in the world to him right now."

A long pause.

Play?

He'd gotten a part in the school production of *Annie* that, flush with excitement over his first experience holding a girl, he'd neglected to tell me about.

Margaret described Sam's role as being the biggest of any of the freshmen kids: the lead villain, Rooster Hannigan. There would be four performances, starting December 5 and ending December 12.

"Will you be home in time for Sam's play?" she softened.

I promised I would.

CHAPTER THIRTY-TWO

ENDURANCE TESTS

In Upstate New York the leaves had started changing colors. Indian Summer would give boaters a last outing on Cayuga Lake and Sam and Casey would begin thinking of what they wanted to be for Halloween.

In Los Angeles it was just another month of uninterrupted sunshine.

Except on Stage 16 at Warner Bros.

The one-line schedule for the next month read EXT. ANDREA GAIL – MAIN MOTION BASE – STAGE 16. This would include the sequence in which our brave cast dies at sea. If the filming didn't kill them first.

The first couple of days would supposedly be the easiest. This day was a continuation of the scene in which, under steady rain, a spirited Andrea Gail crew accidentally catches a shark and hauls it on board.

Filming was going a little slowly. It took awhile to get the animatronic shark looking right. Then there was a delay of another hour as another of our camera cranes ripped a hole in the blue screen, which had to be patched. All this was taking place on relatively calm seas – which meant the gimbal was only rocking gently, not sending men flying at contortionist angles, dodging nautical detritus.

Wolfgang, the masterful commander, focused on keeping up morale.

"Alright, I'm getting excited now," he rubbed his hands together as he paced, watching his crew struggle with re-animating the fish. The director couldn't help glancing at his watch as he returned to the playback monitors where he conferred with our script supervisor, Diane Dryer, and first assistant Alan Curtiss.

"Is there anything else we can be shooting now?"

I'd dined with Diane the previous night. A streetwise Brooklynite who pulled no punches and suffered no fools, she offered a candid assessment of the upcoming weeks' work.

"We've now fallen a coupla days behind and we're getting into areas where we don't know what the fuck we're doin'." Also, she said, the tank on Stage 16 was too small for the crane platforms John Seale needed to give his cameras proper movement and perspective. The filmmakers would have very little time to correct this for the big scenes upcoming.

During one of our filming breaks, Diane and I walked over to Stage 23 to visit our mutual friend Ken Regan, who was in L.A. working as stills photographer on the Clint Eastwood picture. He was supposed to have joined us for dinner – before getting a last minute invitation from Warren Beatty.

"Clint is racing through this movie," he said. "I'm liable to be outa work two weeks early."

I felt a little envious.

Over the weekend, construction crews built a moveable, floating platform on which a Super Technocrane was mounted. Now, while an operator remotely spun the crane head, grips swimming alongside could also steady the crane body's movement around the water.

On Wednesday, the rogue wave hit.

"Brilliantly directed," Wolfgang shouted through a microphone. "Mark, not too bad."

Wahlberg, who'd done a fine take – warning his mates, then ducking against the side of the boat – laughed.

Wolfgang was keeping everyone loose.

"I think we print that one. Let's bring in second team."

It was nearly time for 11:00 soup, a Petersen tradition that was never more appreciated than on this movie. The cast, soaked thru to their wetsuits, climbed into rafts that piloted them out of the tank. There were heated tents in which they could change out of their damp clothes but most headed straight for the soup cart. The crew stood aside out of respect, not rank.

Back on board the Andrea Gail, the actors were re-harnessed so that the tilting of the boat and the impact of the waves didn't knock them overboard. Again and again on this and ensuing days they would be blasted with walls of water and jolted to the end of their tether, sliding or tumbling. Kneepads and wetsuits notwithstanding, the physical punishment was brutal. Stunt coordinator Doug Coleman stood by to coach them, Wolfgang to cheer them on.

"Alright, everybody, boys and girls, I'm getting excited again. Alan are we ready?"

And the rumble of the Ritter fans would commence.

Clooney was coming down with the flu. A couple of the other actors were already so sick that, in most other jobs, they'd have spent the day in bed.

Wahlberg had an ear infection – or so he thought. Whatever it was, it was bothering him enough that all agreed he be given time off to see a specialist.

Part of the problem was that the water was heated for comfort, which made it a breading ground for germs. The other part was sheer physical exhaustion.

Wahlberg returned from the doctor that afternoon, his hearing vastly improved and his earache gone after the removal of an earplug that had apparently been driven in by a pounding wave and forgotten about until the pain became too unbearable to ignore.

Meanwhile, the waves kept pounding.

And the press kept hounding.

I caught a bounce pass from Waldo Sanchez, Clooney's longtime friend and hair stylist, on my way past the basketball hoop near George's trailer and sank a ten-foot jumper. My second shot bounced off the rim. Clooney rebounded and put it in with a little spin shot off the glass.

I continued towards the camera truck to talk with our stills photographer when Mark Wahlberg burst out of his trailer. He spotted me over his shoulder. I waved. He stopped and turned.

"I'm not doing any press ever again!" he snapped.

What had happened to turn our easy-going young star into a petulant prima donna?

"Did you see this month's *Us Magazine*? All they did was talk about the time I'd been in jail and all that crap. Nothing about the movie. I never even met this guy."

He stomped off toward the stage. I reversed direction and headed for the studio newsstand where I bought a copy of the magazine.

The story, written by someone named Chris Heath, did appear to focus on Mark's bad-boy background and have nothing current in it save the mention of Wahlberg's role in *Three Kings*, which would be opening next week. It's not uncommon for writers to use "banked" material from a previous story but usually only to supplement a recent interview.

I had dinner that night at the home of L.A. Times columnist Patrick Goldstein. I told him about Mark's reaction to the *Us* story and he suggested, if it was true Wahlberg had never even met the writer, he should send a letter to the editor.

The next day I passed along Patrick's suggestion.

"Yeah, I dunno. Lev says I should just shake it off and remember never to talk to the guy again."

Again?

But I didn't ask that question.

It was good advice on the part of Wahlberg's manager. The sad truth of media biz is you only make a story more important by fighting it.

On my way to lunch, Wolfgang phoned.

"I've just gotten a call from my son in Germany," our director began. "He read in a newspaper that my movie is $40 million over budget. This is not good. We have to stop this."

Then again, sometimes you have to fight back.

I had a fairly useless meeting with John Dartigue and senior v.p. of international publicity Mic Kramer, then spent the afternoon trying to find out which German publication had run the over-budget story. I also contacted Reuters newswire to try to arrange a phone interview with our director and wrote some items for Liz Smith's syndicated column that included subtle mention of what a good time we were all having in a fun-filled, smoothly running production. Slowly, over time, the mistake didn't so much get corrected as disappeared. *Film on Budget* is a really dull news story.

George and Mark had reluctantly agreed to do four five-minute interviews with foreign television press next week. I felt bad even asking.

The feeling went from bad to worse with a follow-up call from Mary Hunter informing me that the international publicity department wanted to double the number of foreign TV journalists. That stretched the subjects' time from twenty to forty minutes, which is often impossible to find between scenes.

"The last time we talked, I said three or four was pushing it," I tried not to shoot the messenger. "This stuff on stage is killer. All the actors have come down with flu or bronchial infections or stage one Plague. Dartigue's loaded me up with more domestic publicity than these guys can handle and we're deferring most of those for the boat work in Dana Point."

A few minutes later, Mary's boss, Mic Kramer, called and told me there would now be eight visiting journalists. Deal with it, he said.

I decided not to tell the actors about the change. That might have been a mistake. Or maybe George would have blown up at me anyway.

I was in Clooney's trailer with Waldo who was telling me about his new girlfriend – recently split from director Renny Harlin - when George dragged himself in, rubbing his temples.

"Gimbal trouble," he raised his eyebrows, then limped into the bedroom to lie down.

Filming of the Nightmare on Stage 16 was nearing completion. By the end of the week, we would be moving to Stage 20 for interiors of the Crow's Nest and most of our Andrea Gale gang would be getting a few much needed days off. Next Friday would be the only day they were all working – which meant the only day we could set up the international television interviews. I'd sent memos to Wolfgang and the principal cast alerting them to this but didn't approach them in person to confirm. Given the mood of the moment, I didn't want to have my head handed to me by a movie star with a migraine or a director with a gimpy gimbal. They'd all signed off on the concept. Let it go at that.

The fateful Friday came and Mary Hunter arrived at Stage 20 with nine - another Japanese outlet had been added - international television journalists, all needing five minutes apiece with Wolfgang and our stars. We set up a video camera in a quiet place by the side of the stage and waited for breaks in the filming.

Mark hid in his trailer between scenes and never did come out to talk to the reporters. Wolfgang took his turn shortly after 11:00 soup; Diane Lane filled in for Wahlberg. But the journalists were all waiting for George.

After lunch, Clooney was sitting with Waldo in a golf cart near the stage while the grip and electric departments were inside relighting the next shot. I checked with the a.d.s who told me George had about thirty minutes before they would need him in front of the cameras. We could at least begin the near hour-long process.

I approached our star.

"Why are they here today? I don't remember talking to you about this."

Well, I sent you this memo, then you were off a few days...

"I'm not going to do it. Tell them you got it wrong. I'm not talking to them."

I returned to the anxiously awaiting horde and pulled Mary aside.

"He's not in the mood, right now."

"But some of my people have planes to catch. I can't keep them around all day."

"Then let them catch their planes. George'll show up when he's ready."

Part of this was a bluff, part was knowing the actor with whom I was dealing. Sure, I'd screwed up by not confirming this with him. Sure he was still feeling like he'd been run over by the mechanical boat he'd been riding for the last three weeks. But I was gambling that maybe I had one small favor left in the bank.

Only two of the reporters departed early.

At around 5:00, while cameras were being re-set for the last shot of the day, Clooney found me in a corner of the stage looking like somebody had shot my dog.

"Alright, let's do it," he relented.

The journalists got their interviews. Mary Hunter embraced me like I was a hero. It was embarrassing. Sloppy job, Mr. Publicist. My lame excuse was that I was as worn down as the rest of the crew. We were all at the point of just wanting to get this movie over with. But there was still a month to go.

CHAPTER THIRTY-THREE

THIS MASQUERADE

It had been a slightly frustrating Halloween for Casey. Margaret had made a costume to his exact specifications, which required mounting a small cardboard box atop a larger one and drawing a face on the smaller one. Unfortunately, he couldn't wear it to church where all the other kids were in costumes, because he couldn't sit down.

Halloween night came and the brothers went trick-or-treating. Sam, as Dr. Evil from *Austin Powers: The Spy Who Shagged Me,* garnered comments ranging from "Where's *Mini-Me?*" to "Oh, I saw that movie. You were very funny." Casey drew remarks ranging from "And who are you?" to "What have we here?" He was, as anyone should have been able to tell, Marvin the Paranoid Android from *The Hitchhiker's Guide to the Galaxy.* It got no better when he tried to provide hints in the form of Marvin's famous line, "I'm so depressed." One parent who knew him called us to inform, "I think Casey may be upset about something."

Back in L.A. - where every night is a costume parade and every day trick or treat – publicist Dave Fulton and I were having dinner at La Scala in Burbank, near the studio.

John Dartigue was at a table by himself.

"I've heard he's here almost every night," Dave told me.

Lonely town, Hollywood.

Walking home along Sunset, I spotted a tall, familiar figure, head bent under a fedora hobbling on a silver-handled walking stick and carrying the leash attached to a black wolfhound. It was producer Daniel Melnick.

I shouted to him.

He made a half-turn, positioned to make an unsteady run for his life.

He flipped through memory cards: *Not an enemy*. His face relaxed.

Melnick was once the player of players in Hollywood. Former president of Columbia Pictures, mentor of the first female studio head Sherry Lansing, renowned for his high stakes poker parties with the likes of Johnny Carson, Steve Martin and Neil Simon and former son-in-law of composer Richard Rodgers, he was Hollywood Royalty.

He hadn't produced a major movie since 1991's *L.A. Story*, he admitted, but he was "back in the saddle again," having just finished *Blue Streak* with legendary pain-in-the-ass Martin Lawrence. This was small potatoes for a man who'd made *Straw Dogs, All That Jazz* and *Altered States* and taken some big risks with commercial uncertainties like *Making Love*, the first big studio gay love story, and *Punchline*, a serious look at the unfunny side of standup comedy.

"They just don't make the kind of movies I use to make any-more," he said as our brief exchange ended.

Blue Streak would be the last film to which Melnick's name was ever attached.

Hard town, Hollywood.

David Mickey Evans was about a half-hour late for lunch and apologized profusely. But he had a good excuse.

"I had a meeting with these assholes about a movie," he began.

David had sold the first million-dollar script, *Radio Flyer*. He later wrote and directed the kids' classic *The Sandlot* and another profitable kidflick, *First Kid*. Then he hit a dry spell with his own projects. He was now trying to get traction as a director-for-hire.

His meeting was about a proposed Paramount feature, based on a popular children's novel *How to Eat Fried Worms*. Dave liked the script but had objections to the worm action.

"They had 'em all gooped up in chocolate and peanut butter and shit," he explained. To illustrate his point at the meeting, he'd brought along visual aids.

"I walk into the office with these three executives, carrying a cooler and a box. I dump the contents of the cooler on one of their desks and they all start freaking out 'cuz it's a pile of manure filled with about 500 night crawlers. I figure these guys have never seen a worm before. I ask if anybody wants to hold one and they all kinda go like this..." holding his hands in front of his face. "One of 'em had to run out of the room. One of the others says, 'you're not going to eat one, are you?' I said I wasn't planning to – unless it would get me the job. Then I said, 'But the movie's not about worms, it's about *fried* worms. Y'ever try to fry a worm?'"

Taking a small Coleman stove out of the box, he proceeded to demonstrate.

"When you fry 'em up, the little suckers pop all over the place."

The rest of the meeting, he thought, went pretty well.

Two weeks after our lunch, Dave reported he didn't get the job. Apparently, Paramount ran a background check and an executive at another studio had alleged that he'd yelled at a child actor on *The Sandlot*.

Unforgiving town, Hollywood.

Returning from work one night last week, I'd reached into my coat pocket and found a pair of old, cold hand-warmers. I became fixated on trying to remember if they were from this movie, the last one, one last year, two years ago. It was irritating as a song title on the tip of your tongue. Silly? But you see, film people retrace their personal history through the movies they've done: Winter, 1984? *Body Double*, L.A., Ann was dying; February, 1987? *Jaws, the Revenge* in the Bahamas, right after Casey was born; Fall, 1992? *Lost in Yonkers*, started in Cincinnati two weeks after we moved to Ithaca.

At a certain point though, the demarcations start to bleed into one another and you have to think too long about what movie you were working on when your third child was born or when the roof fell in on your kitchen remodeling or when your second wife first asked for a divorce. Each movie was precious both for the uniqueness of the experience and as a life marker. And then, no telling when it happens, the sum of these parts are welded into a career and the parts themselves are no longer so unique, no longer such reliable place holders, somehow less than what they once had been.

And still, you can't resist adding another credit to this amorphous mass. And another. And another. And the career grows. And the parts become more solidly welded.

An old friend had come to town for a press junket and I met him for lunch at a Hollywood hangout on the corner of Crescent Heights and Santa Monica Boulevard called The Silver Spoon.

Gino Salamone was an icon to radio and television audiences throughout greater Milwaukee. He was a favorite of actors on the junket circuit for an interview style that approached the silliness of celebrity with the indulgence of a confessional priest in a brothel. He was also a walking encyclopedia of film history.

Gino, his friend Dino, commissioner of the Oklahoma State Film Office, and I were escorted to the patio and seated near a long stretch of tables pushed together with 12 chairs - many filled with familiar, aged faces. Among the character actors I recognized were Robert Forster (from *Jackie Brown*) and Dick Miller (the original *Little Shop of Horrors*). Seated at the head of the table was Shelly Winters.

"Wasn't this a scene from *Sunset Boulevard?*" Gino quipped.

I couldn't believe my luck. I'd been curious about the Marilyn-Shelley connection to the modern art installation I called home ever since Howard first told me about the possibility. Figuring there was only a one-in-four chance my apartment had once been theirs, I'd dismissed the likelihood of ever finding out. Until now. The one thing that distinguished my apartment from the other one upstairs were brackets that once fitted an awning over the balcony. I suddenly *had* to know.

Shelley wore a 75th Academy Awards baseball cap to shield her from the sun. Her neck was wrapped in a colorful scarf and her eyes shielded by aviator sunglasses. I'd always imagined her a physically imposing woman. She was a sparrow.

The conference table was animated but most of the conversation seemed to take place at the end opposite Shelley. She was the jewel among them but not the center of attention. Still, it was apparent the court would not leave before the queen. When she finally turned towards her attendant - a sturdy-looking woman standing near a wheelchair - the others began rising from their seats to disburse.

Nearly knocking Gino's coffee cup into his lap, I sprang on her like a fundamentalist pamphleteer.

Miss Winters, I've long been an admirer of your work.

"Thank you," not giving much besides a polite nod.

And I think I may be living in the apartment you used to share with Marilyn.

"Ahh," she brightened. "On Holloway."

Yes – I brightened - but I'm not sure if it's the exact apartment.

"The one upstairs."

Narrows it to two.

"…With the awning."

Eureka!

She tilted her head. A little smile appeared.

"Oh, we had a lot of fun there."

I left with Gino and Dino before she got up. I didn't want to see Shelley Winters rolled out in a wheelchair.

I'd see her again when I slept in my apartment on Holloway that night - and in memory many times thereafter: *A Place in the Sun, The Night of the Hunter, The Diary of Anne Frank, Lolita, A Patch of Blue, Alfie, Bloody Mama* and always, always swimming to the rescue in *The Poseidon Adventure*.

Those memories are what the hard work of making movies is for.

Amazing town, Hollywood.

My brief return to Ithaca for Thanksgiving weekend was bracketed by the boys' endearments, "We're so glad you're home" and "We don't want you to go." In-between, there were moments of "We were doing fine 'til you showed up."

One of Casey's chores was loading our trashcans in a garden cart and wheeling it down our L-shaped, 900-foot long driveway. It was a job he found tolerable, even manly – until Dad came home. Grumbling that this chore was taking him away from a very important computer program, he loaded the bins with a huff and a thump. "Now what?"

But Margaret and I were in mid-discussion about remodeling the basement and I told him, "Hold on a sec."

This lit the fuse. It was one thing having to be *nice* because Dad's home for such a short stay and you want everything to go smoothly but to compound that with wasting his valuable time... He exploded and took off down the drive, stumbling, yanking the cart behind him - a blind kid on a kamikaze mission to meet a tree trunk. Sam jumped on his bicycle and peddled after his brother – circling, cautious not to interfere lest he catch the brunt of Casey's wrath. I caught up with them at the bend where the cart had gone into a shallow ditch. Casey was sitting on the handle.

"So, what just happened back there?" I calmly inquired.

"I was trying to do this stupid job and you yelled at me."

I explained I was trying to talk to his mom and needed a minute to think of something. "Maybe, because you couldn't see what my expression was, you couldn't tell that I wasn't mad. Does that ever happen?"

He yanked the cart out of the ditch and continued herky-jerky towards the road. It was adding insult to injury to now have to listen to "one of Dad's talks."

I followed and he slowed a bit. At the end of the drive he unloaded the trashcans.

"There. Are you happy?"

Not yet. I picked him up and put him in the garden cart. Around the bend, Sam abandoned his bike and jumped in beside his sibling. Gershwin joined us as I jogged the last hundred feet while they clutched the rails, shouting "faster."

A weekend can be the microcosm of a year. A weekend at home was a microcosm of my life - in instructive moments.

Mind-emptying hours spent cutting and stacking firewood, trimming the weeds around our posted "no hunting" signs, filling potholes of displaced gravel along the driveway reminded me how much I missed my house.

Sitting up nights in the music room sharing classics from the sixties, listening to Casey's keyboard compositions and Sam's saxophone serenades reminded me how much I missed my boys.

Taking autumn trail walks with Margaret along gorges, beside waterfalls, having a cup of coffee while waiting to have snow tires put on the car, sharing a glass of wine after the boys had gone to bed, reminded me how much I missed... sex.

"Not tonight," she'd said. "It just takes me a while to get used to your being home."

Yes, a weekend can be a reflection of something larger. But a weekend is also only a weekend. We needed time. Somehow. Some-time. Who makes the sacrifice to make that happen? Somebody needs to. Both bodies have to. But how?

Sam woke up and joined me in the music room while I was making a tape of songs-to-feel-sorry-for-myself-by. I asked if he was at all nervous about the opening of *Annie* next week.

"Not really," he said after a moment's contemplation. "Except I hope the chorus doesn't mess up their choreography when I sing *Easy Street*."

I still had a lot to give thanks for over turkey that weekend.

CHAPTER THIRTY-FOUR

THE LAST VOYAGE

It was with some regret that I said goodbye to my alligator coffee table, motion sensor frog and Marilyn's ghost, packed my two suitcases and headed out of Hollywood.

Had I learned to love L.A.? What I'd learned was, L.A. isn't a city that imposes a structure on you like New York, San Francisco, Boston, but a do-it-yourself environment: little pieces of the hills, the beaches, the canyons that become your personal city. It is a liquid place that fills whatever container you put it in.

I'd filled mine with friends, work, a little Hollywood folklore, a few favorite restaurants and a crazy-quilt of kitsch that was my home for the better part of four months. Yes, I'd learned to love that. But as I drove south along the 405 Freeway, it all became Brigadoon, dissolving in the rearview, and my only thoughts were about getting through the last ten days of this movie in the next place it took me before I could return to where I lived.

While Seattle was exploding with protests over the World Trade Organization, Orange County was worrying about which yachts were going to have the best Y2K parties when the calendar changed and their computers froze.

The Marriott Laguna Cliffs Resort and Spa was Orange County at its Muffy-ist. From its turreted residential wings with private balconies overlooking green acres that dropped off into the Pacific, to the mountains of throw pillows in rooms with plastic plants, it was in timeless oblivion to any impending cataclysm of the New Millennium.

Our first night there, the production threw a crew party in the lounge. A hundred and fifty scruffy art department, catering, costume, camera, transport, maritime, makeup and effects geeks were a stark contrast to the country club plaid that lined the lobby. Many of those filtered into the bar to see what carnival was in town. Many of them stayed when they saw, amongst the carnies, a nattily dressed George Clooney.

Eventually, all his cronies and colleagues drifted away and George was surrounded by a group of newfound friends. It was only after some of the women began pulling and pushing in a competition for photos that he said, "gotta go." It was an abrupt departure. *Snooty Movie Star Spurns Fans.*

The main crew boat, Deanna Lee, left the docks at 6:00 a.m. for the twenty minute ride to where our Andrea Gail – having limped up the Pacific Coast after breaking down around Nicaragua - awaited the first day's filming. Thirty-mile-per-hour winds made the seas choppy but the big boats rode the waves without anyone losing breakfast. Less lucky were crew who had to shuttle between the picture boat and equipment trucks at our parking lot base camp via rubber Zodiacs that skimmed the ocean surface in bounding, high speed sprints.

I awoke early but chose to stay behind and finish some paper-work. I printed out a copy of the press schedule for next week and had some ham and eggs in the cafe. Then I walked to the docks and waited for a boat to fetch me. Soon, a Zodiac came bouncing across the breakers – with Gail Katz, clinging on.

Our producer looked ghostly as the pilot helped her ashore. Yes, she had gotten sick on the Andrea Gail. But she wasn't the only one.

"All sorts of people had to go over to the catering boat to lie down," she gasped. "Most of them are still there. I just needed to be on land."

I climbed in with Lyn from wardrobe, carrying a new shirt for Wahlberg, and the boat sped off. It didn't take long for me to re-gret having had breakfast.

On board the picture boat, we were shooting a dialogue scene between George and Mark. The sea had quieted a bit but not enough to prevent Wahlberg from going to the rails after almost every take.

My sole reason for going out today was to check conditions for next week's visiting journalists. It was clear I should suggest they take Dramamine and go easy on their morning meal.

I had lunch with Wolfgang and briefed him on the upcoming press visits. He nodded approval.

"I'll bet you're looking forward to going home," he smiled.

I said I was and told him about Sam's play.

"I know. You told me before."

I took the catering boat, Sum Fun, back to shore in late after-noon and asked the front desk to send any calls straight to voice-mail. I slept for nearly four hours – ignoring the blinking red light.

When I awoke, the reviews were in:

"He was incredible," said one critic.

"'Easy Street' was a show stopper," proclaimed another reviewer.

"He's on top of the world," his mother reported.

They were all talking about Samuel Nelson Harris "stealing the show" (Diane Wallace, Boynton Middle School PTA).

I called back to say "*sehr eindrucksvoll*," knowing they were already asleep.

On Monday morning I hitched a ride to base camp with George and waited while he went through "the works" (hair, makeup and wardrobe). We boarded a Zodiac RIB, a 24-footer with both the trademark inflatable buoyancy tube and a rigid hull, a far smoother ride than the all-rubber boats.

We crawled onto the bow in front of the pilot's windscreen and stretched out, feeling the sea breeze and the sun just beginning to warm the air.

"You're going to enjoy the ride from up here," George told me. "And this sure beats going with The Cowboy."

The Cowboy was the pilot of a 12-man inflatable who got his kicks revving it up to top speed and flying over waves so that the rubber bottom would come down in a bone-jarring bounce. This was a Norwegian Cruise Liner by comparison.

I brought up the tourist gang-tackle at the bar the other night and he said he left not because they all wanted photos but because some of the women were getting "mean." George had no use for mean people.

He'd had a famous near-incident with director David O. Russell on *Three Kings* when he allegedly saw the director roughing up an underperforming background actor. Co-workers reportedly had to hold Clooney back to stop a fistfight.

"If I could spend my career only working with guys like Soderbergh, the Coens and Wolfgang, I'd be a happy man," he concluded.

We were soon out where there were no other boats, the sun reflecting hypnotically off gentle swells and a long strip of island the only sight on the horizon. I guessed it was Catalina.

"Never been there. Is it nice?"

There's a place on earth where George Clooney hasn't been?

I said I'd heard there was going to be a big End of the Millennium party there.

"You going?"

I was going nowhere outside of Ithaca for as long as I could help it.

He said he had rented a hotel in Carmel, California for about 75 friends.

"I throw a party at home, 100 people I don't know drop by. Somehow there are always guys with cameras and the pictures show up in the tabloids. Happens every time."

At the Sum Fun, we transferred to a rubber dingy that ferried us to the Andrea Gail where we could see Wolfgang and all the crew waiting. As we got within shouting distance, the blasting beat of ZZ Top's *Tush* screamed across the waves and the crew cheered as they sighted Captain Billy who did a little arm-waving boogie from his seat. The music kept pulsing as we climbed on board, with Wolfgang leading an impromptu disco at the rail.

According to our music supervisor, Maureen Crowe, there had been some debate as to what hard-pounding tune should be blaring over the loudspeakers during the next scene, in which the jubilant longliners begin to haul up a motherlode of swordfish. John C. Reilly had argued for AC/DC; someone else suggested working class Springsteen. Maureen put this one on just as they'd spotted our boat. Wolfgang shouted, "That's it!" and *Tush* became our anthem.

I rode the Sum Fun back to base camp after lunch and was reading contentedly on the calm sea when the pilot came on the loudspeaker, alerting all aboard to come to the prow. We were surrounded by dolphins. It was one of the biggest pods our captain had ever seen, "probably over 1,000 of 'em," sounding and diving, leaping out of the water almost close enough to touch.

"They're as curious about you as you are about them," he announced. "Watch them when they come up. They're lookin' at you."

They paced themselves alongside our boat and stared up with unmistakable curiosity. To them, *I* was George Clooney.

Thankfully, none of the dolphins had cameras.

My first press victim at sea was *Premiere's* Christine Spines. The last time I saw her was at the Crow's Nest, pounding down shots with Dave McVeigh. The Nancy Drew act had ended and she'd become one of the gang by the time she poured herself into an airport taxi around dawn.

The Andrea Gail was on the move this morning, about seventeen miles from shore. Our ride out on the lunch boat, which was delivering the morning soup, took about 45 minutes because we had trouble finding the picture vessel.

Once aboard the Andrea Gail, we took positions on the pilot's deck to watch the action below. After about an hour, I noticed my charge wasn't looking too well.

Did you take Dramamine, like I suggested?

"No." She "forgot."

It probably didn't help that, while observing the morning's scene - the fishermen pulling in empty hooks from a fruitless day - she was also observing Wahlberg puking his guts out. Mark's resistance had improved: he was now only throwing up between camera setups, not after every take.

Having arrived in late morning, we didn't have long to wait before lunch break. My visitor regained stability on the flat-bottomed Sum Fun where she enjoyed a mealtime conversation about Anthony Minghella with Diane Dryer who'd worked on three of his movies, including the recently released *The Talented Mr. Ripley,* which Christine greatly admired.

The talented Ms. Spines seemed back to her feisty journalistic self when we took one of the pilot boats back to the Andrea Gail. But while kneeling with crew behind an upper deck railing to hide our shadows from the shot, I noticed she was no longer getting up each time the director called "cut." I asked if she'd had enough. She gave two short nods.

The principal actors were released when the scene was finished. Normally, Christine would've asked to talk with them. But talking would've required opening her mouth. I got her on the next boat out.

Karen Allen returned for a day at sea in the Mistral.

Over dinner, we ran the gamut of topics from small town living to great people of the passing Century. None of it got too personal. She did ask if I was looking forward to seeing Margaret: not if I was looking forward to going home but to seeing my wife.

Yes, I answered honestly.

We closed the restaurant and I walked her to her room for a platonic goodnight kiss at the door.

In an alternate universe...

Rick Lyman of *The New York Times*, by way of Gary, Indiana, rode the soup boat out to set with me the next day. This was my first time meeting Rick. I liked his easy humor, Midwest directness and the fact he didn't get seasick.

Once on board the Andrea Gail we watched a dramatic scene in which John Hawkes' character confronts the captain with news that the ice machine has broken beyond repair. A desperate return into the heart of the storm is now their only option.

Rick interviewed Wolfgang at lunch. George was still running a fever but held to his agreement for an interview, which the journalist considerately kept short.

Wahlberg had a much-needed day off.

On the phone that night, Margaret's voice was the balm it had always been. "I'm counting the hours 'til you get home," her silky contralto sang to me, "and we can have some real time together."

Time together at home. For the first time in a full year I allowed myself to sink into the warm tub of that imagining.

On December 10th, I was out at sea with the EPK crew when I got a call from Jeff Ressner of *Time Magazine*.

"Ya think we could put off tomorrow's visit for a day. I've got an interview with Angelina Jolie tomorrow night and I'd like to conserve my energy."

I kept my cool and told him that would not be possible.

"I'm sure you're man enough to handle the Andrea Gail crew during the day and Angelina at night." I added, "Take Dramamine."

I rode one of the pilot boats back to shore with our lovely young production assistant, Jasa. She had decisions to make now that this movie was nearing the end.

"I'd love to move back to San Francisco but it's a choice between living where I want and doing what I want," which was "something creative" in the film business.

"One thing I do know: I don't want to end up one of those people who has pictures of their cats in the production trailer and no one to come home to."

If this business is hard on men, it's a hundred times harder on women.

Still, she'd summed up all our fears, men and women on the bounding boat of location life: we all want someone to come home to and we all secretly fear that the life we leave behind might leave us.

I'd warned Jeff Ressner of *Time Magazine* that the actors wouldn't have the stamina for long interviews.

"That's alright, I can always get more on the phone with them later," he said. "But I have to talk to them. An actor won't take your call if you haven't already talked to them." He was a pro.

Jeff arrived at around 9:00, after a two-hour drive in rush hour traffic. I offered him the choice between going immediately to the set and having breakfast in the hotel. He chose the latter.

Did you remember the Dramamine?

"I don't get seasick."

Famous. Last. Words.

A grey Zodiac called the Viking Explorer had just pulled away as we reached the docks. Our second a.d., a droll Dutchman named Basti, cheerfully offered to radio it back.

Basti was a bit of a rascal – and maybe slightly sadistic. The boat he called back was piloted by The Cowboy.

"Better hold on to your hats," our pilot grinned. "We'll be going thirty-to-forty knots an hour." He would later claim – with that same aw-shucks smile – we were only going twenty.

Jeff and I grabbed onto the inside ropes, put our feet in the floor stirrups, I held my hat, he held his breath and we were off.

The picture boat was twelve miles out, across the choppiest seas we'd seen since Gloucester, with wind whipping up whitecaps. Every time the Explorer flew over a wave, all four passengers – which included two terrified wardrobe assistants – came out of their seats. A lens popped out of the reading glasses around my neck. I grabbed it before it became fish food.

Jeff started off laughing, whooping, enjoying the spine-crunching thrill ride. About halfway through our fifty-minute journey he wasn't laughing anymore.

Cowboy unloaded us onto the Deanna Lee, the tug that was our most stable, comfortable boat. Foregoing any macho pretense, Jeff flung himself onto a bench seat in the cabin where he lay down.

As queasy as my guest appeared, he was dancing a fisherman's fandango compared to another Deanna Lee passenger.

Apparently Mark Wahlberg had attempted to drown his viral invaders in vats of alcohol the previous night. Looking like the victim of a vampire attack, he sprawled on a bench with one foot pressed to the floor. The morning work, it was reported, saw him heaving his guts out before *and* after every take.

"I've never seen anyone so sick," Wolfgang said.

I took a seat outside and read a book for fifteen minutes. Jeff came out twice to vomit over the rail.

"If I throw up, I throw up," he managed to mutter. "It won't embarrass me."

Thirty minutes later, Wahlberg and makeup wizard Ken Diaz were transferred to a small Zodiac and gently transported to the picture boat.

Jeff said he was ready to go to work too.

"The Andrea Gail sways like a pendulum," I warned. "You sure you're up to it?"

Time Magazine don't hire no wimps. He was ready to rock and roll.

Aboard the Andrea Gail, Wolfgang offered Ressner a seat near the monitors where he watched an hour of filming before lunch was called. Most of the crew took pilot boats to the Sum Fun but the director remained on the hero vessel to watch Alan Curtiss and John Seale set up the next shot. Meals were delivered and Wolfgang said he'd be happy to do his interview with Jeff while he was eating.

Jeff picked up his tape recorder and Wolfgang picked up his barbequed chicken leg. Then, in the middle of Petersen's detailed response to the second question...

"Would you mind holding this," Jeff asked, handing the director his tape recorder.

Wolfgang continued talking into the recorder between bites of chicken while Ressner went to the rail to eject the remainder of his morning pancakes. Then he calmly came back and continued his interview.

"Well, that's a first," exclaimed Wolfgang. "Was it something I said?"

Good to his word, Jeff didn't appear the least bit embarrassed.

Towards the end of lunch, George gave him fifteen minutes.

"All I need is Mark and I'm done," he said in an undisguised challenge.

You saw him earlier, Jeff. He's in no condition to do an interview.

"Well, I can come back tomorrow."

In my entire career, no other words have made my blood run colder.

I approached Wahlberg who was seated, head down, on an apple box in front of the wheelhouse.

"I have a huge favor to ask." And I explained.

An eternity passed between my explanation and his response. His bleary eyes met mine and a head that must have felt like a watermelon bobbed slowly up and down.

I brought Jeff over, tape recorder at the ready. He squatted beside the actor and began his interview. Fortunately, neither of them wanted to drag it out.

I escorted *Time Magazine* to the waiting pilot boat. Looking back as I climbed off the Andrea Gail for the last time, I caught Mark's eye and mouthed a "thank you." He gave a little finger wave and lowered his head back between his knees.

A production van delivered me to Los Angeles International Airport two hours early for my scheduled takeoff. I didn't mind the wait.

I'd saved my nausea for the U.S. Air flight to Philadelphia and, around midnight, deposited vegetarian lasagna in one of the business class restrooms. I managed three twenty-minute naps and at 5:30 a.m. Eastern Time, changed planes to a twin prop 24-seater that would fly me the final hour home.

I stared out the window as dawn broke over the patchwork greenery of Upstate New York farmland. The crooked finger of Cayuga Lake rolled into frame and ten minutes later we landed.

It was icy cold when I crossed the airfield to the small terminal. Margaret and the boys were waiting. My sons came up to greet me first. Then I hugged Margaret. She squeezed until our bodies fused, the quilt of down jackets melting away until I could feel her heartbeat and she mine.

It wasn't the moment to tell her I'd been offered a new job starting in a month.

I got a few hours sleep that afternoon and awoke to dress for the closing night's performance of *Annie* at Boynton Middle School. There was a mistake on an entrance that Sam covered well. His *Easy Street* solo brought down the house.

More riveting to me even than his performance was his appearance. In a Depression Era suit that could have fit two of him, slicked back hair that revealed his genetically acquired high forehead and an eyeliner-drawn, pencil-thin moustache, I swear, he looked just like my father.

THE END

EPILOGUE

S ee Ya On the Next One:

This book really began with my separation from Margaret at the end of 2003.

Before that, I'd started writing about how you keep a marriage together while living in a small town and working on the road. It was a lot more about life in Ithaca, a place I truly loved and hoped, like Ulysses, to live out my days.

Wasn't gonna happen.

I moved back to L.A. in 2005, the year of our divorce.

Nineteen-ninety-nine was the end of the first full century of movie-making. There have been many endings since:

Bill Bonanno died in January of the year I finished my first draft of this book, 2008. I like to think he might've gotten a few laughs out of the Italy chapters. He had a great laugh.

Of course, Oliver Reed never saw his last movie. The British Academy recognized his stellar performance with a Best Supporting Actor nomination in 2000.

Richard Harris left this world as Albus Dumbledore, The First. But I'll always think of him as the philosopher emperor – firing a revolver into the Bahamian surf.

My dear friend Ken Regan died just days before this was published. A great photographer, an even greater human being. We all thought he would live forever.

David Hemmings is back in the company of his friend John Lennon, joining him in December, 2003. They may still be arguing the merits of weed over booze.

Sound mixer Ken Weston won an Academy Award for *Gladiator* but he couldn't make it to the ceremony. He died of kidney cancer a few weeks later.

The soundman on *Perfect Storm*, Keith Wester, also got an Oscar nomination in 2000. He died in November of 2002, six nominations and no statuettes later.

Ethyl Shatford Spencer left the Crow's Nest for good a month after *The Perfect Storm* crew left Gloucester.

Assistant director Alan B. Curtiss' wife Kathy died of cancer the year after *Perfect Storm* was released. Alan nursed her through to the end. He's now happily remarried.

Producer Dick Berg passed in September, 2009. *Rated X* was not among the credits noted in any of his obituaries.

The inimitable Daniel Melnick left the Hollywood shark pool in October, 2009. Patron to such directors as Sam Peckinpah and Roman Polanski, he was always kind as an uncle to me.

My best dog Gershwin died in the summer of 2003, at the age of eight. His early death reminded me to make the most of life.

Charlie Sheen had the Godzilla of public relapses – but the lively sparkle I so enjoyed lasted through nine seasons as star of one of the top shows on television. Now he's back in *Anger Management*. No cooler cat has had more lives.

Shelley Winters is again sharing a balcony with Marilyn Monroe, as the entire list of the famous men they wanted to bed serenades below.

And Steve Levinson gave up trying to hide Mark Wahlberg's *Entourage*.

Every film crew veteran has one list of actors and directors with whom they'd eagerly work again and one you couldn't pay them enough to repeat the experience. Since 1999, I've worked twice more with Ridley Scott (*Hannibal, American Gangster*), Wolfgang Petersen (*Troy, Poseidon*) and Russell Crowe (*American Gangster, State of Play*) and three more times with George Clooney (*Syriana, The Men Who Stare at Goats, The Monuments Men*). My never-again list is very short and includes no one mentioned herein.

Those whose names and stories appear in these pages were only a fraction of the colleagues with whom I worked, played, laughed and lamented during the course of this year. Please believe that in editing this opus, the many laudatory things I wrote about all of you had to be cut.

Some thanks:

To my beautiful, brilliant and loving wife Nicola, a journalist who invaded the set of a movie on which I was working, got her story and won my heart – after many months of chasing her. But that's the next book.

Thanks to my editor Susan Salter Reynolds who helped me through the final draft when my eyes were crossing after the ten-thousandth reading. And to former L.A. Times book review editor Sonja Bolles who thought enough of this book to steer me to Susan.

I don't believe it's possible to write a book alone. You can feed yourself and change your own printer cartridges but you need a support network to cheer you on – even if they're only voices in your head. I was fortunate in finding some live voices.

To former New York Times film editor Linda Lee who encouraged me to write about this job I do so love. Also, my Brazilian confidante and correspondent, psychologist Ana MacDowell Gonzalves without whose encouragement and counseling I might not have made it through my divorce, let alone all these pages.

To Tex Roselle Brown, a creative writing teacher at Poly High who gave my life direction. To all teachers who care enough to lift the tollgate of possibilities.

Deepest thanks also to my friend Paul Lomartire who introduced me to author and film historian Scott Eyman, whose belief in this work spurred me on. Overdue thanks to Megan Crawford of CAA who commissioned me to write a website journal for the movie *Hannibal* while she was at MGM, providing the blueprint for this work. To Rob Friedman who gave me my first shot at a unit publicity job and to director Joe Dante who hired me for *Gremlins*, my first movie. Also to Barry Glasser and Elisabeth Landon Sarrow who brought me into this business and Arthur Wilde who made me want to be a unit publicist.

My friend and attorney Roger Armstrong served in two capacities: as legal advisor and as one of my first readers. In the latter role, he provided an invaluable reality check – having been a unit publicist himself once – and much needed encouragement. Thanks, Roger.

Additional thanks to my insightful web designer/creative consultant Nancy West *(endetail@aol.com)*, my talented illustrator Steve Carver and my publishing guru Jim Lawrence.

I did not make many people aware I was writing this but I thank those who read an early chapter or two for their valuable ideas - most of which I resisted before the light bulb went on. Those who gave valuable feedback after plowing through a whole draft included friends and colleagues, Peggy Klaus, Kathleen McInnis, Marsha Robertson, Donald Buckley, Patti Hawn, Dean Silvers, Phil Caruso, Karen Gehres, Luisa Bonello, Andy Lipschultz, Mitchell S. Waters and John Hackett.

Brilliant writers who provided insights and guidance included, Nancy Slonim Aronie, Bob Spitz, Blake Bailey, Stephen Silverman, Karen Krizanovich and former Washington Post editor R.B. Brenner who told me to put away my detailed journals and just tell the story. Special thanks to former publishing and film executive Michelle Abbrecht for her notes and the assessment that I may need to start thinking about a new career after this is published. Longhaul trucking?

Neglected in these pages, though ever dear to me, my mother whose inner strength overcame her physical frailty and who lived a long and full life – until age 87 - with too many stories untold. And Sis, thanks to you too, for being such a stalwart.

A deep thank you to the International Alliance of Theatrical and Stage Employees and Local 600, the cameraman's union. In union there is strength and, in these Orwellian political times, we need unions more than ever.

Last, not least, to Steven Spielberg who gave me Arthur Knight's *The Liveliest Art* in the summer of 1969.

photo by Kevin de la Noy

Rob Harris is the author of *The Hannibal Journal* and a former freelance television writer whose credits include Laverne & Shirley. He tried other things: social work, horse ranching, art therapist in a mental hospital, delivery services, songwriting, movie trailer writing and ad copy. But unit publicity was the only job that worked out. He's had to find a new job every three months for the last thirty years. He is a three-time nominee for the Publicists Guild Lifetime Achievement Award and one of the few unit publicists to have been voted into the Academy of Motion Picture Arts and Sciences and the British Academy of Film and Television Arts. He is married and has two rock-star sons. He currently lives in London – though his heart is in New York and his house is in Los Angeles.

Robhar11@mac.com
www.lifeinthemovies.com

38422674R00200

Made in the USA
Columbia, SC
10 December 2018